Mathematical Fun, Games and Puzzles

D0289981

By
JACK FROHLICHSTEIN

INSTRUCTOR IN MATHEMATICS,
HANCOCK JUNIOR HIGH SCHOOL, LEMAY, MISSOURI

Dover Publications, Inc.
New York

Mathematical Fun, Games and Puzzles is a new
work, first published by Dover Publications, Inc.,
in 1962.

International Standard Book Number: 0-486-20789-7
Library of Congress Catalog Card Number: 75-5011

Manufactured in the United States by Courier Corporation
20789723
www.doverpublications.com

PREFACE

Mathematical Fun, Games, and Puzzles is written for the non-mathematician as well as for those who love mathematics. People who disliked mathematics in school should derive much enjoyment from the reading and active participation in this book. No great knowledge of mathematics is necessary for comprehension of its ideas; the book is written on the level of the average person with a vocabulary commensurate to his own. It is written informally, and unfamiliar technical words have been avoided. Most puzzle books require the reader to be able to understand college or high school mathematics. The material is good, but too hard for the average person. The material in this book requires only a knowledge of arithmetic through the eighth grade, and its organization dovetails the topics presented in junior high school texts. This is the first puzzle book of its kind to be organized in this manner, and to be written for the upper elementary mathematics level. However, people who have had college and high school mathematics will also greatly enjoy this book. This book is written for all.

Presented in this book are 334 puzzles, 20 games, 37 fun novelties, and 27 fun projects. This collection is the result of many years of research, use, and interest in the field. The author has taught in the field of junior high mathematics for ten years, and feels that the material presented here represents the best available from the realms of mathematical puzzles, games, and fun that all can enjoy regardless of their mathematical background. Many of these puzzles, games, and fun sections are original, but the majority of them are restatements of exercises or ideas which have been known for many years. Some were brought to the author by his students.

It is the author's hope that this book will be not only fun but educational as well. It will offer you a chance to review your elementary mathematics in a new and refreshing way and will give you a new and fresh approach to mathematics, leading you to conclude that mathematics can be fun and enjoyable — other than mere drill in fundamentals.

Now, to explain the most important feature of this book, its organization. Instead of being organized under the three main headings, Puzzles, Games, and Fun sections as most puzzle books are, this book is organized in such a way that it dovetails very closely the normal headings to be studied in upper elementary mathematics texts. A glance at the Table of Contents will readily disclose that there are eighteen chapters, with many subdivisions under each. Thus you may pick Puzzles, Games or Fun sections from any topic you so desire. A teacher or student, therefore, can use this book as a supplement to his regular text, or for additional material, since the material presented here is not normally found in a mathematics textbook on the upper elementary level. Not all sections, of course, contain all three parts. The chapter on Graphs, for example, contains Puzzles and Fun, but no Games. Sometimes there are subdivisions (as those on Geometrical Drawings and Topology under Geometry), and each of these contains Puzzles, Games, and Fun sections.

The puzzles in this book are of different kinds. Some take a lot of good thinking, and call for very intelligent solutions. Many require tricky answers. Many even have silly solutions. Some are just advanced or tough problems on topics of the kind found in upper elementary texts. In many of these puzzles, you will be surprised when you look up the answer in the back of the book. However, you should try to solve the puzzle before looking up the answer. You can derive much enjoyment by trying these puzzles on your friends.

The mathematical games in this book can be played with your friends. In many of them, you alone will know the winning technique. This consistency of brilliance in winning will greatly arouse your friends, who will consider you a mathematical whiz. Other games are in the form of solitaire, where only one can play.

The Fun section of this book is indeed an unusual one. The Fun section is subdivided into two main parts — Fun Novelties, of which there are thirty-seven, and Fun Projects, of which

there are twenty-seven. The novelties are merely statements of
mathematical oddities, novel methods, and short cuts. For
example, many short cuts for multiplication are given. New and
novel ways of doing old procedures are shown, such as finding
the day of the week for any date of any year. The oddities are
just stated for your pleasure.

The Fun Project section is completely different; these sections stress the uses of mathematics in everyday living. Many
people say, "Why do we learn mathematics?" These sections
will give you a better and a clearer picture of the way you can
use mathematics every day. Some are in the nature of puzzles
and games. Others call for some experimenting on your own.
The material, however, is different from that usually found in
standard upper elementary textbooks on mathematics. For
example, there are projects dealing with the Mobius strip and
map coloring; projects dealing with guessing games in geometry; things to do, such as making geometric solids. But most
important, there are projects dealing with the uses of mathematics in everyday life: investing $1,000 in the stock market;
using algebra in cooking and scale drawing; working with
maps; learning how to make your own budget, and so on.
Finally, there are projects just for learning something new:
how to find the square and cube roots of numbers; mathematical logic; sign numbers; and working with formulas.

The answers to all the puzzles, and to those games which
need answers, are found in the back of the book. The Fun
sections do not require answers.

Finally, the Puzzles, Games, and Fun sections are rated,
according to difficulty, "easy," "average," or "difficult." This
is just to help you. However, don't let the easy ones fool you.
They can still be tough.

If any of you are teachers, incidentally, these ratings will help
you use this book in junior high school classes: the "easy" projects are for use in the seventh grade; the "average" and some
of the "difficult" ones are for use in the eighth grade; the
"difficult" Puzzles, Games, and Fun sections are for use in
ninth-grade general mathematics classes and algebra. The
material presented in Chapter XVIII on Algebra should be

used in ninth-grade algebra classes, but may be used in eighth-grade classes in which some algebra such as the simple equation has been studied.

This is not a standard textbook, however, and the teacher should not feel bound by these divisions. This book is for you, the reader, and the author hopes you will find enjoyment here and perhaps be encouraged to make your own collection of puzzles and interesting material on mathematics.

One final word: approximately ten of the puzzles under the Arithmetic section of the book also appear in the Algebra section. They were repeated so that you might realize that many arithmetic puzzles may be solved more easily by algebra. The puzzles appear to be the same, but the method of solving them is completely different.

The author thanks his fellow teachers, friends, and students, for their kind assistance in gathering the material for this book. In particular, I would like to thank Arthur Christ and Francis Otterson.

And now you are ready for the puzzles, games, novelties, and projects. Have fun.

University City, Missouri   JACK FROHLICHSTEIN
June, 1961

CONTENTS

Mathematical Fun, Games and Puzzles

A NOTE ON THE ORGANIZATION OF THIS BOOK

This book contains the following types of enrichment material:

Puzzles	numbered consecutively from		1 to 334
Games	,,	,,	,,	1 to 20
Fun Novelties	,,	,,	,,	1 to 37
Fun Projects	,,	,,	,,	1 to 27

The nature and use of each of these enrichments is explained in the author's preface, page viii.

The **Answers to Puzzles** begin on page 211.

Not all Games require answers, but those that do are answered in the **Answers to Games** section which begins on page 296.

The Fun Novelties and Fun Projects do not require answers.

Chapter I

INTRODUCTION AND HISTORY OF MATHEMATICS

PUZZLES NOS. 1, 2

Easy

1. Why is the number 13 considered unlucky? Where did the superstition originate? Many hotels omit the number 13 in marking their floors and numbering their rooms.

2. Odd numbers were once considered masculine and even numbers were considered feminine. Can you think of the reason why?

FUN PROJECT NO. 1: HISTORY OF PUZZLES

Average (Read, Review, and Learn)

No one knows how old the word "puzzle" is; what we know as puzzles are as old as the spoken language. The origin and early history of most types of puzzles are unrecorded.

Sam Loyd (1841–1911) was a genius in the invention of puzzles of all kinds. H. E. Dudeney (1847–1930) was an English mathematician who interested himself in puzzles and published several collections of his own inventions.

There are many kinds of puzzles and the word "puzzle" means different things to different people. The history and background of puzzles is very nebulous indeed.

A BRIEF HISTORY OF ARITHMETIC

Necessity drove man to figuring. As families grew into tribes and tribes into nations, a system of trade sprang up. Clay was traded for herbs. As nations grew and the volume of trade increased, they felt the need of selling on credit. A nation raising grains or herbs might need clay for pottery, but the harvest might be some time off. So it bought the clay, giving a promise to pay in grain when the grain was harvested. Written records became necessary, and accounting was born. Coins or tokens were made to represent certain definite values.

Many examples of the first written numerals can be found. Of interest here are the numerals found in the Great Pyramid tombs in Egypt. Painted on the walls were 1, which was represented by a vertical line; 10 represented by a kind of horseshoe; 100, by a corkscrew shape; 10,000, by a pointing finger; 100,000, by a frog; and 1,000,000, by a man looking astonished.

Primitive man could count only to 5, probably because he had 5 fingers. For numbers greater than 5, he would say, "Five skins and one skin," when he meant 6. This was the first addition. Some said, "One fruit, two fruits, many fruits," being unable to count above 2. For greater numbers, they would say "Two and one more, and one more, and one more, and one more," and so on. This is still the only method of computation among primitive tribes all over the world.

As trade grew, systems for larger numbers were devised. The decimal system is one of these. Ten was the base because man has 10 fingers and 10 toes and he used these in his early counting. The Babylonians had 60 as their basis, the Aztecs 20. The Eskimos and the American Indians of the West Coast today count by 20, using the sum of their fingers and toes as a basis. The Israelites spoke of the average life span of man as "three score years and ten" because it was easier to count 20 (a score) three times and then add half a score (10), than it was to count to 70. This was plain addition.

Remember:

$$A \text{ decade} = 10 \text{ years}$$
$$A \text{ score} = 20 \text{ years}$$
$$A \text{ century} = 100 \text{ years}$$

Remember Lincoln's *Gettysburg Address* starts off with "Fourscore and seven years ago . . . ," which was 87 years ago.

Since subtraction is merely the taking away of something,

primitive man even today holds up 5 fingers, then turns down 3 of them, leaving 2. In Roman numerals, IV means "subtract 1 from 5." This statement, rather cute, is found in an old eighteenth-century book on arithmetic: "Note that IV signifies four as IX signifies nine which takes, as it were, by stealth or pulls back one from 10. So that, in fact, I stands behind X and picks his pockets and I stands behind V and picks his."

Ancient multiplication was a matter of repeated additions. Division, even in the early times, was done by means of repeated subtractions. To divide 9 by 3, the ancients are believed to have subtracted 3 from 9, giving 6, then 3 from 6, leaving 3; then 3 from 3, leaving 0, showing that 3 goes into 9 three times, with no remainder.

Ancient man had little need, in his trading, to resort to fractions. When these people encountered difficulty in handling parts of a broken object, they created various measuring systems for designating subunits.

One word, "inch," is a relic of the Roman system. The Romans clung to 12 as a basis of their division of measures because it is easily divisible by 2, 3, 4, and 6. This permitted the taking of simple fractional parts. They divided the foot into twelfths.

As we said previously, every system of counting has its own base, ten being the one most often used. The Babylonian system used 60 as its base; from this we get our minutes and seconds, but in time and in angles. It is also assumed that the Babylonians divided the circle into 360 equal parts because of the early idea that a year consisted of 360 days, and because their scientists knew that the radius employed in stepping around a circle divided it into 6 equal arcs, thus making 60 a mystic number.

Four or five hundred years ago, the only way they knew to tell time was by a sun dial. The time was indicated by the edge of the shadow cast upon the graduated surface by an inclined pointer or rod. On a cloudy day, it was useless, but on sunny days they could tell time within an accuracy of ten minutes.

Inches, feet, and yards were not always used as units of measure. Arms, hands, feet, and even noses were used in early times. A "hand" was the width of a man's hand. He measured a horse with his hand by putting one hand above the other until he counted how many hands high the horse was. If his hands were large and wide, the horse would not measure as many hands high as it would if the man had smaller hands. That led to much confusion. Today a "hand" means 4 inches.

In early times, a "span" was the distance between the tip of your little finger and the tip of your thumb when you stretched them as far apart as you could. The span of an adult hand is about 8 or 9 inches. A "foot" meant the length of the foot of whoever was doing the measuring.

Another common early measure was the "pace." This was the length of a step and was about 30 inches.

About four hundred years ago, an emperor decreed that a rod would be the total length of the left feet of 16 men as they left church services on a Sunday morning.

The yard was fixed by an English king who decreed it should be the distance from the tip of his nose to the end of his thumb. A woman measuring a piece of cloth by placing one end at the tip of her nose and holding the cloth with her other arm outstretched measures almost a yard.

Many of the ancient measures are in use today. Finally, it was decided to have a foot mean a certain distance — 12 inches. Now we have a metal bar with notches cut in it to mark the length of a foot; it is kept in the Bureau of Standards in Washington, D.C., at a fixed temperature to prevent its expanding with heat or shrinking with cold. Our foot rulers are made as nearly the same length as the standard foot as possible.

In old England, when a man owed money, he would record the amount by cutting notches in a stick called a "tally stock," which he gave to his creditors. Sometimes dishonest creditors would cut extra notches before they presented the tally stock for payment. So the system was changed; after the notches were made, the tally was split down the middle and the notches on the creditor's half had to correspond with the notches on the debtor's half.

Banks kept records of deposits by the tally system. Their

depositors held tally stocks corresponding to those in the bank. From this came the modern word "stockholder."

Until 1543 the British Government also kept records of transactions by the tally system. After the system was discontinued, the basement of the House of Commons remained cluttered with vast accumulations of these dry sticks for nearly two centuries. Finally it was decided to burn them. The stove became overheated and a fire ensued which burned down both the House of Commons and the adjacent House of Lords.

This is but a very brief history of arithmetic.

Chapter II

WHOLE NUMBERS

Reading and Writing Whole Numbers

PUZZLES NOS. 3-5

Easy

3. What letter equals 4 in the alphabet? Can you find another example?

4. Make a walking man out of the following, using two straight lines: H030

Average

5. What plant stands for the number 4?

FUN NOVELTY NO. 1

Average

Can you read very large numbers like this:

$$6,000,000,000,000,000,000,000$$

This is read as 6 hexillion or 6 sextillion. In science, where we deal with outer space and the universe, being able to read and handle these large numbers is a great advantage.

After billions comes trillions, quadrillions, quintillions, hexillions or sextillions, septillions, octillions, nonillions, decillions, and so on. There is no such number as zillions. The largest number imaginable is represented by a symbol called infinity which looks like a horizontal 8.

∞

Infinity is not definitely defined. Think of the biggest number possible, and then keep going until you come to infinity. Infinity is a number without bounds or limits.

To continue — after decillions comes undecillion, duodecillion, tredecillion, quattuordecillion, quindecillion, sexdecillion, septendecillion, octodecillion, novemdecillion, vigintillion, and so on. Six vigintillion would be written:

6,000,000,000,000,000,000,000,000,000,000,000,000,000,000,000,000,000,000,000,000,000 (6 followed by 21 periods or 63 zeros)

GAME NO. 1

Easy

1. Bet anyone that he can't correctly name the next highest number to every number which you will give him. When he takes you up, name a lot of numbers starting with two digits and gradually going up to three digits and finally four digits. For example:

43 — he will say		44
87 — he will say		88
123 — he will say		124
412 — he will say		413
893 — he will say		894
2,341 — he will say		2,342
3,633 — he will say		3,634
5,099 — he will probably say 6,000 (if he is like others)		

Say all the numbers correctly, like "three thousand six hundred thirty-three." When you come to the catch number 5,099, say "five thousand ninety-nine" or "five thousand and ninety-nine." The numbers you take make no difference, but always give the catch number as your last number. Always start low and work up gradually, pausing between numbers to imply that you are thinking hard and demanding a quick response from your friend in each case.

Addition of Whole Numbers
PUZZLES NOS. 6–38

Easy

6. One day the teacher asks this simple question: "Is it correct to say seven and five IS thirteen — or seven and five ARE thirteen?"

7. In this magic square you must use the digits 1 through 9, each one once only. Make a sum of 15 in all directions — horizontally, vertically, and diagonally. (There are many solutions.)

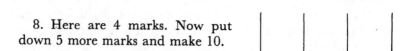

8. Here are 4 marks. Now put down 5 more marks and make 10.

9. Give the following sum in addition: Can you strike out 6 of these digits so that the total of the remaining numbers shall be 20?

```
111
777
999
———
```

10. How can 2 and 1 make 4?

11. Take the digits 1 through 11 and arrange them in the circles shown, so that they add to the same result in all directions. (Add the 3 circles together on the same straight line. The sum should equal all the other straight line totals.)

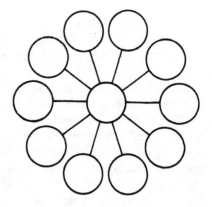

12. If a farmer had 39 haystacks in one corner of a field, 15 haystacks in another corner, 10 in another, and 5 in the last, how many haystacks would there be altogether?

13. How can you use eight 8's to make a total of 1,000?

$$8 \; 8 \; 8 \; 8 \; 8 \; 8 \; 8 \; 8 = 1,000$$

14. If a wagon wheel has 18 spaces between the spokes, how many spokes does it have?

15. (a) How can you use seven 4's to make 100?
    (b) How can you use sixteen 4's to make 1,000?

16. When do 11 and 2 more equal 1?

17. Using the numbers 1 through 7, place a different number in each circle in such a way that all connecting lines

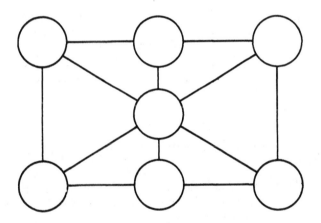

containing three of the numbers add up to 12. The sum of all straight lines must be 12 in each individual addition.

18. A clerk had only 10 vacant rooms left in a hotel. There were 11 men who went into the hotel at the same time, each wanting a separate room. The clerk, settling the argument, said: "I'll tell you what I'll do. I will put two men in Room 1 with the understanding that I will come back and get one of

them a few minutes later." The men agreed to this. The clerk continued: "I will put the rest of you men as follows:

the 3rd man in Room 2
the 4th man in Room 3
the 5th man in Room 4
the 6th man in Room 5
the 7th man in Room 6
the 8th man in Room 7
the 9th man in Room 8, and
the 10th man in Room 9."

Then the clerk went back to get the extra man he had left in Room 1, and put him in Room 10. Everybody is happy. What is the fallacy of this plan?

19.

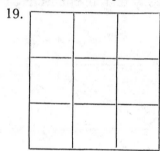

Using the numbers 1, 2, 3, 10, 11, 12, 19, 20, and 21 only once, place them in the squares in such a way that the sum of all horizontal, vertical, and diagonal lines is 33.

20. Can you write 24 with three equal digits, none of them being 8?

21. Here are simple addition problems in disguise. Put a digit in for each letter. All identical letters must have the same digit, but all different letters must be replaced by different digits:

```
(a)   Y      (b)  ON      (c)  MA      (d) XXX
      Y           ON          +A           +B
     +Y           ON          ──          ────
     ──           +ON         AM           BAAA
     MY           ──
                  GO
```

All problems can be logically worked.

22. If a group of soldiers are lined up as follows:

> 2 soldiers in front of a soldier
> 1 soldier behind a soldier
> 1 soldier in the middle

how many soldiers are there?

23.

Square I
1 3 5 7 9 11
13 15 17 19 21 23
25 27 29 31 33 35
37 39 41 43 45 47
49 51 53 55 57 59

Square II
4 5 6 7 12 13
14 15 20 21 22 23
28 29 30 31 36 37
38 39 44 45 46 47
52 53 54 55 60

Square III
8 9 10 11 12 13
14 15 24 25 26 27
28 29 30 31 40 41
42 43 44 45 46 47
56 57 58 59 60

Square IV
2 3 6 7 10 11
14 15 18 19 22 23
26 27 30 31 34 35
38 39 42 43 46 47
50 51 54 55 58 59

Square V
16 17 18 19 20 21
22 23 24 25 26 27
28 29 30 31 48 49
50 51 52 53 54 55
56 57 58 59 60

Square VI
32 33 34 35 36 37
38 39 40 41 42 43
44 45 46 47 48 49
50 51 52 53 54 55
56 57 58 59 60

Tell a person that you can guess his age, using these magic squares. Ask him to indicate all the squares in which his age appears. Suppose he is 30 years old; he would say that his age appears in Squares II, III, IV, and V. Immediately you could tell his age. How?

Instead of using a person's age in the problem, just ask someone to pick a number and, by the same procedure, you will indicate the number he chose.

Average

24. This is a classic problem which may be found in many textbooks. It is really an addition problem in disguise. You must replace each letter by a digit, using 0–9. The same digit must be used

```
      S  E  N  D
      M  O  R  E
   ─────────────
   M  O  N  E  Y
```

to represent the same letter. For example, if 3 is used for the letter E, then 3 must be used for all E's and

```
      S  E  N  D                        S  3  N  D
      M  O  R  E   taking out E becomes  M  O  R  3
   ─────────────                      ─────────────
   M  O  N  E  Y                      M  O  N  3  Y
```

However, you must use a different digit for different letters. The problem is not all guesswork, but can actually be figured logically. If you use a 6 for an N, for example, you may not use a 6 for an S. After you substitute all the letters for numbers, you will have a perfectly valid problem in addition. (Hint: There is one place at which you should begin this problem.)

25. Using the numbers from 1 to 9 once and once only, write them in such a way that by addition they add to a value of 99999. *How?* 123456789 = 99999.

26. Here is a tricky problem. You must make a sum of 100 exactly, using only these five numbers:

16   17   23   24   39

You may use any of these numbers as many times as you like, but you must use them only to make a sum of 100.

27.

Column I	Column II	Column III
1	4	7
2	5	8
3	6	9
6	15	24

Now, each of these columns adds to a different sum. Can you move one number from one column into another column so that each column will total the same amount?

28. Can you use the same digit eight times and get an answer of 1,000? Use any digit from 1 to 9, but the digit you decide upon must be used throughout the addition problem. (To make the problem easier, the teacher may tell you what digit to use.)

29. A student who was failing science was told by his teacher when the class was on a field trip to a farm, "If you can find an ear of corn in this cornfield with 15 horizontal rows of grain on it, I will pass you." The boy husked all the corn in the field, but did not find an ear with 15 rows. He failed his science class. Why can't an ear of corn have 15 rows of grain?

30. How may the first 16 digits be arranged so that the sums of the vertical, the horizontal, and the two diagonal rows equal 34? (There are many different solutions.)

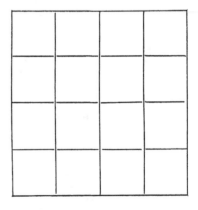

31. Can you find five odd numbers which add up to 20? You may use the same number more than once. Remember, odd numbers are 1,3,5,7,9, etc.

Example:

These five odd numbers add to 21 — but the answer must be 20!

$$\begin{array}{r} 5 \\ 5 \\ 3 \\ 1 \\ 7 \\ \hline 21 \end{array}$$

32. Take the ten digits

0, 1, 2, 3, 4, 5, 6, 7, 8, and 9

and make up an example in addition using three of the digits on the top line, and another three of the digits on the second line. Then, add the two numbers together to get an answer using the other four digits not used in the addends. Thus, every digit is used once and once only in this addition problem:

$$\begin{array}{ll} \text{x x x} & \text{addend} \\ \underline{\text{x x x}} & \text{addend} \\ \text{x x x x} & \text{sum} \end{array}$$

There is more than one answer to this puzzle. Can you find as many as three different answers?

33. Using the digits 1, 2, 3, 4, 5, 6, 7 once only, make an addition problem in which the sum will be 100. The digits may be used individually or combined.

Example:

$$\begin{array}{r} 12 \\ 7 \\ 63 \\ 4 \\ 5 \\ \hline 91 \end{array}$$

Wrong answer:

The sum must be 100.

Difficult

34.

There are 72 prisoners arranged in a jail as shown. In each cell are 9 men, and 3 cells on each corridor, or 8 cells altogether. Every hour, the guard walks down each corridor and counts the number of men in all three cells, or 27 men in each corridor. The corridors on the ends count as being in two different corridors, as the diagram shows. The guard did not bother to note the number of men in each individual jail, as sometimes the men would stay in a neighboring cell instead of their own, but always within the same side or corridor. So, on some occasions, there might be 11 men in one cell and only 7 in another as 2 men switched cells. But the guard was always careful to see that there were a total of 27 men on each side or corridor. One day the prisoners managed to get an extra set of keys which would open all 8 cells. They figured out a method by which 4 men could escape every night and when the guard counted each side, he would still get the sum of 27 men. The men had to be rearranged in their cells for this technique to work.

Again the next night, 4 more prisoners escaped and those remaining arranged themselves in their cells in such a way that the guard could still count 27 men each way.

How did the prisoners rearrange themselves in the cells, and for how many nights could they continue to permit 4 prisoners to escape before the formula ran out?

35.

T	H	I	S	This is really an addition problem
		I	S	incognito. You must replace each
V	E	R	Y	letter by a digit, using 0–9. The
E	A	S	Y	same digit must be used to repre-

sent the same letter. Put in the numbers for the letters to get a perfectly valid addition problem. (There are 12 solutions.)

36. A fox ate 100 grapes in 5 days, each day eating 6 more than on the previous day. How many did he eat on each of the five days? (This also appears under Algebra.)

37. Can you arrange the numbers 1, 2, 3, 4, 5, 7, 8, 9 into two groups, so that each group will add up to the same sum? Each group must be composed of four numbers.

38. Find four consecutive odd numbers which, when added together, make 80.   (This also appears under Algebra.)

FUN NOVELTY NO. 2

Easy

This trick is demonstrated on the blackboard by a teacher who claims to be very fast in the addition of whole numbers — in fact, so fast that he can write down the answer to the problem immediately after drawing the line. For example, the teacher asks the students to give him a five-digit number.

Student's number	21,343
Student gives another number	59,268
Teacher says, "Now it's my turn"	40,731
Student's number	64,999
Teacher's number	35,000
	221,341

The teacher gives this answer right away, pretending to have added the numbers very quickly. He tries another example:

Student's number	611
Student's number	517
Teacher's number	388
Student's number	135
Teacher's number	482
Student's number	876
Teacher's number	864
Student's number	982
Teacher's number	123
Teacher's spontaneous answer	4,978

How can the teacher do this? How can he add so quickly? Are teachers just naturally brilliant?

ANSWER: The idea is for the teacher, at his turn, to choose numbers in such a manner that a combination of two numbers will add to 9. How does he get the answer 221,341?

Student's number	21,343*	(Leave this number for later)

Student's number	59,268	⎫	59,268	
		⎬	40,731	(all 9's)
Teacher's number	40,731	⎭	99,999	
Student's number	64,999	⎫	64,999	
		⎬	35,000	(all 9's)
Teacher's number	35,000	⎭	99,999	
	221,341			

Take the first number * above (21,343) which was not added to 9's. Now, to get the answer, the teacher takes this number and subtracts from it the number of groups of 9's he has. In the foregoing problem the teacher has two sets of 9's:

$$\begin{array}{r} 21,343 \\ 2 \\ \hline 21,341 \end{array}$$

Now, the two groups or 2 which the teacher subtracted must be put back at the beginning of the number; he sets the 2 in front of 21,341 and has the answer, 221,341.

This puzzle can be worked another way. After the student gives the teacher the first number of 21,343, the teacher tells him he can predict the answer before the rest of the numbers are given.

The teacher can control the amount of addends in the addition problem. As in the example above, he knows that there will be 2 groups of 9 and he knows the first number is 21,343; he takes away 2, places it in front, and has 221,341, which is the answer regardless of what addends are selected.

From personal experience the writer recommends using the first method; the students will think the teacher is a rapid adder but the second method may make them suspicious of a trick to the problem.

The teacher can switch techniques and keep the students from guessing how the puzzle works. He can put his groups of 9's in different places, separating the two addends that total 9 from each other. He should also use a different number, as the basis of his final answer.

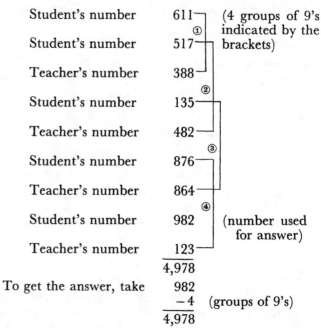

Student's number	611	(4 groups of 9's indicated by the brackets)
Student's number	517	
Teacher's number	388	
Student's number	135	
Teacher's number	482	
Student's number	876	
Teacher's number	864	
Student's number	982	(number used for answer)
Teacher's number	123	
	4,978	

To get the answer, take

$$982$$
$$\underline{-\ 4}\quad\text{(groups of 9's)}$$
$$4,978$$

The teacher may use as many digits as he desires in a number (say, 7,865,463, etc.) and as many addends as he likes, but should always keep track of the number of groups of 9's in the problem. He will always have an odd number of addends unless the student selects a number with all 9's to begin with. If this happens, the teacher may claim he does not choose to take his turn — he would really have to use all 0's.

Example:

Student	6,135	(number used for answer)
Student	2,364	
Teacher	3,864	
Student	9,999	
(teacher skips turn)		
Student	4,136	
Teacher	5,863	
	32,361	

Other examples:

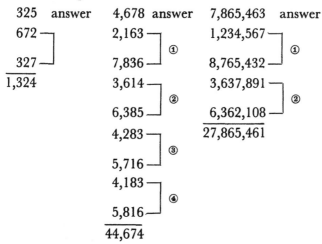

325	answer
672 ⌐	
	①
327 ⌐	
1,324	

4,678	answer
2,163 ⌐	
	①
7,836 ⌐	
3,614 ⌐	
	②
6,385 ⌐	
4,283 ⌐	
	③
5,716 ⌐	
4,183 ⌐	
	④
5,816 ⌐	
44,674	

7,865,463	answer
1,234,567 ⌐	
	①
8,765,432 ⌐	
3,637,891 ⌐	
	②
6,362,108 ⌐	
27,865,461	

You will enjoy trying this yourself, making up experiments of your own, and even doing a bit of bragging to your friends, claiming to be a whiz in addition.

FUN NOVELTY NO. 3

Easy

This addition gives the same result when you turn the paper and problem completely upside down.

$$\underline{5,074}$$
$$986$$
$$818$$
$$969$$
$$989$$
$$696$$
$$616$$
$$\overline{5,074}$$

(The 9's become 6's and vice versa when the problem is turned upside down.)

FUN NOVELTY NO. 4

Average

In the year 1540 people added columns in this manner:
Add each column separately, writing the several results and
adding the partial sums. Be sure to get the 10's in the 10's
column, the 100's in the 100's column, etc.

$$
\begin{array}{r}
9,279 \\
1,389 \\
4,479 \\
6,321 \\
\hline
\end{array}
$$

28 –	from column 1
24 —	from column 2
12 ——	from column 3
20 ———	from column 4

Answer $\overline{21,468}$

You need not worry about "carrying over" with this procedure,
but you must get the digits in the proper columns.

For very long columns of numbers in addition, this method
would be practical because some of us have difficulty keeping
everything in our minds. This method does not require you to
keep so much in your mind, as each separate column is an
individual problem in itself.

GAMES NOS. 2–4

Easy

2. I have used this game many times in my teaching, in
classes, at parties, and so on. It is very simple to play but
requires good concentration by the participants. The more
participants the better, but at least 20 should play.

The participants sit around in a large circle — or in rows as in a classroom — and number off (or count off). Player No. 1 sits in the first seat, the seat of honor; No. 2 is in back of him, No. 3 in back of No. 2, and so on. Player No. 1 starts the game

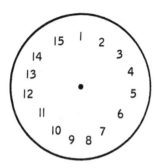

by calling out any number; however, he cannot call a number beyond the number of players (if 15 are playing, 15 is the highest number he can call). The player whose number has been called immediately and without hesitation calls out another number. When a player's number is called, he or she must call the number of another player. The game continues until someone misses which he does by:

(a) calling his own number,

(b) not speaking, or hesitating too long,

(c) stuttering or not making clear the number he is calling,

(d) calling a "wrong" number — such as 23 when only 20 are playing.

To be effective, the game must move fast. One person must be the judge, to avoid arguments. When a person misses, he goes to the end of the line or circle and everyone above his number moves up one seat. Everyone then must concentrate on a new number, which can become confusing because the players will always be changing their numbers. Every time someone misses, those with higher numbers move up one. Now, the one in seat No. 1 is the leader — the object is to dethrone the leader by making him miss. Players in the higher-numbered seats try to make the lower-numbered people miss so they can work up to No. 1. Player No. 1 usually concentrates so hard that he eventually says his own number; also, everyone puts pressure on No. 1.

The person who remains in seat No. 1 the longest or is in it at the end of the time allotted for the game is the winner.

After the players become accustomed to the game, the judge makes sure that the players' responses are fast, otherwise the game will suffer. In this way the players miss every few seconds and will be moving around so fast their heads will swim! After a player misses, the others need a little time to renumber themselves (not aloud). A person in seat No. 20 can reach seat No. 1 rather quickly.

For example, let's take the game with fifteen players. Player No. 1 calls 8, No. 8 calls 10, No. 10 calls 13, No. 13 calls 1, No. 1 calls 4 — No. 4 hesitates too long (more than two seconds) and loses. Player No. 4 goes to the end of the line and becomes No. 15 and all players above 4 (5, 6, 7, 8, 9, 10, 11, 12, 13, 14, and 15) move up one number or seat. Numbers 1, 2, and 3 do not move.

The game continues with twelve players having new numbers. Player No. 1 calls 3, No. 3 calls 4, No. 4 calls 1, No. 1 stutters and calls two numbers together — he must go to the end of the line, becoming No. 15, and everyone else moves up one. We now have a new king or queen for No. 1.

The new No. 1 calls 13, No. 13 calls 15, No. 15 calls 16 — but there is no 16! He would go to the end of the line but he is already there. So nobody moves.

Try this game at parties. All adults and children will love it.

Average

3. This is a good game which can be played in several different ways.

Game A. The rules are simple. The player who reaches 100 first is the winner. The first player starts at 0 and may add any number from 1 to 10. The next player builds on the first player's score, also by adding any number from 1 to 10. The game continues, each player taking his turn until 100 is reached. The player reaching this number wins. For example:

> Player A — starts with 6
> Player B — adds 7 and makes 13
> A — adds 10 and makes 23
> B — adds 8 and makes 31
> A — 40
> B — 48
> A — 58
> B — 60
> A — 65
> B — 75
> A — 80
> B — 88
> A — 89
> B — 99
> A — 100 — wins

A player can not add more than 10 or less than 1. However, the teacher will always get to 100 first (or any person knowing the tricks). Can you see how this is done? Try this game and you will begin to see a set pattern. (To learn how to win, look at the Answers.)

Game B. Now the tables are reversed and the player who reaches 100 first *loses*. Remember, you do not want to reach 100. The rules are the same as in Game A. You must add from 1 to 10 onto the total at each turn. For example:

> Player A — starts with 3
> Player B — adds 10
> A — 20
> B — 23
> A — 33
> B — 40

Player A — 46
Player B — 49
    A — 59
    B — 68
    A — 78
    B — 88
    A — 89
    B — 99
    A — must say 100 and loses

When 99 is reached, the next player must add 1 to make 100, and he loses. You have to add 1 and no more than 10. Again, there is a pattern which forces the second person to lose. Can you see the pattern? (See Answers.)

Game C. You may play "100 wins" by adding on any number from 1 to 9 (instead of 1 to 10). This changes the pattern for winning. Can you see the pattern?

Game D. You may play "100 loses" by adding on any number from 1 to 9 (instead of 1 to 10). This requires a new pattern. What is it?

4. This game is lots of fun and is played like tic-tac-toe, *but* instead of using X's and O's, you use the digits 1 through 9. Two can play, and no trick is involved in winning this game. The game follows the pattern of tic-tac-toe; one player, at his turn, uses any of the odd digits, 1, 3, 5, 7, 9, and the other uses even digits, 2, 4, 6, 8. The one using the odd digits has an extra one and always goes first. The player who can make a straight row — vertically, horizontally or diagonally — add to the sum of 15 first wins. Naturally, each player tries to keep the other from scoring.

Example: *A* has 1, 3, 5, 7, 9.
B has 2, 4, 6, 8.

The tic-tac-toe nine square diagram is used.

A goes first, using a 7. (A number can be used only once in the game.) Numbers 1, 3, 5, and 9 are left.

B places a 2, leaving 4, 6, 8.

		2
		7

A blocks B by using 1 and prevents his using 6 on his next turn and scoring.

		1
		2
		7

B plays a 6.

6		1
		2
		7

A plays a 5 in the middle square.

6	5	1
		2
		7

B plays an 8 to stop A from scoring.

8		1
6	5	2
		7

However, A can still play his 9 and make 15 diagonally.

8		1
6	5	2
9		7

Therefore A wins.

Sometimes neither player wins or makes a sum of 15. Then the game ends in a tie. In the next game, A and B should change numbers, B taking 1, 3, 5, 7, and 9, and A taking 2, 4, 6, and 8.

Subtraction of Whole Numbers

PUZZLES NOS. 39–54

Easy

39. How can you make 7 even?
40. How many times can 19 be subtracted from 190?
41.   5 X 0 9

    X 6 X X   Replace the X's with the missing num-

    3 1 6 0   bers.

42 (*a*). Two men in the Army had a potato-peeling contest to see who could peel the most potatoes in a given time. One peeled two hundred thirty-six potatoes, and the other peeled three hundred and won. How many potatoes did both peel altogether? (This problem is more effective if you state it orally to your friends.)

(*b*) If you have twenty (six or sick) sheep, and one dies, how many are left? (Must be posed orally.)

43. Here is a fast-disappearing word. It has nine letters. If you take away six letters, only one will be left. What is the word?

44. Three men entered a hotel and asked for a room, but the clerk said there was only one room available but that he would put dividers in the room. The room would cost $30. Each man paid $10. After the clerk thought the situation over, he decided that he had overcharged the men and called the bellboy and instructed him, "Take this five dollars back to the three men. Tell them I overcharged them and that they should divide this five dollars among themselves." The bellboy thought that dividing $5 among three men would be fairly difficult and, being dishonest, kept $2 for himself. Then he returned $1 to each man so, actually, the cost to each man was $9. Now, 3 times 9 is 27 and the $2 the bellboy kept makes $29. What happened to the other dollar?

45. What word spelled with four letters still has five left when three of the letters are taken away?

Average

46. How can you take 1 away from 19 and leave 20?

47. There is a frog at the bottom of a well 20 feet deep. The frog climbs upward 5 feet in the daytime. During the night, it goes to sleep and slips back 4 feet. At this rate, how many days will it take the frog to get out of the well? How did you arrive at your answer?

48. A teacher has 24 students in her class. She divides the students into three groups, 11 in the first, 7 in the second, and 6 in the third, in order that she can work individually with each of the separated groups. However, she later decides that all groups must have an equal number of students, or 8 in each group. The students objected to being separated and agreed that the only way they would move to another group would be if the group they were moved into had the same number of students as the number being shifted. For example, the teacher could form a group of 11, move 6 students and place them with the other group of 6 students; or move 7 students and place

them with the other group of 7 students. Also, because the students disliked being moved around, the teacher had to make the fewest shifts possible. She made only three moves to get all three groups equal in number, with 8 students in a group. How did she move the students?

49. How can you subtract 45 from 45 and have 45 as the remainder?

50. A word I know, six letters it contains;
Subtract just one and twelve remains.
What is the word?

51. II − IIII = II.
This reads 2 minus 4 equals 2 which, as anybody knows, is wrong—and it doesn't make sense. Now, change the position of just one stick (or line) to make the problem absolutely correct.

52. Under addition, you had this puzzle:

You made a good addition problem of it by substituting the digits 0 to 9 for the letters. Now, try the same idea in a problem similar to this, but in subtraction of whole numbers:

```
    S  E  N  D
 +  M  O  R  E
 ───────────────
    M  O  N  E  Y


    S  P  E  N  D
 −  M  O  R  E
 ───────────────
    M  O  N  E  Y
```

The same digit must be used to represent the same letter, and different digits for different letters. Remember, this time it is subtraction.

At Christmas time, here is another subtraction problem to try:

```
    S  A  N  T  A
 −  C  L  A  U  S
 ───────────────
    X  M  A  S
```

Difficult

53. Two farmers were taking their sheep to the market and one said, "Give me one of your sheep, and I'll have as many as you have." The other replied, "Yes, but if you give me one of your sheep, I'll have twice as many as you have." How many sheep did each farmer have in the beginning? (This puzzle is also under Algebra.)

54.   9 8 7 6 5 4 3 2 1

Using + signs and − signs only, place them anywhere between these numbers in order to get 100 as the answer. For example: $9+8+7\ 6+5\ 4-3\ 2+1 = 116$. Of course, this is not correct because the answer must be 100. You may use as many + and − signs as you like.

FUN NOVELTY NO. 5

Easy

A. Write three high digits in a line		8 4 6
B. Reverse the digits		6 4 8
C. Subtract B from A		1 9 8
D. Reverse them again and add		8 9 1
		1, 0 8 9

On high numbers, the answer will always be 1,089 no matter what three digits you take. In step C, always subtract the smaller number from the larger; also, when subtracting, you must always have three digits in the answer — otherwise the process will not work and your answer will be 198 instead of 1,089.

$$
\begin{array}{r}
5\ 5\ 4 \\
4\ 5\ 5 \\
\hline
9\ 9 \\
9\ 9 \\
\hline
1\ 9\ 8
\end{array}
$$

If the numbers are the same when reversed, your answer will be 0.

Example:
$$
\begin{array}{r}
9\ 8\ 9 \\
9\ 8\ 9 \\
\hline
0 \\
0 \\
\hline
0
\end{array}
$$

Try 375:
$$
\begin{array}{r}
5\ 7\ 3 \\
-3\ 7\ 5 \\
\hline
1\ 9\ 8 \\
+8\ 9\ 1 \\
\hline
1,\ 0\ 8\ 9
\end{array}
$$

Using 2 digits only, your answer will be 99 — as long as the two digits are different. Try 26:

$$\begin{array}{r} 6\ 2 \\ -2\ 6 \\ \hline 3\ 6 \\ +6\ 3 \\ \hline 9\ 9 \end{array}$$

FUN NOVELTY NO. 6

Easy

Another method of subtracting whole numbers is by using addition. You subtract by adding. That is how subtraction is actually taught in European schools. To subtract

8 4 6 1 (minuend)
5 7 3 9 (subtrahend)

you take the subtrahend and ask, "What number added to each individual digit will give you the minuend?" For example, 9 and what number add to 11? (Think of 1 as an 11 since you could not add any number to 9 and get 1. Also, you could borrow 1 from the tens digit to make the 1 in the units digit 11.)

The answer is 2.

$$\begin{array}{r} 8\ 4\ 6\ 1 \\ 5\ 7\ 3\ \boxed{9} \\ \hline \boxed{2} \end{array}$$

Now, $9 + 2 = 11$, which leaves 1 to carry to the tens column. Then $3 + 1$ to carry and how much more make 6, the top digit? Again, the answer is 2.

$$\begin{array}{r} 8\ 4\ 6\ 1 \\ 5\ 7\ \boxed{3}\ 9 \\ \hline \boxed{2}\ 2 \end{array}$$

Now, take the hundreds column. There is nothing to carry from the tens, so think $7 +$ what number equals 14? (4 counts as 14.) The answer is seven.

$$\begin{array}{r} 8\ 4\ 6\ 1 \\ 5\ \boxed{7}\ 3\ 9 \\ \hline \boxed{7}\ 2\ 2 \end{array}$$

The last step is the thousands column. There is 1 to carry, so

think $5+1$ to carry and how much more adds to 8, the top
digit? The answer is 2.

$$
\begin{array}{cccc}
 & 8 & 4 & 6 & 1 \\
5| & 7 & 3 & 9 \\
\hline
2| & 7 & 2 & 2
\end{array}
$$

Remember: you add the subtrahend and difference to get the
minuend.

$$
\left.\begin{array}{cccc}
8 & 4 & 6 & 1 \\
5 & 7 & 3 & 9 \\
\hline
2 & 7 & 2 & 2
\end{array}\right\}
$$

8 4 6 1 answer trying to add to

5 7 3 9⎫
———   ⎬ add
2 7 2 2⎭

$9+2 = 11$ (1 to carry)
$3+2+1 = 6$
$7+7 = 14$ (1 to carry)
$2+5+1 = 8$

This method is very useful in checking subtraction. When you
write checks, you must keep track of the balance in your
account in the bank on your check stubs. This requires many
subtractions and a mistake would give you the wrong balance
in your account. If you would check your subtractions by
adding, you would avoid embarrassing errors.

FUN NOVELTY NO. 7

Average

A man was recently discharged from his job because his
employer decided the man was not worth the $5,000 a year he
was getting. The employer reasoned this way:

365 days in a year	365
Sleep 8 hours a day (1/3 day)	-122
	243 days left
You rest 8 hours a day (includes your meals at home, recreation, reading, etc.)	-122
	121 days left
52 Sundays	-52
	69 days left

52 Saturdays	− 52
	17 days left
1/2 hour for lunch (in 50 weeks amounts to 5 days, 2½ hours a week)	− 5
	12 days left
Annual vacation of two working weeks	10
	2 days left
Christmas and New Year's Day	− 2
	0 days left

and the boss concluded, "You do no work at all, and you want me to pay you?"

GAMES NOS. 5, 6

Easy

5. This is an oral game. An elevator operated in a hotel was checked to determine the number of riders. A hotel may bill a rider for the number of times he uses the elevator. A person interested in this statistical operation made his own problem and gave it to his friend. It was like this — listen carefully:

The elevator took on 6 people on the first floor and proceeded to the third floor where 3 people got out and 2 got in. On the next floor, 1 person got on and 5 people got out. On the seventh floor, 1 person got off and 8 people came in. The elevator went down to the fourth floor where 2 people got out. On the third floor, 6 people got on and 2 got off. Back up to the eighth floor, 3 more people got on. Down to the fifth and 1 person got off. Down to the second, and 4 people got off and 3 came on.

Now, the quizzer might ask, "How many people are still on the elevator?" This is, no doubt, what the listeners have been counting. However, the quizzer surprises the listeners by asking how many stops the elevator made after starting from the ground floor. Or, he might ask how many floors were skipped, how many were stopped at, or the total floors covered by the elevator. Or, if he mentions the elevator operator's name in relating the story, he might ask the others what the elevator operator's name was. (See Answers to Games, p. 298.)

Average

6. This game is played by two people. Put 20 dots on the blackboard or on paper. Each player is to erase 1, 2, or 3 in his playing turn. You need not choose a number and stay with it; for instance, you might erase 1 on your first turn, 2 on your second, 1 on your third, and 3 on your fourth turn. The player who takes the last dot loses. The one who knows a certain trick will win every time. Try the game and see if you can find the trick.   (See answer, p. 298.)

Multiplication of Whole Numbers

PUZZLES NOS. 55–72

Easy

55. What two whole numbers multiplied together = 31?

56. How much is $9 \times 8 \times 7 \times 6 \times 5 \times 4 \times 3 \times 2 \times 1 \times 0$?

57. Why is twice 10 like 2 times 11?

58. On one shelf of a bookcase are 4 books, each of which contains 248 pages. How many pages are between the first and last book?

59. Tom is carrying a bag of apples. Jim is carrying 10 bags. All the bags are the same size, but Tom's load is 30 times heavier than Jim's. Why?

60. Each of the Smith brothers has as many sisters as he has brothers. But each of the Smith sisters has twice as many brothers as she has sisters. How many brothers and sisters are there in the Smith family?

61. How can you express 30, using three equal digits? You may use addition, subtraction, or multiplication. Can you get three different answers using a different digit for each new answer? Remember, the answer in each case must be 30.

62. Write in the missing numbers in these problems:

```
(a)      8 . . 9              (b)              . . .
      ×      . 8                        ×      2 6
        ─────────                         ─────────
         6 4 0 7 2                          2 3 0 4
       4 . . 4 5                          . . .
       ─────────                         ─────────
       4 . . 5 2 2                        . . . 4
```

Average

63. If three cats can catch 3 rats in 3 minutes, how many cats can catch 500 rats in 500 minutes?

64. (*a*) In how many ways may a family of 10 persons seat themselves at the dinner table?

(*b*) How many changes can be made in the arrangement of 5 differently colored Easter eggs, laid in a row?

65. This is a multiplication problem in which some numbers are omitted. Can you write in the missing numbers?

```
            . . 3
     ×    2 . .
     ─────────
       . 1 . 7
       . 7 .
     . 1 4 .
     ─────────
     . 2 5 . . 7
```

66. Write in the missing numbers in this multiplication problem:

```
          . . 7
     × 3 . .
     ─────────
       0 . 3
       . 1 .
     . 5 .
     ─────────
     . 7 . . 3
```

67. Fill in the missing numbers in this multiplication problem. Can you find two different solutions?

```
          . . 5 .
     ×          . .
     ─────────────
       . . . . .
       . . . .
     ─────────────
     8 6 4 5 7
```

Difficult

68. A farmer had his own zoo collection. When the census taker asked him how many birds and how many beasts he had, the farmer replied, "Well, I have 36 heads and 100 feet altogether." The census taker had to figure how many of each

the farmer had. How many birds and how many beasts were there?

69.   6 5 7 4 3 = 26. Write in a +, −, or × sign between each of the above numbers, to reach the proper answer of 26. For example: $6 \times 5 - 7 \times 4 + 3 = 5$, but this is not the correct answer — it should be 26.

70. Figure out the missing numbers:

```
        . . 3
    × . . 3
    ─────────
        3 . .
      . 3 .
      . . 3
    ─────────
    . . . . .
```

71. Write in the missing numbers in this multiplication problem:

```
          3 5 7
    ×       . .
    ─────────────
          . . . .
        . . . .
    ─────────────
      . 5 3 5 .
```

72. Complete this multiplication problem:

```
        . . 7 .
    ×   . 7 .
    ─────────────
      . . . . . .
      . . . 2 .
    8 . 5 .
    ─────────────
    . . . 5 . .
```

FUN NOVELTY NO. 8

Easy

Take all the digits, 1 through 9, omitting 8. Now, what digit, 1 through 9, including 8, don't you like? Suppose it's 5. Take $9 \times 5 = 45$ and multiply (omitting 8)

$$
\begin{array}{r}
1\ 2\ 3\ 4\ 5\ 6\ 7\ 9 \\
\times\ 4\ 5 \\
\hline
6\ 1\ 7\ 2\ 8\ 3\ 9\ 5 \\
4\ 9\ 3\ 8\ 2\ 7\ 1\ 6 \\
\hline
5\ 5\ 5\ 5\ 5\ 5\ 5\ 5\ 5
\end{array}
$$

The result is all 5's — the digit you disliked. The procedure is to take the digit you do not like and multiply it by 9. Then multiply the result by 1 2 3 4 5 6 7 9 and your answer will always be in the digit you do not like, repeated 9 times. Suppose you don't like 3:

$$
\begin{array}{r}
1\ 2\ 3\ 4\ 5\ 6\ 7\ 9 \\
\times\ 2\ 7\quad (9 \times 3) \\
\hline
8\ 6\ 4\ 1\ 9\ 7\ 5\ 3 \\
2\ 4\ 6\ 9\ 1\ 3\ 5\ 8 \\
\hline
3\ 3\ 3\ 3\ 3\ 3\ 3\ 3\ 3\ 3
\end{array}
$$

FUN NOVELTY NO. 9

Easy

Some people in schools always have trouble with the multiplication tables. Two of the most difficult combinations for them to remember are 9×6 and 8×7. Here is a device which may help them.

When you multiply by 9, or any multiple of 9, the sum of the digits in your answer must always add up to 9 or a multiple of 9. Example:

$$
\begin{array}{cc}
9 & 8 \\
\times 6 & \times 7 \\
\hline
54 = 9 \qquad & 56 = 11 \\
\text{(add digits)} & \text{(not 9)}
\end{array}
$$

If a student thought $8 \times 7 = 54$, he knows he is wrong because he is not multiplying by 9, and 54 adds to 9. On the other hand, when he multiplies 9×6 and gets 56, he knows he is wrong because 56 adds to 11. In using multiples of 9, the answer should always add to 9. Try larger numbers:

$$\begin{array}{r} 83 \\ \times\,9 \\ \hline 747 \end{array} = 18 \text{ which is a multiple of 9}$$

Other numbers from the times table:

$$\begin{array}{r} 7 \\ \times\,9 \\ \hline 63 \end{array} = 9 \qquad \begin{array}{r} 8 \\ \times\,9 \\ \hline 72 \end{array} = 9 \qquad \begin{array}{r} 9 \\ \times\,9 \\ \hline 81 \end{array} = 9$$

FUN PROJECT NO. 2

Easy

This trick will give you practice in addition, and you will be able to correct yourself. Steps:

(*a*) Take any two numbers with different figures, like 87; you may also use like figures (except 99).

(*b*) Double the number.

(*c*) Add 4.

(*d*) Multiply by 5.

(*e*) Add 12.

(*f*) Multiply by 10.

(*g*) Subtract 320.

(*h*) Cross out the zeros in your answer or remainder.

(*i*) The number left should be the same one you started with, provided you made no mistakes.

Example: Take the number 38:

$$\begin{array}{r} 38 \\ \times\,2 \\ \hline 76 \\ +\,4 \\ \hline 80 \\ \times\,5 \\ \hline 400 \\ +\,12 \\ \hline 412 \\ \times\,10 \\ \hline 4,120 \\ -\,320 \\ \hline 3,800 \end{array}$$

(strike out your 0's) $3,8\cancel{0}\cancel{0} = 38$

This trick will also work for three-figure numbers, four-figure numbers, etc.

Example:

$$
\begin{array}{r}
4{,}316 \\
\times\,2 \\
\hline
8{,}632 \\
+\,4 \\
\hline
8{,}636 \\
\times\,5 \\
\hline
43{,}180 \\
+\,12 \\
\hline
43{,}192 \\
\times\,10 \\
\hline
431{,}920 \\
-\,320 \\
\hline
431{,}6\cancel{0}\cancel{0} = 4{,}316
\end{array}
$$

FUN NOVELTY NO. 10

Easy

For those who have difficulty with the tables, especially when required to multiply higher combinations like 8 × 7, 9 × 8, etc., here is a novel method which can be understood by all. In this method, a person need not know his 7's, 8's, or 9's multiplication tables.

To multiply 8 × 7, for example, the work will look like this:

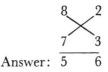

Answer: 5   6

(*a*) First, make a big X or crossed lines on your paper.

(*b*) Next, write the two numbers you are going to multiply at the left-hand side of the lines (like 8 and 7 in the example).

(*c*) To get the numbers you write at the right-hand side of the lines, subtract the top number from 10 (mentally) and the bottom number from 10 (also in your mind), respectively. In the example, $10 - 8 = 2$, so you write 2 to the right of the 8; $10 - 7 = 3$, and you write 3 at the right of the 7.

(*d*) To find the ten's figure in the answer, determine the difference between the figure on either diagonal line ($8 - 3 = 5$ one way, and $7 - 2 = 5$ the other). The tens figure is 5. You will always get the same difference, no matter what diagonal you use.

$$8 \quad 2 \quad (10 - 8 = 2)$$
$$7 \quad 3 \quad (10 - 7 = 3)$$
$$\overline{5} \qquad (\text{difference } 8 - 3 = 5$$
$$7 - 2 = 5)$$

(*e*) To find the units figure in the answer, merely multiply the two right-hand figures together — they will always be simple combinations like 3×2, 2×4, etc. (In the example, $3 \times 2 = 6$, so 6 is the unit's digit.) The final answer is 56.

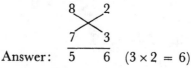

Answer: 5   6 $(3 \times 2 = 6)$

Here is another example:

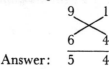

Answer: 5   4

FUN NOVELTY NO. 11

To multiply the following by 3:

$$\overline{1,034,482,758,620,689,655,172,413,793}$$
$$\times 3$$
$$\overline{3,103,448,275,862,068,965,517,241,379}$$

simply take the 3 off the end in the multiplicand and move it to the front to get the answer. In other words, the answer is the same as the multiplicand except that the 3 on the right end is moved to the left end. Try the multiplication and see if you agree.   .

FUN NOVELTY NO. 12

What happens if you multiply all the digits, except 8, by 9?

$$
\begin{array}{r}
1\ 2,\ 3\ 4\ 5,\ 6\ 7\ 9 \\
\times\ 9 \\
\hline
1\ 1\ 1,\ 1\ 1\ 1,\ 1\ 1\ 1
\end{array}
$$

FUN PROJECT NO. 3

Average

The "Lattice Method of Multiplying" is an old method which was used in the schools of England over 400 years ago, for multiplying whole numbers. To multiply 348 by 734, for example:

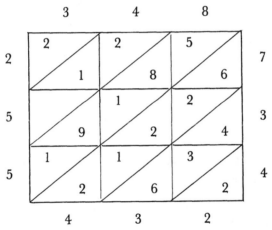

The multiplication was done on a form similar to the above. The multiplicand was written on top and the multiplier was written at the right-hand side (348 and 734, respectively).

Each of the factors is multiplied and the complete product recorded in the appropriate square; e.g., multiply the 8×4 squares to get 32, which is recorded in the square that is common to the column for 8 and the row for 4. Numbers recorded to the right of the diagonal lines are units numbers; those recorded to the left of the slant lines are tens. Example:

8 × 4   8   (column)

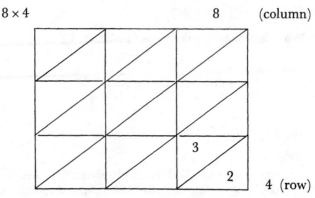

4 (row)

You need go only as high as the tens digit because $9 \times 9 = 81$, and those are the highest two factors you would need to multiply. Multiply 4×4, 4×3, 3×8, 3×4, 3×3, 7×8, 7×4, and 3×7 in any order. Put the results in the proper squares to complete the multiplication. The result should match the example given.

Now, to get the answer to the problem, the sums of the figures in the diagonal columns are then obtained, beginning at the lower-right corner. The right-hand diagonal column has only one figure: 2. Therefore, 2 is written as the sum at the bottom. The next diagonal column contains 6, 3, and 4, which add to 13. Write 3 and carry 1 to the next column. After all diagonal columns are added and placed on the bottom and left-hand side, you merely read the number appearing for the answer. Example:

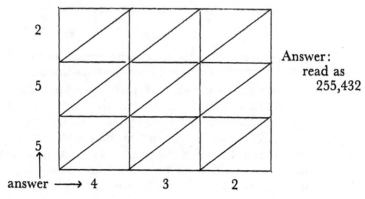

Answer:
read as
255,432

Check by multiplying 348 × 734 the regular way.
Here is another example: multiply 1,345 × 719:

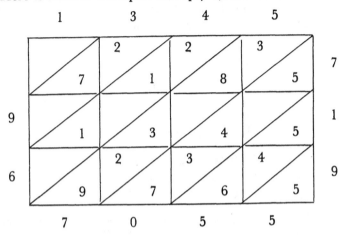

The answer is 967,055.

Try other problems until you can multiply rapidly and with ease, using this method. This affords you excellent practice with the multiplication tables.

FUN PROJECT NO. 4

Average

This is a shorter and faster method of multiplying whole numbers. It takes practice to become proficient in this procedure, and necessitates merely an understanding of our system — all additions are done in the mind. Example:

Step 1. Multiply units digits together. Write the 0 in the units column and carry 2 to the tens column.

$$
\begin{array}{r}
8\ 3\ 4 \\
\times 7\ 1\ 5 \\
\end{array}
$$

$$
\begin{array}{r}
8\ 3\ 4 \\
| \\
7\ 1\ 5 \\
\hline
0 \\
\end{array}
$$

Step 2. To find the tens digit in your answer, multiply 3×5 and 1×4 and add these together (ones × tens = tens) to get 19, and add the 2 you carried. This gives you 21; write down the 1 and carry 2 to the hundreds column.

$$
\begin{array}{ccc}
8 & 3 & 4 \\
 & \diagdown\!\!\diagup & \\
7 & 1 & 5 \\
\hline
 & 1 & 0
\end{array}
$$

Step 3. To find the hundreds digit in your answer, multiply

$$5 \times 8 \quad \text{(ones × hundreds)}$$
$$7 \times 4 \quad \text{(hundreds × ones)}$$
$$1 \times 3 \quad \text{(tens × tens = hundreds)}$$

Add all these results together to get 71, plus 2 to carry from the tens digit, giving the grand total of 73. Write down the 3 and carry the 7 to the thousands column:

$$
\begin{array}{ccc}
8 & 3 & 4 \\
\diagdown\!\!\times\!\!\diagup & & \\
7 & 1 & 5 \\
\hline
3 & 1 & 0
\end{array}
$$

Step 4. To get the thousands digit in your answer:

$$\text{multiply} \quad 1 \times 8 \ \text{(tens × hundreds)}$$
$$7 \times 3 \ \text{(hundreds × tens)}$$

and add these results together to get 29, plus 7 to carry from the hundreds digit, making a grand total of 36. Write down the 6 and carry the 3 to the ten thousands column

$$
\begin{array}{cccc}
 & 8 & 3 & 4 \\
 & & \diagdown\!\!\diagup & \\
 & 7 & 1 & 5 \\
\hline
6 & 3 & 1 & 0
\end{array}
$$

Step 5. To find the last 2 digits in your answer, multiply

7×8 (hundreds × hundreds) and get 56, plus 3 to carry, giving you 59.

$$
\begin{array}{r}
8\ 3\ 4 \\
| \\
\times 7\ 1\ 5 \\
\hline
5\ 9\ 6,3\ 1\ 0
\end{array}
$$

Check the regular way. Although this method seems lengthy, with practice you'll find it is faster than the regular method. Practice this method until you can do it with accuracy and speed.

FUN NOVELTY NO. 13

Average

Here is a quick way to multiply two-digit whole numbers which meet certain qualifications; e.g., 34×36 can be computed faster by this method. This procedure works only if the units digits of both factors add to 10 and the tens digit are the same.

$$
\begin{array}{r}
3\ 6 \\
\times 3\ 4 \\
\hline
\end{array}
$$

In this example, $6 + 4 = 10$, and the tens digit is 3. Now, to get the answer, merely multiply the tens digits together, but always thinking of one of the like digits as being one higher in value. In this case, think of one of the 3's as a 4; then multiply $3 \times 4 = 12$ and place 12 below in the answer. Multiply the units digit as they appear, changing nothing ($6 \times 4 = 24$), and place the result below in the answer:

$$
\begin{array}{r}
\text{(think of 3 as 4} \qquad 3\ 6 \\
\text{when multiplying)} \qquad \times 3\ 4 \\
\hline
1\ 2\ 2\ 4
\end{array}
$$

Let's take another example:

$$
\begin{array}{r}
8\ 2 \\
\times 8\ 8 \\
\hline
\end{array}
$$

The tens digits are both 8's and the units digits add to 10 ($8 + 2$), so the short method will work in this problem.

```
(think of 8            8 2
   as a 9)            ×8 8
            Answer: 7 2 1 6
```

Another example:

```
(think of 9 as a 10)     9 5   (9's are alike)
                        ×9 5   (5+5 = 10)
                        9 0 2 5
```

Check these examples by regular multiplication.

Remember, this trick works only when the factors of the multiplication problem contain two digits each. The answer must always have 4 digits, and there must be two digits obtained from the multiplication of the tens digits, and two digits from the multiplication of the units digits.

```
        x x
        x x
      _____
      x x x x
```

You are probably wondering if this is important. Well, it is important whenever the units digits are 9 and 1, which add to 10, but give only one digit in the answer when multiplied $(9 \times 1 = 9)$. Now, I just said you must have two digits together. Thus, to correct for this, put a 0 in front of the 9 (09) in the answer. This happens only when the units digits are 9 and 1. Example:

```
      8 1              3 1              9 1
     ×8 9             ×3 9             ×9 9
     _____            _____            _____
     7 2 0 9          1 2 0 9          9 0 0 9
```

Check by long multiplication.

FUN PROJECT NO. 5

Average

Here is a quick way to multiply by 11 — you can do it in your mind. You can also multiply 11 by any number of digits; however, the greater the digit, the more difficult to do mentally. Let's start with an easy one, multiplying 11 by a two-digit number:

$$
\begin{pmatrix}
\text{x} & \text{x} \\
\times 1 & 1 \\
\hline
\text{x} \quad \text{x} & \text{x}
\end{pmatrix}
$$

The answer will most likely consist of three digits. To get the units digit in the answer, merely copy the same units digit in the other factor of the multiplication problem (other than 11). To get the hundreds digit in the answer, copy the tens digit from the same factor. To get the middle, or the tens digit in the answer, add the two digits in this same factor (not 11). Example:

$$
\begin{pmatrix}
3 & 5 \\
\times 1 & 1 \\
\hline
3 \quad 8 & 5
\end{pmatrix}
$$

$$
\begin{array}{r}
3 \quad 5 \\
\times 1 \quad 1 \\
\hline
3 \; [8] \; 5
\end{array}
$$

(found by adding $3 + 5 = 8$ from the top factor

$$
\begin{array}{r}
7 \quad 2 \\
\times 1 \quad 1 \\
\hline
7 \; [9] \; 2
\end{array}
$$

$(7 + 2 = 9$ from top factor)

When you add the digits of the non-11 factor, the result might be larger than 9. If this be the case, merely carry the 1 to the next digit in the answer or hundreds digit. Example:

$$
\begin{array}{r}
3 \quad 7 \\
\times 1 \quad 1 \\
\hline
4 \quad 0 \quad 7
\end{array}
$$

$(3 + 7 = 10$, so put down the 0 and carry the 1)

(This should be a 3, but 1 to carry makes 4)

$$
\begin{array}{r}
9 \quad 8 \\
\times 1 \quad 1 \\
\hline
1 \quad 0 \quad 7 \quad 8
\end{array}
$$

$(9 + 1$ to carry $= 10)$ $9 + 8 = 17$ (carry 1)

Try your own examples and check by regular multiplication.

Now, let's try something a little more advanced, and multiply 11 by larger-digit factors. The procedure is the same, but one must be careful about their carrying. Example:

$$\left(\begin{array}{ccc} 3 & 4 & 5 \\ & \times 1 & 1 \\ \hline 3 & & 5 \end{array}\right)$$

Now, to get the middle digits, first add the tens and units digits to get the tens digit in the answer. Next, add the hundreds digit and tens digit to get the hundreds digit in the answer.

$$\left(\begin{array}{ccc} 3 & 4 & 5 \\ & 1 & 1 \\ \hline 3 & 7 & 9 & 5 \end{array}\right) \qquad \left(\begin{array}{ccc} 6 & 2 & 7 \\ & 1 & 1 \\ \hline 6 & 8 & 9 & 7 \end{array}\right)$$

$(3+4 = 7)$ $(4+5 = 9)$ $(6+2)$ $(2+7)$

Again, there is the problem of carrying when two digits add to 10 or more. Merely carry 1 to the next digit in the answer as you did with the two-factor multiplication. Let's see some examples:

$$\begin{array}{r} 8\ 7\ 5 \\ \times 1\ 1 \\ \hline 9\ 6\ 2\ 5 \end{array}$$

Answer:

The 2 in the answer is found by adding $7+5 = 12$. Put down the 2 and carry 1 to the next digit. Next, $8+7 = 15$, plus 1 to carry $= 16$. Put down 6 and carry 1 to the last digit. Bring down the 8 from the top factor, and add the 1 carried which makes 9.

Another example:

$$\begin{array}{r} 4\ 8\ 9\ 2 \\ \times 1\ 1 \end{array}$$

Answer: $5\ 3\ 8\ 1\ 2$—(just bring down)

$(9+2 = 11)$

$(4+1 = 5)$ $(9+8 = 17,\ \text{plus}\ 1 = 18)$

$(4+8 = 12,\ \text{plus}\ 1 = 13)$

This method is very simple to use.

FUN PROJECT NO. 6

Average

Here is a quick way to multiply like numbers together, when the numbers end in a 5 and have two digits (numbers like 15, 25, 35, 45, 85, 95, etc.). To multiply 65 × 65, for example:

$$
\begin{array}{r}
6\ 5 \\
\times 6\ 5 \\
\hline
4\ 2\ 2\ 5
\end{array}
$$

(*a*) Multiply the units digits together (5 × 5 = 25) and put 25 in the answer (it will always be 25), as the two right-hand figures.

(*b*) To get the two left-hand figures in your answer, multiply the tens digits together, and add the tens digit to this product to get the two left-hand figures which go in the final answer.

$6 \times 6 = 36 \quad +6 = 42$ (put 42 in answer)

$$
\begin{array}{r}
6\ 5 \\
\times 6\ 5 \\
\hline
4\ 2\ \ \ 2\ 5
\end{array}
\quad 5 \times 5 = 25
$$

$6 \times 6 = 36 \quad +6 = 42$

Try another example.

FUN NOVELTY NO. 14

Average

Here is the way some Russian peasants still multiply. To multiply 49 × 28, they double 28 and halve 49. The process is continued until you get down to 1 on one of the factors (the one you halve). The fractions are ignored each time.

49	24 (half)	12	6	3	1
28	56 (double)	112	224	448	896

Now, to get the answer, merely add the figures in the lower row, which stand under odd numbers, thus:

$$28 + 448 + 896 = 1,372$$

Try another: 123×85

Halve	123	61	30	15	7	3	1
Double	85	170	340	680	1,360	2,720	5,440

Add:
$$\begin{array}{r} 85 \\ 170 \\ 680 \\ 1,360 \\ 2,720 \\ 5,440 \\ \hline 10,455 \end{array}$$

Our way is much shorter.

FUN NOVELTY NO. 15

Average

Notice the interesting pattern which appears in these multiplications. Take two like numbers:

$$\begin{array}{r} 40 \\ \times\, 40 \\ \hline 1,600 \end{array}$$

Now take two numbers, one above 40 and one below 40:

$$\begin{array}{r} 41 \\ \times\, 39 \\ \hline 369 \\ 123 \\ \hline 1,599 \end{array}$$ Down 1 (1 less than 1,600)

Take two numbers, one 2 above 40 and one 2 below 40:

$$\begin{array}{r} 38 \\ \times\, 42 \\ \hline 76 \\ 152 \\ \hline 1,596 \end{array}$$ Down 3 (3 less than the

last answer, 1,599)

Take two numbers, one 3 above 40 and one 3 below 40:

$$
\begin{array}{r}
37 \\
\times\, 43 \\
\hline
111 \\
148 \\
\hline
1,591 \\
\end{array}
$$

1,591   Down 5 (5 less than last
answer of 1,596)

Now you begin to see a pattern with each answer being 1, 3, 5, 7, etc. (odd numbers) less than the previous answer, depending upon how many numbers away the present factors are from the beginning factors (40, in this example). To begin with, both factors must be the same in the multiplication problem, and all deviations from the beginning must be exactly the same. Try this in other factors:

$$
\begin{array}{r}
63 \\
\times\, 63 \\
\hline
189 \\
378 \\
\hline
3,969 \\
\end{array}
\qquad
\begin{array}{r}
64 \\
\times\, 62 \\
\hline
128 \\
384 \\
\hline
3,968 \\
\end{array}
$$

(each factor 1 away from 63)

3,968 (down 1)

(each factor 2 away from 63)

$$
\begin{array}{r}
65 \\
\times\, 61 \\
\hline
65 \\
390 \\
\hline
3,965 \\
\end{array}
\qquad
\begin{array}{r}
66 \\
\times\, 60 \\
\hline
3,960 \\
\end{array}
$$

(each factor 3 away from 63)

3,960 (down 5)

3,965 (down 3)

You might even be able to predict the answer to the problems without multiplying — just note the pattern.

$$
\begin{array}{r}
83 \\
\times\, 77 \\
\hline
\end{array}
$$

We know $80 \times 80 = 6,400$. We know the pattern goes down 1, 3, 5, 7, 9, etc., and that the factors are 3 away from 80. Thus, $1 + 3 + 5 = 9$ away from the answer of 6,400 — deduct 9 and the answer is 6,391.

FUN NOVELTY NO. 16

Average

The reappearing multiplicand:

$$2{,}178 \times 4 = 8{,}712 \qquad 1{,}089 \times 9 = 9{,}801$$

FUN NOVELTY NO. 17

Average

These would be classified under mathematical oddities. Notice the interesting patterns in these multiplications:

(a)
$$11 \times 11 = 121$$
$$111 \times 111 = 12321$$
$$1111 \times 1111 = 1234321$$
$$11111 \times 11111 = 123454321$$
$$111111 \times 111111 = 12345654321$$
$$1111111 \times 1111111 = 1234567654321$$
$$11111111 \times 11111111 = 123456787654321$$
$$111111111 \times 111111111 = 12345678987654321$$

(b)
$$1 \times 9 + 2 = 11$$
$$12 \times 9 + 3 = 111$$
$$123 \times 9 + 4 = 1111$$
$$1234 \times 9 + 5 = 11111$$
$$12345 \times 9 + 6 = 111111$$
$$123456 \times 9 + 7 = 1111111$$
$$1234567 \times 9 + 8 = 11111111$$
$$12345678 \times 9 + 9 = 111111111$$
$$123456789 \times 9 + 10 = 1111111111$$

FUN NOVELTY NO. 18

Average

Turn completely around:

$$
\begin{array}{r}
123{,}456{,}789 \\
\times\, 8 \\
\hline
987{,}654{,}312 \\
+\, 9 \\
\hline
987{,}654{,}321
\end{array}
$$

GAMES NOS. 7–12

Easy

7. This is one of the oldest arithmetic games; it probably goes by the name of "Buzz." The rules are: Any number may be "it" — the number which you must not say but for which you substitute the word "buzz." Usually, 7 is "it," and you substitute "buzz" for all 7's, all multiples of 7, or whenever a 7 appears.

This game may be played by the whole class in a school, by a few people, at parties, etc — the more the merrier. Someone starts the game by saying "1," the next one says "2," and you go right around the group. When someone fails to substitute "buzz" in its proper place, or puts it in the wrong place, or just says the wrong number, he or she is out (if the students are standing around the room, the one who misses takes his seat.)

The counting should go: "1, 2, 3, 4, 5, 6, *buzz*, 8, 9, 10, 11, 12, 13, *buzz* (14 is a multiple of 7, i.e., 7×2), ... 55, *buzz* (56 = 7×8), *buzz* (57), 58, 59, 60, 61, 62, *buzz* (7×9), 64, 65, 66, *buzz*, 68, 69, *buzz* (70), *buzz* (71), *buzz* (72), *buzz* (73), *buzz* (74), *buzz* (75), *buzz* (76), *buzz buzz* (for 77), *buzz* (78), *buzz* (79), 80, 81, 82, 83, *buzz* (84), 85, etc."

When the game reaches the higher numbers and the players are required to remember the multiples of 7 faster, they begin to miss quickly. When you reach numbers like 256, it is more difficult to picture mentally if 7 divides evenly into 256. The faster the players are required to answer, the more difficult the game grows. The person remaining in the game is winner.

Variety is obtained by using other numbers for "it." For example, 3 would be rather difficult because you would have more buzzes: "1, 2, *buzz*, 4, 5, *buzz*, 7, 8, *buzz*, 10, 11, *buzz*, *buzz*, 14, *buzz*, 16, 17, *buzz*, 19, 20, *buzz*, etc."

8. This is a way of guessing not one, but three numbers someone has in mind. The teacher says:

(*a*) Think of any three numbers less than 10.
(*b*) Multiply the first number by 2.
(*c*) Add 5 to the product.
(*d*) Multiply the sum by 5.

(*e*) Add the second number.
(*f*) Multiply by 10 the last result.
(*g*) Add the third number.
(*h*) Tell the answer you have obtained.

The teacher then names the numbers he first had in mind and the order in which he thought of them. How does the teacher do this? (See Answers to Games, p. 298.) Example:

Suppose the numbers were 3, 4, and 5:

(*a*) 3, 4, 5
(*b*) $\begin{array}{r} 3 \\ \times 2 \\ \hline 6 \end{array}$
(*c*) $\begin{array}{r} +5 \\ \hline 11 \end{array}$
(*d*) $\begin{array}{r} \times 5 \\ \hline 55 \end{array}$
(*e*) $\begin{array}{r} +4 \\ \hline 59 \end{array}$
(*f*) $\begin{array}{r} \times 10 \\ \hline 590 \end{array}$
(*g*) $\begin{array}{r} +5 \\ \hline \end{array}$
(*h*) $\overline{595}$

The teacher claims your numbers were first 3, second 4, and third 5.

9. This game will give a person's age as well as the month in which he was born. Here are the steps:

(*a*) Take the month of your birthday, counting January as 1, February as 2, etc.

(*b*) Multiply by 2.
(*c*) Add 5.
(*d*) Multiply by 50.
(*e*) Add your age.
(*f*) Subtract 365 for the days of the year.
(*g*) Add 115.
(*h*) Tell the sum of *g*.

The result tells your age and the month in which you were born. Example: Suppose I was born in April and I am 32 years old.

$$
\begin{array}{r}
\text{April} = 4 \\
\times 2 \\
\hline
8 \\
+5 \\
\hline
13 \\
\times 50 \\
\hline
650 \\
+32 \\
\hline
682 \\
-365 \\
\hline
317 \\
+115 \\
\hline
432
\end{array}
$$

432   4 for April and 32 is the age.

Average

10. This is a card trick combined with mathematics, so you need a deck of cards. A teacher tells her class to:

(*a*) Pick a card from the deck without letting anyone see it.

(*b*) Double the numerical value of the card (i.e., the 8 of spades counts as 8, a Jack is 11, a Queen is 12, a King is 13, and an Ace is 1).

(*c*) Add 1.

(*d*) Multiply by 5.

(*e*) Add 6, 7, 8, or 9, depending upon the suit of the card (use this as your guide: clubs = 6, diamonds = 7, hearts = 8, and spades = 9).

(*f*) Tell the teacher your answer.

The teacher will immediately tell you the first card you

picked. How does the teacher do it? Suppose your card was the 8 of hearts:

(a)	8
(b)	× 2
	16
(c)	+ 1
	17
(d)	× 5
	85
(e) Heart = 8	+ 8
	93

(f) The teacher will immediately say your card is the 8 of hearts — how does she know? (See answer, p. 299.)

11. This is one of the best numerical manipulation games of all. A person will select a word from any textbook of the reading variety, then

(a) The person selects any page from the book, then any line from the top 9 lines of the page; next, he selects a word from any of the first 9 words on the line he selected. This is the secret which the teacher will uncover.

(b) Multiply the page number by 2.

(c) Multiply by 5.

(d) Add 20.

(e) Add the number of the line on which the word appears.

(f) Add 5.

(g) Multiply by 10.

(h) Add a number equal to the position of the word in that line (i.e., in the last sentence, "equal" is the fourth word, so add 4).

(i) The teacher asks for the result and immediately reads from the book the word you selected.

Suppose we take a sentence from (say) page 287, "The earliest book on arithmetic printed in England was the Grounde of Artes, by M. Robert Record, Doctor of Physics; first issued in 1540, it was republished in numerous editions until 1699."

Take the word "editions" which appears here on (say) line 4 and is word number 7 on this line.

(a)   287
(b)   × 2
      ―――
      574
(c)   × 5
     ―――
    2,870
(d)   + 20
     ―――
    2,890
(e)   + 4 (line)
     ―――
    2,894
(f)   + 5
     ―――
    2,899
(g)   × 10
    ―――――
   28,990
(h)   + 7 (seventh word on line)
   ―――――
(i) 28,997 (result)

The teacher will then identify the word as "editions" from the number given. How does she do it? (See answer, p. 300.)

12. This game is quite similar to previous games — it will give the exact day, month, and year of a person's birth, as well as his present age.

(a) Count January as 1, February as 2, March as 3, etc. Write the day you were born, putting the figures together to form one complete number; e.g., if you were born April 19, the number would be 419 (4 for April and 19 for the day). If you were born September 6, the number would be 96 (9 for September and 6 for the date).

(b) Multiply this number by 2.
(c) Add 5 to the result.
(d) Multiply by 50.
(e) Add your age.
(f) Tell your result.

The teacher then promptly tells the person his age and date of birth. How does he know? (See answer, p. 301.)

Let's try another. Suppose the date of birth is April 19, 1939:

$$
\begin{array}{rl}
(a) & 419 \\
(b) & \times 2 \\
\hline
 & 838 \\
(c) & +5 \\
\hline
 & 843 \\
(d) & \times 50 \\
\hline
 & 42{,}150 \\
(e) & +20 \\
\hline
 & 42{,}170 \\
\end{array}
$$

(f) From this result the teacher tells you your age and the date and year of your birth.

Division of Whole Numbers

PUZZLES NOS. 73–90

Easy

73. Six ears of corn are in a hollow stump. How long will it take a squirrel to carry them all out if he takes out 3 ears a day?

74. A mother had 5 potatoes and 6 children. How can she divide the potatoes equally? (Do not use fractions.)

75. If it takes one minute to make each cut, how long will it take to cut a 10-foot pole into 10 equal pieces?

76. If you had in your dresser drawer 18 green socks and 20 red socks, and you reach into the drawer at night with no light on, how many socks must you take out to be sure of getting a matching pair?

77. Can you make eight 8's equal 1,000, using division?

78. Fill in the missing numbers in this division problem.

```
        x x
      ____
5x)1 x x x
   x 5 x
   _____
     x x x
     4 0 0
```

Average

79. This is one of my favorite puzzles. How can you put 21 pigs in 4 pigpens and still have an odd number of pigs in each pen? You may put the same number of pigs in each pen, but the number in each pen must always be odd. Example:

I	II	III	IV
5	5	5	6

wrong

Although this does add to 21 pigs, pen IV has 6 pigs in it; this is an even number and, thus, it is wrong. How can this problem be solved?

80. How can you divide 12 in half and get 7?

81. If you divide 349 by 7, you will have a remainder:

```
       49
     ____
7)349
   28
   ___
    69
    63
    ___
     6 (remainder)
```

How can you rearrange the dividend in such a way that it will be divisible by 7?

For example: Take 349, make it 394, then divide:

$$\begin{array}{r} 56 \\ 7)\overline{394} \\ 35 \\ \hline 44 \\ 42 \\ \hline 2 \end{array}$$

This does not work because you still have a remainder. You have to use the digits 349 but you can rearrange them. How can the division by 7 be accomplished and still have no remainder?

82. Seven good friends dine in the same restaurant. All are eating there today; however, all do not eat in this restaurant every day.

> The first man eats there every day.
> The second man eats there every other day.
> The third man eats there every 3 days.
> The fourth man eats there every 4 days.
> The fifth man eats there every 5 days.
> The sixth man eats there every 6 days.
> The seventh man eats there every 7 days.

When the friends again all appear in this restaurant on the same day, they will have a big celebration. How many days from today will this celebration take place?

83. What number leaves a remainder of 1 when divided by 2, 3, 4, 5, or 6 and no remainder when divided by 7?

84.   1 2 3 4 5 6 7 8 = 9. Using all digits from 1 to 8 and all 4 processes — addition, subtraction, multiplication, and division — get a result of 9. The digits 1 to 8 must be used exactly as appear above, and one operational sign must be put between each digit. Example:

$$1 + 2 \times 3 \div 4 \times 5 + 6 - 7 \times 8 = 9$$

This is wrong, of course, because the answer is not 9. To get the answer, the problem must be worked in the order in which the digits appear rather than by the correct rules of algebra.

85.

```
            1 x x
      215)x x x x x
         x x x
        ─────
         x 5 x 9
         x 5 x 5
        ─────
           x 4 x
           x 4 x
          ─────
```

This is a division problem with some numbers omitted. Can you supply the missing numbers?

86.

```
          x 5 2 x
      x)x 4 x x 9
```

What numbers are omitted in this problem? Fill them in.

Difficult

87. A group of friends planned to meet for lunch each week. There were 21 friends in all, and the restaurant could not accommodate more than 5 at any one time because of the size of the table and because all friends wanted to sit together. They decided that 5 different groups would meet each week, so long as they did so without forming exactly the same group of 5 on any two occasions. How long will it take before all possible combinations of 5 friends would have lunched together?

88. When membership in the United Nations had grown to 82 members, there was talk of enlarging the 11-member U.N. Security Council. Five countries had permanent seats on the Council. The other six representatives were elected for two-year terms. If no member were elected more than once, how long would it have been before every U.N. member nation had had an opportunity to be represented on the Security Council?

89. Solve or simplify the following:

$$6 \times 8 \div 12 + 3 \times 24 - 12 \div 6 + 8 = \quad ?$$

(This problem is also under Algebra.)

90. A man lost an important paper, bearing figures he had worked out. He found the paper, but all the figures but one

were illegible. However, from this one figure he managed to reconstruct the problem. Can you?

```
           x x 8 x x
        _____
  x x )x x x x x x x x
       x x x
       _____
             x x
             x x
             _____
             x x x
             x x x
             _____
```

Put in numbers for the x's to make a perfectly good division problem.

FUN PROJECT NO. 7: A NEW WAY TO CHECK PROBLEMS

Easy

Another way to check the four fundamental processes is by casting out 9's. Most textbooks do not describe this method. We shall talk about checking problems here, showing you how to check additions, subtractions, multiplications, and divisions of whole numbers by casting out 9's.

A. Addition

Normally, to check addition, we add in the reverse direction. When we speak of casting out 9's, we generally mean to discard all sums adding to 9. We add the individual digits of each number, and keep adding until only one digit remains; if this is a 9, we cast it out and have 0. We check our problem's casting-out-9's with the answer's casting-out-9's to see if they agree. This is the general procedure for all four fundamental procedures. Now, in addition, we cast out 9's in each individual addend, add these results, and again cast out 9's to come up with one digit remaining. We also cast out 9's in the sum. If both results agree, most likely the addition has been done properly. This can best be illustrated by an example. Check the following problem by casting out 9's:

$$634 = 6+3+4 = 13 = \qquad (\ 4)$$
$$237 = 2+3+7 = 12 = \qquad (\ 3)$$
$$891 = 8+9+1 = 18 = \qquad (\ 0)$$
$$483 = 4+8+3 = 15 = \qquad (\ 6)$$
$$\underline{649} = 6+4+9 = 19 = 10 = \qquad (\ 1)$$
$$\overline{2{,}849} = 2+8+4+9 = 23 = 5 \qquad \overline{(14)} = 5$$

Both addends and sum agree, both giving 5 as their check.

$$1{,}938 = 21 = \qquad (\ 3)$$
$$6{,}203 = 11 = \qquad (\ 2)$$
$$1{,}004 = \qquad (\ 5)$$
$$8{,}921 = 20 = \qquad (\ 2)$$
$$\underline{7{,}115} = 14 = \qquad (\ 5)$$
$$\overline{25{,}181} = 17 = 8 \ \text{(final sum)} \qquad \overline{(17)} = 8 \ \text{(final sum)}$$

Both agreed with 8. If the sums do not agree (maybe one is 8 and the other is 7), you may be sure you have made a mistake in your addition somewhere. You always add the digits in each number, regardless of whether the process is subtraction, multiplication, division, or addition. Try other problems and check by this method.

B. Subtraction

To subtract, follow the same procedure except that you add the subtrahend to the remainder to get the minuend in casting out 9's, just as you do in checking ordinarily in subtraction problems.

$$9{,}831$$
$$\underline{6{,}398} = 26 = \qquad (\ 8)$$
$$\overline{3{,}433} = 13 = \qquad (\ 4)$$
$$\overline{9{,}831} = 21 = (3) \qquad \overline{(12)} = (3)$$

$$9{,}000$$
$$\underline{3{,}416} = 14 = 5$$
$$\overline{5{,}584} = 22 = 4 \Big\} = 9 = (0)$$
$$\overline{9{,}000} = \ 9 = (0)$$

Both give 0, thus the problem checks.

C. Multiplication

To check multiplication, we can reverse the factors. We can divide one factor into the product, to get the other factor, or we can cast out 9's. Few people check multiplication by division, but this is a very good method of checking, and also offers you an opportunity to practice on your division. Most people check by interchanging the factors.

```
   638        Check by interchanging:
 × 211
   638                              211
   638                            × 638
  1276                            1688
 134618                            633
                                  1266
                                134618
```

Check by division:
```
                           638
                   211)134618
                       1266
                        801
                        633
                       1688
                       1688
```

To check by casting out 9's, add the digits of both factors, and add the digits of the product. Multiply the result of the factors found by casting out 9's, and add this result until one digit remains. This should agree with that of the product. Let's take the above example:

```
   638 = 17 = ( 8)
   211 =      ( 4)   (8 × 4)
   638          (32) = (5)
   638
  1276
 134618 = 23 = (5) — agrees
           1987 = 25 =   ( 7)
            654 = 15 = × ( 6)
           7948            (42) = (6)
           9935
          11922
        1299498 = 42 = (6)
```

D. Division

We normally check division by multiplying the quotient by the divisor, which gives the dividend. In casting out 9's, we multiply the same way after casting out 9's in the divisor, dividend, quotient, and remainder. Any remainder is added just as it is in regular check of division.

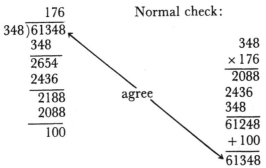

```
        176          Normal check:
    348)61348
        348                              348
        ────                           × 176
        2654                           ─────
        2436                            2088
        ────                           2436
        2188         agree              348
        2088                          ─────
        ────                          61248
         100                         + 100
                                     ─────
                                     61348
```

Casting out 9's:

```
              176 = 14 = (5)
          348)61348 = 22 = (4)              6
(15) = (6)    348                         × 5
              ────                         ────
              2654                          30 = (3)
              2436                  Remainder = (1)
              ────                              (4)
              2188
              2088
              ────
               100 = (1)
```

Casting out 9's, the figure is 4 on the dividend and 4 from the other part of the check. Thus, we know the problem has been correctly worked.

```
9 = (0)    210       = (3)
       162)34171     = 16 = (7)           3
           324                          × 0
           ────                         ────
           177                            0
           162                          + 7
           ────                         ────
           151                           (7)
             0
           ────
           151 = (7)
```

The work of casting out 9's can be further shortened by skipping any 9's or figures whose sum is 9.

The shortened method may be illustrated by an example previously given (in multiplication):

$$
\begin{array}{r}
1987 = (\ 7)\longrightarrow 1\ \underline{9}\ 8\ 7\ \ (\text{only 7 is left}) \\
\times 654 = (\ 6)\longrightarrow (5 \text{ and } 4 = 9, \text{ just skip them}) \\
\hline
7948 \quad (42) = (6) \\
9935 \\
11922 \\
\hline
1299498 = (6)\ (\text{forget all 9's and } 8+1 = 9; \text{ only 2 and 4} \\
= 9 \qquad\qquad\qquad \text{are left, which equals 6})
\end{array}
$$

(forget)

The casting-out-9's method is a novel means of checking problems.

FUN NOVELTY NO. 19

Easy

28. What happens when you divide 987654312 by 8?

$$
\begin{array}{r}
123456789 \\
\hline
8\overline{)987654312}
\end{array}
$$

So, when you divide by 8, the numbers go in order from 1 through 9.

FUN NOVELTY NO. 20

Average

29. Seven boys agreed to work together and share their earnings. When they had accumulated $28, the leader took out his 1/7 share, $13. The other boys argued that $28 \div 7$ is not 13 but 4. The leader said, "I'll prove you are wrong and $28 \div 7$ is 13." Now, watch:

$$
\begin{array}{r}
13 \\
7\overline{)28} \\
7 \\
\hline
21 \\
21 \\
\hline
\end{array}
$$

Steps: (*a*) 7 will not divide into 2, will it? So,

    (*b*)   1
          7)8

    (*c*) $1 \times 7 = 7$.

    (*d*) Subtract and get 21.

    (*e*) Now, 7 goes in 21, 3 times, so the answer is 13.

The boys still did not believe him, so the leader said, "Look, I will prove it to you another way."

$$7 \times 13 = 28$$

Steps: $7 \times 3 = 21$
         $7 \times 1 = \underline{7}$
                28

    13
      7
   —
    21
      7
   —
    28

Or, check it another way.

Let's add 13, seven times: 13
                          13
                          13
                          13
                          13
                          13
                          13
                          —
                          28   because

$21 + 1 = 22 \rightarrow$ [1] 3   Steps: Adding the 3's column gives
$22 + 1 = 23$ 1 3   21, and then going to the 1's
$23 + 1 = 24$ 1 3   column and adding the 1's
$24 + 1 = 25$ 1 3   on, one by one, the total is
$25 + 1 = 26$ 1 3   28.
$26 + 1 = 27$ 1 3
$27 + 1 = 28$ 1 3
                ✓2 1

Answer $= 28$

The leader then walked away with his share, $13.

GAME NO. 13

Average

13. This computation will give you your telephone number:

(*a*) Take 60.
(*b*) Divide by 2.
(*c*) Add your telephone number digits.
(*d*) Subtract 25.
(*e*) Multiply by 3.
(*f*) Subtract 15.
(*g*) Multiply by 2.
(*h*) Divide by 6.
(*i*) The answer is your telephone number.

Example: Suppose my telephone number is 1-1111.

(*a*) Take 60.

$$2\overline{)60}$$
$$30$$

(*b*) Divide by 2 = 30.

(*c*) Add 1-1111 = 11,141.

$$11,111$$

(*d*) Subtract 25 = 11,116.

$$\overline{11,141}$$
$$-25$$

(*e*) Multiply by 3 = 33,348.

$$\overline{11,116}$$
$$\times 3$$

(*f*) Subtract 15 = 33,333.

$$\overline{33,348}$$
$$-15$$

(*g*) Multiply by 2 = 66,666.

$$\overline{33,333}$$
$$\times 2$$

(*h*) Divide by 6 = 11,111.

$$6\overline{)66,666}$$

(*i*) My telephone number is 1-1111.

$$\overline{11,111}$$

Try this on your friends.   (Also shown under Algebra.)

Averages

PUZZLES NOS. 91, 92

Easy

91. The speeds of the cars in a hot-rod race were timed after 3 miles, 4½ miles, and 6 miles. One car averaged 140 mph for

the first 3 miles, 168 mph for the next 1½ miles, and 210 mph for the final 1½ miles. What was his average speed for the 6-mile run?

Average

92. The teacher was angry with Carl. She did not have time to record the students' grades in the grade book last week and she asked the students to keep track of their own homework grades.

This week, when the teacher asked the students to report their grades, Carl could not find his homework papers. He said, "Gee, teacher, I must have lost them!" The teacher retorted: "Well, Carl, just how do you expect me to give you a grade on your report card?" Carl answered, "I do remember this: The grades on four of the six homework papers were 100, 84, 72, 60, and the average of all six papers was 69. The other two papers had identical grades, but I can't remember them."

Can you help Carl and the teacher by ascertaining the grades on the other two homework papers?

FUN PROJECT NO. 8: ELEMENTARY STATISTICS (CENTRAL TENDENCY)

Average

Can you find the mean, mode, and median of these scores on tests taken by a student in school?

64 68 70 73 73 73 75 76 77 82 85 87 92

Most of you probably can't unless you have had some Statistics. The mathematics used in the first course in Statistics given in college requires no more than simple mathematics through the eighth grade. Statistics is the science of collecting and classifying numerical facts in order to show their significance.

The three chief methods for finding the most typical or representative score for a particular group of scores are the mean, median, and mode. The mean is the arithmetical average of a group of numbers. The median is found by finding the middle number in a group of numbers. The mode is the

number appearing most frequently, or the most typical score.
In the example:

$$
\begin{array}{rl}
64 \\
68 \\
70 \\
73 \\
73 & \text{(mode)} \\
73 \\
75 & \text{(median)} \\
76 \\
77 \\
82 \\
85 \\
87 \\
92 \\
\hline
13\,\overline{)995} \\
\hline
76\tfrac{7}{13} & \text{or } 77 \text{ (mean)}
\end{array}
$$

The mean score of these 13 grades is 77 and is found by adding
all 13 numbers and dividing by 13 and rounding off to the
nearest whole number. The median of this example is 75 as
there are six scores above and six scores below 75. If there
were only 12 scores, the median would be represented by the
two numbers in the middle, maybe 76 and 74; then 75 would
be the median. The mode is 73, as it appears three times.

The mean or average is the most used procedure; however,
extreme scores at either end will throw off the central tendency. When extreme scores appear, the median is better as it
is not affected by extreme scores. The mode is rarely used by
itself, but helps in giving a more complete picture of central
tendency.

Most statistics are used for a large number of scores or
frequencies, and statistical methods are very helpful in handling 100 scores or a greater number.

Try this: Take the hourly temperatures given in your daily
newspaper of a particular day and find the mean of these
temperatures as well as the median and mode.

Making Change
PUZZLES NOS. 93–98

Easy

93. I have 2 coins whose sum is 55 cents. One of them is not a 50-cent piece. What coins are they?

94. A man owed $63. He paid his debt with 6 bills. He did not use one-dollar bills. What bills did he use?

95. (*a*) It takes 20 nickels to make one dollar. How can you make $1.00 using 21 coins?

(*b*) How can you make $1.00 using 50 coins?

Average

96.

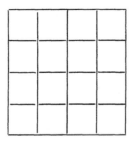

Using 4 pennies, 4 nickels, 4 dimes, and 4 quarters, place them in the squares above in such a manner that no two like coins are next to each other horizontally or vertically on the same straight line. You may use

1 for a penny
5 for a nickel
10 for a dime
25 for a quarter

and in this way you do not need coins. Also, no two like coins should be on the same straight line on the main diagonals only (corner to corner). You may have two like coins together diagonally on the same straight line, as long as they are not on the main diagonal.

97. In how many different ways can you make change for a dollar?

Difficult

98. Two girls were selling candy. They had $1.07 in change to begin. Their first customer said that before he could buy anything, he needed change for half a dollar. One of the girls looked in the change box and said they didn't have the change. Then the customer asked if they had change for a quarter, but again the girl couldn't make change. The customer asked if they had change for a dime — the answer was no again. The girls said they had seven coins in all, but could not even change a nickel. What are the coins the girls had?

GAME NO. 14

Easy

14. You have 5 coins arranged like this:

● ○ ● ○ ●
1 2 3 4 5

The object is to bring three like coins together in a line at the side of the two unlike coins, like this:

You must move two coins next to each other on every move; these two coins may be placed alongside or between the other coins. You can make only four moves.

Chapter III

FRACTIONS

Reducing Fractions

PUZZLES NOS. 99, 100

Easy

99. What fraction is the same, even if you turn it completely upside down?

Average

100. Can you reduce these fractions:

(*a*) 76/95
(*b*) 85/102

FUN NOVELTY NO. 21

Easy

In reducing fractions, you must determine which numbers will divide into both the numerator and denominator evenly. There are many tests of divisibility which can help in the reducing of fractions; here are a few:

(*a*) Any whole number is divisible by 1.

(*b*) If the last digit of a number is divisible by 2, then so is the number itself; all even numbers (2, 4, 6, 8, 0) are divisible by 2. Example: both the numerator and denominator of $\frac{22}{26}$ are divisible by 2 because 2 and 6 are even numbers.

(*c*) Any number is divisible by 3 if the sum of its digits is divisible by 3. Example: $\frac{24}{36}$ is divisible by $\frac{3}{3}$ because 24 = 2 +4 = 6 and 36 = 3 + 6 = 9, and 2)6 and 3)9. Therefore 24/36

————— —————
   3   3

may be reduced by 3/3 for an answer of 8/12 = 2/3.

73

(*d*) Any number may be divided by 4 if the last two figures, the tens and units digit together, are divisible by 4. Example: $\frac{332}{512}$ is divisible by $\frac{4}{4}$ because 32 and 12 are both divisible by 4. Thus 332/512 = 83/128.

(*e*) Any number is divisible by 5 whose right-hand figure is 5 or 0. Example: 125/330 is divisible by 5/5 because the last digits are 5 or 0. Thus, 125/330 = 25/66.

(*f*) Any number may be divided by 6 which is even and the sum of its digits is divisible by 3. Example: 72/108 is divisible by 6/6 because 72 and 108 are even numbers and $7+2 = 9$ and $1+0+8 = 9$, which are divisible by 3. Thus 72/108 = 12/18 = 2/3.

(*g*) The number 7 is skipped here because the directions are too complex to be of much help.

(*h*) Any number is divisible by 8 when its three right-hand figures are divisible by 8 or when there are three 0's. Example: 3432/5000 is divisible by $\frac{8}{8}$ because 432 is divisible by 8 $\left(\frac{8)432}{54}\right)$ and 5000 has three 0's as its last figures. Thus, 3432/5000 must be divisible by 8/8: 3432/5000 = 429/625.

(*i*) Any number is divisible by 9 if the sum of the digits of such a number is divisible by 9. Example: 378/1998 is divisible by 9/9 because $3+7+8 = 18$ and $1+9+9+8 = 27$, and 18 and 27 are divisible by 9. Thus, 378/1998 = 42/222 = 7/37.

(*j*) Any number is divisible by 10 if its right-hand figure is 0. Example: 3020/6310 is divisible by 10/10 because both numbers end in 0's; thus 3020/6310 = 302/631.

(*k*) Any number is divisible by 11 if the difference of the sums of the figures of the odd and even orders is 0 or divisible by 11.

even digits

/　/　/

6　3　6　3　8　3

/　/　/

odd digits

The number 636383 is divisible by 11 because $6+6+8 = 20$ and $3+3+3 = 9$ and $20-9 = 11$ which is divisible by 11.

Similarly, 5313 is divisible by 11 because $5+1 = 6$ and $3+3$ = 6, and their difference is 0.

(*l*) Any number is divisible by 12 if the sum of the digits is divisible by 3 and the two right-hand digits are divisible by 4. Example: 624 is divisible by 12 because $6+2+4 = 12$, which is divisible by 3, and 24 of 6<u>24</u> is divisible by 4.

FUN NOVELTY NO. 22

Average

$$\frac{2\cancel{6}}{\cancel{6}5} = \frac{2}{5} \qquad \frac{1\cancel{6}}{\cancel{6}4} = \frac{1}{4} \qquad \frac{1\cancel{9}}{\cancel{9}5} = \frac{1}{5} \qquad \frac{4\cancel{9}}{\cancel{9}8} = \frac{4}{8} = \frac{1}{2}$$

If you cross off the duplicated digits in these fractions, their values will remain the same. All these fractions actually reduce to the values shown by the normal method of reducing, but here is another way to get the answer without reducing in these special cases. This trick does not always work. Example: $\frac{1\cancel{5}}{\cancel{5}3} = \frac{1}{3}$, which you can see is wrong.

Addition of Fractions

PUZZLES NOS. 101–116

Easy

101. (*a*) How can you make 100 using six 9's?
(*b*) Can you make 100 using only four 9's?

102. The teacher gives a student a sheet of paper $8\frac{1}{2} \times 11$ inches and says, "If you can cut or fold this paper into exactly four pieces, I will give you a quarter." The student does and wins the quarter. Where is the trick in this puzzle?

103. A man on horseback was chased by Indians. Seeing a cave, he rode into it but the Indians saw him and rolled a huge rock into the opening and there was no other way out of the cave. How did he get out?

Average.

104. Two volumes of an encyclopedia are standing side by side, in order, on a bookshelf, Volume I to the left of Volume II. A bookworm eats a hole, starting at page 1 of Volume I, and eats his way in a straight line to the last page of Volume II. If each cover is 1/8 of an inch thick, and each book without the cover is 1 inch thick, how far does the bookworm travel?

105. There is a castle surrounded by water, as shown below.

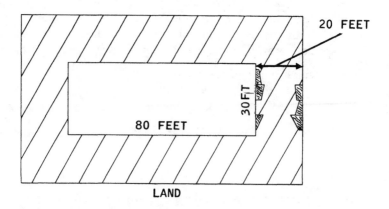

During a storm, the bridge from the land to the castle is washed away. The distance across the water from the land to the castle is 20 feet. A man desiring to cross to the castle found two long boards. One was 19½ feet long and the other was 18 feet long. This posed a problem: How was he to get across the 20 feet of water? His 19½-foot board was not long enough; he could not nail the boards together. He finally figured a way to get across the water. How did he do it?

106. A rich man needed his lawn cut for a big party he was

giving that evening. The lawn was very large. He called an employment agency and three men were sent to him. The first man claimed he could cut the whole lawn in 6 hours; the second man said he could do it in 4 hours, and the third claimed he could cut the grass in 3 hours. It was already mid-afternoon and the grass had to be cut before dinner, so the man said, "I will hire all three of you." Can the men finish the job in time if they all work together? How long will it take them? (This puzzle is also under Algebra.)

107. Rearrange the figures 1, 2, 3, 4, 5, 6, 7, 8, 9, 0 so they add to 100. (This is usually done by using fractions but it can be done without.) How many ways can you use to solve this puzzle?

108. A farmer was asked how many cows he had. He answered, "If one-fourth, one-fifth, and one-sixth of the herd were added together, they would total thirty-seven." How many cows did he have? (Also under Algebra.)

109.   9   9   9   9   9 = 10.

How can you use five 9's to make 10?

110. Can you divide the 9 digits (1 through 9) into two equal parts — one with the odd numbers and the other with the even numbers — so that each part adds to the same total?

Example: $135 + 79 = 246 + 8$
$214 = 254$ (wrong)

Of course, these are not equal. Notice, only the odd digits were used on the left side and the even digits on the right side. You may arrange the digits on each side any way you like. How can you make the two sides give the same result?

111. When Mr. Einstein was asked how many students he had, he replied, "One-half of them study mathematics, one-third of them study geometry, one-seventh of them study chemistry, and there are twenty who do not study at all." How many students did Mr. Einstein have?

Difficult

112. The sum of $2 + 2$ and the product of 2×2 are the same. Cite five more examples of two numbers which give the same result when added and multiplied. You may use whole numbers or fractions.   (Note: $0 \times 0 = 0$ and $0 + 0 = 0$ do not count.)

113. A man passed 1/6 of his life in childhood, 1/12 in youth, and 1/7 in bachelorhood. Five years after he was married, a son was born who died 4 years before his father, at half the age at which his father died. What was the father's age when he died?

114. Can you take the ten figures: 1, 2, 3, 4, 5, 6, 7, 8, 9, and 0 and rearrange them, using one + sign, to make the sum of 1?

115. A man willed his wife 1/3 of his estate, and the remaining 2/3 to his son, should one be born; but in the case of a daughter being born, 2/3 of the estate was to go to the wife and 1/3 to the daughter. After the man's death, twins were born — a boy and a girl. How should the estate be divided in order to carry out the arithmetical relationships prescribed by the will?

116. Can you make a total of 100 using the digits 1 through 9? Use only one + sign in the problem and use each digit only once. Do not use $-$, $\times$, or $\div$ signs.

$$1 \ 2 \ 3 \ 4 + 5 \ 6 \ 7 \ 8 \ 9 = 100$$

Of course, the above work is wrong because the sum is not 100. However, this gives you an idea of what is wanted in this puzzle. You may rearrange the digits anyway you like, and put the + sign wherever you wish, but remember that the sum must be 100.

Subtraction of Fractions

PUZZLES NOS. 117–119

Easy

117. How can you arrange three 8's so that they will equal 7? $8 \ 8 \ 8 = 7$

118. What looks most like half of an apple?

Average

119. Solve the following:

$$25\tfrac{3}{7} - 16\tfrac{3}{8} - 3\tfrac{1}{9} - 2\tfrac{3}{10} = ?$$

Multiplication of Fractions

PUZZLES NOS. 120–133

Easy

120. From what number can you take half and leave nothing?

121. Show how the following can be true:

(*a*) Two-thirds of six is nine.
(*b*) One-half of five is four.
(*c*) Six is one-half of eleven.

122. If a boy and a half can eat a pie and a half in a day and a half, how long will it take 18 boys to eat 18 pies? (A half of a boy is a small boy.)

123. What letter is always nine inches long?

Average

124. How can you add 1/3 of 12 to 4/5 of 7 and get 11 as your answer?

125. Two mothers and two daughters went shopping. After totaling all their purchases, they found they had spent $18 altogether. Yet, each spent the same amount and each spent exactly 1/3 of the total. How was this possible?

126. A farmer died, leaving his 17 horses to his 3 sons. The will stated that 1/2 of the horses must go to his oldest son, 1/3 of the horses to the middle son, and 1/9 of the total horses to his youngest son. But you cannot take 1/2 of 17 horses, 1/3 of 17, or 1/9 of 17, so this posed a problem of how to divide the horses. A kindly friend said that he would lend the boys one

horse. This settled the argument because they now had 18 horses.

$$1/2 \text{ of } 18 = 9$$
$$1/3 \text{ of } 18 = 6$$
$$1/9 \text{ of } 18 = 2$$
$$\overline{17}$$

So when they divided the horses, they found they had used only 17 and had one left over which they immediately returned to their friend. Everyone was happy as they did not really need the extra horse to begin with. Yet they could not divide 17 horses. Where is the fallacy in this problem? What happens to the extra horse?

127. Three men and a dog took a trip in a space ship to a planet called "K." The space ship developed engine trouble and the men found themselves marooned on this planet. Their food supply ran out. There was only one tree on this planet which bore a type of nut. The nuts were the size of apples so the men named them "applenuts." This was the only food they found on the planet. Applenuts were covered with a hard shell, but were soft and chewy inside. The men collected all the applenuts off the tree and were very tired after this chore, so they decided they would divide all the applenuts into three equal parts in the morning.

During the night, one man awakened and, thinking the other two would cheat him, took his 1/3 and, having 1 left over, gave it to the dog. The second man awoke and, also distrusting his companions, took 1/3 of the 2/3 applenuts remaining and had 1 left over which he gave to the dog. About an hour later, the third man awoke and took his 1/3 of the 2/3 of the 2/3 that was left and had one left over which he gave to the dog.

When they got up the next morning, although noting that the pile was much smaller than the night before, none of the men dared to say anything for fear of giving himself away. Each had a guilty conscience. They commenced to divide the remaining applenuts three ways; after dividing them, one was left over, which they gave to the dog.

The question is: How many applenuts were there before the night started?

128. Simplify:

$$\frac{\frac{1}{3} \times 6}{\frac{4}{6} \times \frac{12}{2}} + \frac{3}{4} = ?$$

Difficult

129. Each of these problems is different.

(*a*) What is a third and a half of a third and a half of ten?

(*b*) What is a third and a half of a third, of a half of ten?

(*c*) What is a third and a half of a third of a half of ten?

Being very careful, how many of them can you correctly solve?

130. If $\frac{1}{4}$ of 20 is not 5 but 4, then $\frac{1}{3}$ of 10 should be what? (Also under Algebra.)

131. If 1 watermelon would balance on a scale 2/3 pounds +2/3 of a watermelon, what is the exact weight of 1 watermelon, in pounds?

132. A farmer told two boys they could take apples off his tree, provided neither took more than 20 apples. After a minute, one boy asked, "Have you picked your limit yet?" The other replied, "Not yet, but if I had twice as many as I have now, plus half as many as I have now, I would have the limit." How many did he have? (Also under Algebra.)

133. Joan is 1/6 as old as her father. Joan's father's age, when divided by 2, 3, 4, 6, and 8, leaves one remaining year, but when divided by 5, there is nothing left. How old is Joan?

Division of Fractions
PUZZLES NOS. 134–143

Easy

134. Simplify: $\frac{\frac{3}{7}}{\frac{1}{2}} = ?$

135. Solve the following:

$$\frac{\frac{3}{8} - \frac{1}{12}}{\frac{6}{5} + \frac{3}{10}} = ?$$

Average

136. Can you show four different ways to do this division of a fractions problem: $6 \div \frac{1}{2}$? (Hint: One way, of course, is inversion; but can you arrive at the same answer by three other methods?)

137. A house has a window 8 feet long. If you measured from the top of the window to the ground, you'd find it was 31/42 of the height of the house; but if you measured from the window's lower edge to the top of the house, you would then find the window to be 3/7 of the height of the house. How tall is the house?

138. Solve or simplify the following problem:

$$4\overline{)\phantom{3\overline{)6/8}\qquad +3\overline{)3/16+3}}}$$
$$3\overline{)6/8}\qquad +3\overline{)3/16+3}$$

(Hint: Do not change to decimal but leave as fractions.)

139. $\dfrac{\frac{5}{3} - \frac{3}{7}}{\frac{1}{2} + \frac{1}{11}} = ?$

Difficult

140. Solve the following:

   (*a*) If 3 were equal to 5, what would 4 be equal to?
   (*b*) If 1/2 of 5 were 3, what would 1/3 of 10 be?

(Also under Algebra.)

141. How much is:

$$5 \div 5 \div 5 \div 5 \div 5 \div 1/5 \div 1/5 \div 1/5 =$$

142. A brick weighs 6 pounds plus one-half of its total weight. What is the total weight? (Also under Algebra.)

143. A miller took 1/10 of the meal or flour he ground as his fee. How much did he grind if a customer had exactly one bushel left after the fee had been subtracted? (Also under Algebra.)

FUN NOVELTY NO. 23

Average

The early books on arithmetic gave two ways of dividing fractions. The first method reduced the fractions to common denominators and took the quotient of the numerators. Thus $2/3 \div 3/4 = 8/12 + 9/12 = 8/9$ because $8 \div 9 = 8/9$. In the same way, $33/5 \div 3/5 = 11$ because $33 \div 3 = 11$.

The second method is one of cross multiplication, which involves the same operations that enter into the inverted divisor.

$$2/3 \div 3/4$$

$$\frac{2}{3} \times \frac{3}{4} = \frac{8}{9}$$

$$\frac{33}{5} \times \frac{3}{5} = \frac{165}{15} = 11$$

Chapter IV

DECIMALS

Addition of Decimals
PUZZLES NOS. 144–146

Easy

144. How do you write eleven thousand, eleven hundred and eleven?

145. Jim travels 34.58 miles every day. In his travels, he doesn't notice the traffic lights, for he passes no streets, roads, automobiles, trees, fields or houses. He doesn't fly, walk, run, travel on any animal, ride in any vehicle that runs on wheels, and rarely is seen on a boat. He is not alone in his travels. How does Jim do this?

Average

146. The teacher did not want the students to know his middle initial. The students kept begging him to tell them, and finally the teacher said, "All right. If you figure out this puzzle, you will know my middle initial."

"It is the letter that is not found in the numbers from 1 to 999, but is found in all mixed decimals like 23.68 or 1.7."

What is the teacher's middle initial? How did you arrive at this answer?

The problem may be stated in another way: "It is the letter not found in the numbers from 1 to 999, but is found in all numbers from 1,000 to 1,000,000."

GAME NO. 15

Easy

15. This mathematical calculation will tell you someone's house number and his age. Also, this work will give you your own house number and age, if you like.

(*a*) Take your house number; double it.

(*b*) Add 5.

(*c*) Multiply by 50.

(*d*) Add your age.

(*e*) Add 365 for the number of days in a year.

(*f*) Subtract 615.

(*g*) Point off for dollars and cents (or put in a decimal point).

(*h*) The dollars will be your house number, and the cents will be your age.

Example: 700 is the house number, and I am 30 years old.

$$
\begin{array}{r}
700 \\
\times\,2 \\
\hline
1{,}400 \\
+5 \\
\hline
1{,}405 \\
\times\,50 \\
\hline
70{,}250 \\
+30 \\
\hline
70{,}280 \\
+365 \\
\hline
70{,}645 \\
-615 \\
\hline
70{,}030
\end{array}
$$

70,030 — $700.30

Try this on your friends. (Also solved by Algebra under the Algebra section.)

Subtraction of Decimals

PUZZLES NOS. 147–150

Easy

147. Solve the following twice:

$$6\tfrac{3}{8} - 4.175 = ?$$

(*a*) The first answer should be in decimals.

(*b*) The second answer should be in fractions.

Average

148. A man enters a store and addresses the proprietor: "Give me as much money as I have with me now, and I will spend $10 in your store." The proprietor agrees, and the man spends the money.

He goes into a second store and says: "Give me as much money as I have with me now, and I will spend $10 in your store." The same thing happens.

He goes into a third store and repeats the question, after which he has no money left. How much money did he start with? (Also under Algebra.)

149. A bottle and a cork cost $1.10. The bottle cost $1.00 more than the cork. How much does the cork cost? How much does the bottle cost? (Also under Algebra.)

150. How can you make five 5's equal 6, using decimals and + and − signs?

Multiplication of Decimals

PUZZLES NOS. 151–157

Easy

151. Simplify: $.1 \times .2 \times .3 \times .4 \times .5 \times .6 = ?$

152. What three figures, multiplied by 4, will make precisely 5? Can you give a second answer?

Average

153. When we multiply:

$$\begin{array}{r} 16.5 \\ \times\, 12.5 \\ \hline 825 \\ 330 \\ 165 \\ \hline \end{array}$$

our answer is: 206.25

However, when we multiply:

$$\begin{array}{r} 16\tfrac{1}{2} \\ \times\, 12\tfrac{1}{2} \\ \hline \end{array}$$

$8\tfrac{1}{4}$	$(1/2 \times 16\tfrac{1}{2})$
$6\tfrac{1}{4}$	$(1/2 \times 12\tfrac{1}{2})$
32	(16×2)
16	(16×1)

$$206\tfrac{1}{2}$$

we get 206½ or 206.5, which is not the same as the decimal answer. Where is the fallacy in the fraction problem work? What has happened to the other 1/4?

154. A man went to a machine shop to have a broken chain repaired. He has 5 separate pieces of chain to be welded together, and each piece has 3 links attached. The rate for such a job is: 1 cent to cut a link, 2 cents to weld a link. The machinist claimed he would have to cut and weld 1 link on each of 4 separate pieces to form the 5 pieces into one chain. He also said he could not just weld the separate pieces together but must have one link to put between each separate piece to do the job properly. The drawing explains the work necessary.

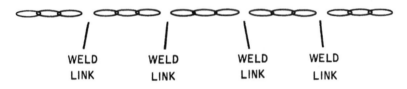

The cost would be 12 cents — 1 cent for each link that was cut to use for welding, and 2 cents for each welding job.

4 links	4 cents
4 welds	8 cents
total	12 cents

The man argued, "No, you are wrong. The cost would be only 9 cents, if you do the job differently." How should the machinist repair the chain so that it will cost only 9 cents?

155. To make sure his son did good work in arithmetic, a father told him one night that he would give him 8 cents for every problem he got right in his homework, and deduct 5 cents for every one he missed. There were 26 problems on the homework assignment. The next evening, the father asked his son how much he owed him and the son said, "You owe me nothing, Pop, we are even." How many problems did the boy do correctly, and how many did he miss? (Also under Algebra.)

156. Jack spent 25 cents for 25 articles of drawing supplies. He bought four different articles:

> Paper at 2 sheets for 1 cent.
> Pens at 1 cent each.
> Pencils at 2 for 5 cents.
> Erasers at 5 cents.

How many of each did he buy?

Difficult

157. A farmer sells chicken eggs, duck eggs, and turkey eggs. A customer wants to buy a total of 22 eggs. He has 22 cents to spend. Chicken eggs cost 1/2 cent each; duck eggs cost 2 cents each; and turkey eggs cost 3 cents each. How many of each kind can he buy? (Also under Algebra.)

Division of Decimals

PUZZLES NOS. 158–164

Easy

158. Simplify and find the answer to the nearest hundredth:

$$.67/3.2$$

Average

159. How may three 7's be arranged so they will equal 20? You may use 7's only, and nothing else.

160. Find the answer to this problem to the nearest tenth:

$$\frac{6.314+7\frac{3}{4}}{6\frac{1}{2}-3.615} \div \frac{1.89}{3.42}$$

161. Mr. Jones has a large fish pond in his back yard. One day, using fish nets, he caught a big lot of fish — altogether 135. Now Mr. Jones wanted to know about how many fish were actually in his pond, so he put tags on the 135 and threw them back in. Later, with the aid of fish nets, he caught 247 fish. In this catch were 35 tagged fish. With this information he determined the approximate number of fish in his pond. Approximately how many fish were there?

Difficult

162. What number, added to itself once or several times, will give a total having the same digits as that number but differently arranged, and after the sixth addition will give a total of all 9's?

163. Can you make 100, using only four 7's and decimals?

164. Using the digits 1 through 9, inclusive, once only, arrange them in such a way that you get the value of 1/2.

FUN NOVELTY NO. 24

Average

The fraction 1/7, when changed to a decimal, gives

$$\frac{.142857142857142857142857}{7\,)\,1.000000000000000000000000}$$

Notice, the same digits 142857 keep repeating themselves when we divide by 7. The division never comes out even.

Now, suppose we take the same digits and multiply them by 2, 3, 4, 5, 6, and 7:

$$142857 \times 2 = 285714$$
$$142857 \times 3 = 428571$$
$$142857 \times 4 = 571428$$
$$142857 \times 5 = 714285$$
$$142857 \times 6 = 857142$$
$$142857 \times 7 = 999999$$

Notice, we always get the same digits when we multiply by 2, 3, 4, 5, and 6. Also, these digits always run in the same order, but starting at a different place.

$$142857 \times 2 = 285714$$
$$/(\text{starts over again})$$
$$142857 \times 5 = 714285$$

Also notice when we multiply by 7, we get all 9's.

Chapter V

PERCENTAGES

Percentage Missing

PUZZLE NO. 165

Easy

165. How much is 10,000 per cent of a penny?

Rate of Per Cent Missing

PUZZLES NOS. 166–169

Average

166. If a piece of jewelry is marked "16-carat gold," is this 100 per cent pure gold? If not, what per cent pure is 16 carat?

167. In a certain high school, 25 per cent of the girls and 50 per cent of the boys attended a football game. If 48 per cent of all the students are girls, what per cent of all the students went to the game?

168. 1/3 is ____ % of 1/2?

169. John borrowed $5 from a friend. When he next sees his friend, he repays the $5 and remarks that this leaves him flat broke. Feeling sorry for John, his friend returns $1 of the $5, stating that he considers the debt paid and they are even. The question is, what per cent of money was gained by the one to whom $1 was returned? Would you say the answer was nearest to 20%, 80%, 120%, 1,000% or 20,000%? Why?

Base Missing *

PUZZLES NOS. 170, 171

Average

170. 30 per cent of 50 is 6 per cent of_____?

Difficult

171. The width of a river is 760 feet at the point where it is spanned by a bridge. 20 per cent of the bridge is on one side of the river, and 16⅔ per cent is on the other side of the river. How long is the bridge?

Percentage Activities

FUN PROJECT NO. 9: PER CENTS IN EVERYDAY LIFE

Easy and Average

Many of you studied percentage in school and know that a per cent is another way of writing hundredths. Did you ever notice how often percentage is used around you in your work, sports, newspapers, in schools, in statistics, and the like?

Look through some newspapers or magazines to see how many times you can find examples of per cent. You will find examples of interest rates, commission, discounts, per cent of increase and decrease, and many more. What are the different ways that they are used? How can you use per cent?

(*a*) Per cents are used throughout sports. Look at the sporting page of the newspaper. How are the batting averages figured? Do you know how to make a chart of your team's standings? Do you understand the ratings of the various sports listed in the

* See Business Math Section for per cent problems on discount, commission, selling price, and interest.

newspaper? For instance, one year Stan Musial's record in the paper looked like this:

	AB	H	Avg. or %
Stan Musial . . .	472	159	.337

AB = at bat; H = hits; Avg. = average, written as a three-place decimal rather than a per cent. To figure Stan's batting average, we divide 472 by 159:

```
           .3368 or .337
      472)159.0000
          141 6
          ─────
           17 40
           14 16
          ─────
            3 240
            2 832
           ─────
             4080
             3776
            ─────
              304
```

Compute your team's standing in any sport. For example:

STANDINGS

TEAM	WON	LOST	PCT.	G.B.
A	18	12	.600	—
B	17	14	.548	$1\frac{1}{2}$
C	15	15	.500	3
D	10	20	.333	8
E	5	24	.172	$12\frac{1}{2}$

Team A is in first place, $1\frac{1}{2}$ games ahead of Team B, who won 1 less and lost 2 more than A. Team C is 3 games behind because they won and lost 3 less. The heading PCT. is the team's winning per cent, and is written as a three-place decimal rather than as a per cent of the games a team won. Compare the number of games won with the total number of games played. For example, Team B's winning per cent is found by comparing 17 won with 31 games played: 17 is _____ % of 31?

$$.548\overline{3} = .548 \quad \text{or} \quad 54.8\% \text{ of games won}$$

$$
\begin{array}{r}
31\overline{)17.0000} \\
15\ 5 \\
\hline
1\ 50 \\
1\ 24 \\
\hline
260 \\
248 \\
\hline
120 \\
93 \\
\hline
27
\end{array}
$$

In sports the winning per cent is traditionally written as .548 rather than 54.8%; it is also easier to say that Stan Musial is batting .337 than 33.7%. We do not even read the decimal point but merely say three-thirty-seven is his batting average.

Check by per cent to see whether the batting averages and standings given in your newspaper are figured correctly.

Figure the batting average of your favorite ball player.

(b) Figuring the per cent of increase and decrease is another big use of percentage. Try these:

(1) Figure the per cent of increase or decrease in your weight during the past year.

(2) Figure the per cent increase or decrease in your savings account in the bank.

Example: You weigh 150 pounds today and weighed 140 last year. What per cent have you gained in weight over the past year? Your increase in weight is 10 pounds. Your original weight was 140 pounds. Thus you must compare 10 with 140.

$$10 \text{ is } \_\_\_ \% \text{ of } 140?$$

$$.071 = .07 = 7\%$$

$$140\overline{)10.000}$$

Your weight has increased 7 per cent.

(3) Figure the per cent increase or decrease in your local school enrollment. This will be quoted many times in the newspaper.

(c) Figure out the per cent of discount you are getting on certain ads in the paper, for example:

> COAT   Was $60.00 — now $50.00 ($10 discount).
> $10.00 is ____% of $60.00?
> 1/6 = 16⅔% discount or the discount is 16⅔% off the original price.

(d) Figure out a budget, using per cents.

(e) Per cents are used in the making of circle graphs.

(f) Maybe someone you know sells newspapers. What per cent of commission does he earn on one newspaper?

> Example: Suppose he keeps 3 cents on every 10-cent paper he sells. 3 is ____% of 10? Then 3/10 = 30% commission he makes on all newspapers he sells.
>
> Many people sell on commission. What per cent do they make? What per cent commission could you make selling magazines, Christmas cards, etc.?

(g) What per cent interest are you getting on your investments and savings account?

(h) What per cent of the time were you absent from work or school during the past year?

(i) What per cent of the time did you make a strike in bowling the last time you bowled? What is your batting average if you play baseball? What per cent of your free throws did you make in basketball? What was the shooting percentage of the team?

(j) In school, students could figure:

(1) Per cent of boys in class; per cent of girls.

(2) What per cent of the whole school enrollment are girls and what per cent are boys?

(3) What per cent of the class is absent today? What per

cent of the whole school enrollment is absent? What per cent have been absent during the month? the year? etc.

These are but only a few of the many ways in which percentage is used in everyday life. Look for more ways.*

* For how to do percentage by algebra see section on Algebra, Using Simple Equations under Fun Project later in the book.

Chapter VI

BUSINESS MATHEMATICS

Discounts

PUZZLES NOS. 172, 173

Average

172. Jones' Department Store is selling coats at a discount of "20 per cent off." Ralph paid $34 for a coat. What was the original price of the coat?

173. A clothing store owner was trying to dispose of out-of-season dresses, and marked a dress down from $40.00 to $35.20. Failing to sell the dress, he reduced the price again to $30.98. Still, he didn't sell the dresses so he reduced the price once again, consistent with his previous reductions. What was the final selling price of the dress?

FUN PROJECT NO. 10: MAKING A DISCOUNT SCRAPBOOK

Average

In the daily newspaper you can find many discount ads. We all read them and sometimes take advantage of them. But do you know how many different reasons there are for discount sales? Do you know the various mathematical devices that advertisers might use to indicate a saving? Many of these sales and devices are displayed in the store windows. You will be surprised at your results in this project, since most of us blindly look at discount ads without paying much attention to the devices, sales, and psychology used on us by the merchants.

To further your knowledge of discounts try this: Cut from the newspapers or magazines advertisements exemplifying certain types of discount sales. The ads should show different types of sales, and the different ways of advertising one, rather than being any ads at all that you might find. You will be able to locate hundreds of discount ads from the newspaper, so to make the assignment more challenging, find specific examples as explained below:

The notebook may be divided into two separate parts.

1. The first part will display all the different types or reasons for discount sales that you can locate. These reasons might be:

(*a*) Anniversary sale
(*b*) Introductory sale
(*c*) Clearance sale
(*d*) Fire sale
(*e*) Damage sale
(*f*) Going-out-of-business sale
(*g*) January white sale
(*h*) Father's Day sale
(*i*) Out-of-season sale
(*j*) Dollar Day sale
(*k*) Big savings sale
(*l*) Annual sale
(*m*) Holiday sale
(*n*) Sale for no particular reason, etc.

You should try to collect at least one ad best exemplifying about 10 of the types you select. Each should be pasted in the notebook and properly labeled according to type.

2. The second part of the scrapbook will have ads showing the various mathematical devices that advertisers use to represent savings to the customers. Some of these are:

(*a*) A certain per cent off, like "20 per cent discount on all items."
(*b*) A fraction off, like "1/3 savings on all items."
(*c*) A listing of the old price and the new price:

Regular price	*Now*
$60	$40

(*d*) All prices greatly slashed:

$$\$60 \text{ to } \$40$$

(*e*) Two-for-one sale or economy sale.

Again, you should try to put into your notebooks one of each type, with each ad properly labeled. On such ads as represented by (*c*) or (*d*) of part 2, where the goods are marked down in price, and the per cent of discount "off" is not given, you can calculate the per cent of discount next to the adds in the notebook. This can be done in 2 or 3 ads of this type.

For example in the above ad:

Regular price	Now
$60	$40

20 is _____% of 60?

20/60 = 1/3 = 33⅓% discount.

Commission

PUZZLES NOS. 174–176

Average

174. If you were offered a job for 30 days at the following rates, would you take it?

$0.01 for the first day
.02 for the second day
.04 for the third day
.08 for the fourth day,

and so on until the thirtieth day, each day's pay being double that of the previous day's pay. How much would you be paid on the thirtieth day?

175. The sales clerks in Sam's Shoe Store receive a salary of $55 a week, plus 1 per cent of all sales over $800 .a week. One clerk earned a total of $80 in one week. What was the total of his sales for that week?

Difficult

176. A farmer sent his three sons to market to sell watermelons. The oldest had 50 watermelons, the next one had 30,

and the youngest had 10. The farmer told his sons they must all sell their watermelons at the same price, and not only that, but they must all bring home exactly the same amount of money, even though each boy had a different number of watermelons to sell. They could not trade or give away their watermelons among themselves. They really managed to come home, each with the same amount of money. How did they do it? (This problem has two possible answers.)

Selling Price *

PUZZLES NOS. 177–179

Average

177. Jimmy sold a horse for $90, bought him back for $80, and resold him for $100. What did he make on the transaction?

178. Mr. Williams purchased a hat for $5, tendering the clerk a $20 bill to pay for it. The merchant could not make the change, and went across the street and got change from a friend. He returned and gave the customer the hat and $15. After the customer had been gone several hours, the merchant's friend discovered that the $20 bill was counterfeit and demanded $20 in good money. The merchant paid his friend for the counterfeit bill. What was the merchant's total loss?

179. (*a*) If the cost is 3/5 of the selling price, the expenses 3 times the profit, and the profit 1/6 of the cost, what per cent of the selling price would be allowed for cost, what per cent allowed for expenses, and what per cent for profit?

(*b*) If the selling price of a coat is $20, how much goes for cost, expenses, and profit?

* See also sections on Banking and Interest, Stocks, Insurance, Taxes, and Budgeting.

Chapter VII

BANKING AND INTEREST

Banking

PUZZLES NOS. 180–185

Easy

180. A bank teller handles many one-dollar bills, but when he was asked how many times the numeral "1" or the word "one" appears on a one-dollar bill, not counting the serial number, he was stumped. How many ones do appear on a dollar bill? (Look carefully.)

181. Any banker should know this one. What has a head and a tail but no body?

Average

182. John put $50 in the bank. During the month he withdraws as follows:

	Withdrawal		*Balance* (what's left)
Jan. 6	$20.00	leaving	$30.00
Jan. 10	15.00	leaving	15.00
Jan. 19	9.00	leaving	6.00
Feb. 3	6.00	leaving	0.00
	$50.00		$51.00

To check his account, he adds the withdrawal column and gets $50.00, which is correct. He next adds his balance column and to his surprise finds it adds to $51.00. The question is: Where did the extra dollar come from? It isn't interest. What is the trouble?

183. If you had one each of every denomination of United States currency issued today, how much money would you have? By currency, I mean both paper money and coins. (Add

all bills and coins issued to get the total.) This leads to the question of which is the largest bill issued by our government (paper money)?

184. According to the American Bankers Association, Americans are now writing checks at the rate of 8 billion a year, exchanging nearly 2 trillion dollars in the process. Experience also shows that many people have only the dimmest notion of how checks work. What do you know about checks? Answer either true or false to the following questions:

(*a*) A check written in pencil is invalid.

(*b*) If your name is misspelled on a check made payable to you, you cannot cash it.

(*c*) An undated check is valid.

(*d*) If someone alters your check and the bank pays more than you intended, the bank is responsible.

(*e*) A check is good for one year after the date written on its face.

(*f*) If the amount of a check indicated in figures differs from the written amount, the check cannot be honored.

(*g*) If a bank finds you have sufficient funds on deposit to pay part but not all of a check, it must pay that part.

(*h*) There is no limit to the amount for which a check may be written.

(*i*) Only the writer of a "counter check" can cash it.

(*j*) The safest form of check is a certified check.

(*k*) If you cross out, erase, or change any part of a check that you write, it is invalid.

(*l*) A check dated on a Sunday is invalid.

(*m*) Once you endorse with your signature a check made payable to you, anyone can cash it.

(*n*) If you endorse a check with your signature and add the words "for deposit only" no one else can cash it.

(*o*) You can endorse a check in such a way that only one person can cash it.

(*p*) You can stop payment on a check by telephone.

(*q*) Any of the owners of a joint checking account can stop payment of any check drawn on the account.

Difficult

185. Mr. Jones gave me a check in full payment for some work which I had done for him. The check was in three figures and for much more than my bill so, naturally, I was quite pleased. Later, Mr. Jones told me he had made a mistake and if I would return the check to him, he would give me the difference between the product of the three digits and their sum, and he assured me that this difference would not be a small number. I agreed. However, I realized later that I had been completely taken in and ended up with nothing. The check was for $0.00. How much was the original check made for?

Interest*

PUZZLE NO. 186

Average

186. Jim lent Carl 25 cents and said he would charge Carl 4 per cent simple interest for the use of his money; he was just kidding. One week later Carl returned the quarter to Jim and Jim said, "Where is my interest?" Carl replied, "There is no interest due when one borrows a quarter for only one week. Figure it out yourself."

Jim found Carl was right. For how long a time would Carl have to keep Jim's quarter at 4 per cent interest for it to earn 1 cent interest? If Carl borrowed 5 cents at 4 per cent interest, how long would it take for the nickel to earn 1 cent interest?

FUN NOVELTY NO. 25

Average

Suppose someone deposited 1 cent in a bank upon the birth of Christ. At 4 per cent interest compounded annually, how much would this 1 cent be worth in the year 1950?

This 1 cent would be worth $\$1.6 \times 10^{33}$, or, expressed as a whole number:

$$\$1,600,000,000,000,000,000,000,000,000,000,000.00$$

This is read: one decillion, six nonillion, and no cents.

* To compute interest by using algebra, see Chapter XVIII, Fun Project 26.

Chapter VIII

HOUSEHOLD MATHEMATICS: BUDGETS*

FUN PROJECT NO. 11: HOW TO MAKE A BUDGET

Average

Everyone should know how to spend his money wisely. A budget is an important step in this direction. A budget is an estimate of the money that can be spent, and the amounts to be spent for various purposes, in a given time. This budget depends mostly on the income received by a person. The smart person will keep records of his spendings, so that he will not spend more than he earns. All budgets will have certain individual differences. A student in school will have different categories from a housewife running a house, or a bachelor living alone paying rent. To explain how to make a budget, however, I would like to start with a simple example, taking a school boy and his expenditures for a typical week.

EXAMPLE:

(*a*) John first keeps a record of his expenditures for a typical week. This record is kept in a cash account such as a book-keeper might keep, and is balanced at the end of the week.

(*b*) At the end of the week, John determines the amount of money spent under each category in his budget.

(*c*) Next, he figures out the per cent spent for each item of his budget.

(*d*) Finally, he could, if he so chooses, make a circle graph showing what per cent of the allowance is spent for each item in the budget.

(*e*) John then will try to follow this budget in the following

---

* For the application of mathematics to cooking, see Fun Project on Cooking, Chapter XVIII, Part B.

103

weeks. If he goes over on one item, he must cut down on another item in his budget.

To illustrate: The classifications in John's budget will be food, transportation, savings, recreation, charity, school supplies, clothing, miscellaneous.

His cash account is kept as follows:

			Received	Spent
Jan.	1	Allowance	$5.00	
	2	Lunch		$0.30
		Hat		1.00
	3	Charity		.10
		Savings		.25
		School supplies		.10
		Lunch		.35
	4	Movie		.25
		Ice cream cone		.05
		Fishing tackle		.30
	5	Lunch		.25
		Ice skating		.30
		Received for work done	1.00	
	6	Transportation		.30
		School supplies		.05
		Clothing		1.50
	7	Church contribution		.25
		Totals	$6.00	$5.35
		Balance on hand		.65
			$6.00	$6.00

Next week, John starts with 65 cents. Now, he classifies each item:

Food	Trans-portation	Savings	Recrea-tion	Charity	School supplies	Clothing	Miscel-laneous
$0.30	$0.30	$0.25	$0.25	$0.10	$0.10	$1.00	$0.30
.35			.30	.25	.05	1.50	
.05			$ .55	$ .35	$ .15	$2.50	
.25							
$ .95							

What per cent of the total $5.35 was spent for each classification?

Food:

$$\frac{.177}{5.35\,)\,0.95} = 18\%$$

Transportation:

$$\frac{.056}{5.35\,)\,0.300} = .06 = 6\%$$

Savings: 5%
Recreation: 10%
Charity: 7%
School supplies: 3%
Clothing: 47%
Miscellaneous: 6%.

Actually, this figures 2 per cent over because of the rounding off to the nearest whole per cent. We now see what approximate per cent of his allowance John should allot for each classification for each week. Now let's make a circle graph of these per cents:

John takes .18 × 360° for lunch:

$$\begin{array}{r} 360 \\ .18 \\ \hline 2880 \\ 360 \\ \hline 64.80 = 65° \end{array}$$

Thus, in making the circle graph, he will measure 65° to represent food, or 18 per cent. All the other items will be figured similarly. We will not complete a circle graph or illustrate it here.

Now, how can John use this budget? Well, for example, suppose the following week John receives $10. Following his budget, how much can he spend on food or lunch?

$$\begin{array}{r} \$10 \\ .18 \quad \text{(18 per cent for food)} \\ \hline 80 \\ 10 \\ \hline \$1.80 \end{array}$$

He can spend $1.80 this week. However, he may prefer to put the extra money into his savings.

This is only a very simple example of how to make a budget.

However, to make a more complicated budget, you will follow the same general procedures.

A housewife would use different categories from those of a student. Her categories might be:

  20% — Rent or shelter
  15% — Clothing
  20% — Food
   8% — Operating expenses (electricity, gas, water, telephone, etc.)
  10% — Recreation
   5% — Education
   5% — Medical expenses
   2% — Charity
  10% — Savings (bonds, insurance, stocks, savings account, etc.)
   5% — Reserve fund (for the unexpected or the leeway needed)

Also a housewife would probably keep her budgets by months, instead of weeks, as shown in the example. Many banks will provide a person with a budget plan to follow:

To make your own budget do this:

(*a*) Keep a record of your expenditures for a typical month or two by a cash account.

(*b*) List and total all items under some category plan similar to that shown above.

(*c*) Find the per cent of the total spent for each category as shown in the example.

(*d*) The figures in (*c*) are the per cents you will use for future months in figuring the amounts you can spend each month.

For example: If you earn $5,400 a year, or $450 a month, and you use the per cents given above, you would figure the amounts you could spend per month for each item:

Rent	*Clothing*	*Food*	*Operating*	*Recreation*
$450	$450	$90	$450	$450
.20	.15	(same as	.08	.10
$90.00	2250	rent)	$36.00	$45.00
	450			
	$67.50			

Education	Medical	Charity	Saving	Reserve
$450	$22.50	450	$45	450
.05		.02		.05
$22.50		$9.00		$22.50

Total
90.00
67.50
90.00
36.00
45.00
22.50
22.50
9.00
45·00
22.50
450.00

If your income is raised, the amounts you could spend each month on each item would also increase. However, the same per cents could be used, unless you decided to change the amount spent on a particular category. You might, for example, be able to save more money now than before. Also, a category like clothing is very seasonal, because you spend more on clothing at different times in the year. You might spend nothing on clothing one month, but twice the normal amount the next month, thus staying within your budget.

A budget should be flexible. The reserve fund gives you a chance to be a little over in one particular category.

You must check each month to see if you are staying within your prescribed limits. It might be necessary to lower or raise your per cents in some categories.

Budgeting is good practice and can be very helpful in your everyday living. Now you should try to make a budget, following the examples given here, according to your own needs and expenditures.

Chapter IX

MEASUREMENT*

Linear Measurement

PUZZLES NOS. 187–191

Easy

187. Your bed and light switch are 12 feet apart:

Bed　　　　←——12 feet——→　　　Light Switch

How can you switch off the light and get into bed before the room is dark?

188. What is bought by the yard and worn out by the foot?

189. What has three feet and can't walk?

Average

190. An employer has a 7-inch bar of gold. He paid an employee 1 inch of gold every night. How can the employer make only two cuts on the 7-inch gold bar and yet pay his employee 1 inch each night for seven nights?

cut　　　7 inches　　　cut

Where would he cut the bar? What are the sizes of the three pieces remaining after the cut? Explain how he would use these pieces to pay 1 inch every night for seven nights.

191. Tom, Dick, Harry, Joe, and Bill are lined up in these positions, midway through a track meet:

Tom is 20 yards behind Dick.
Dick is 50 yards ahead of Harry.
Harry is 10 yards behind Bill.
Joe is 30 yards ahead of Tom.
Bill is 50 yards behind Joe.

* See Chapter I for a brief history of measurement.

At this point in the race, who is winning? Who is second? third? fourth? last? How many yards ahead is each from the boy next to him?

FUN PROJECT NO. 12: MEASUREMENT GUESSING GAMES

Easy

At your next party, whether it be adults or children, try some guessing contests based upon the estimating of distances. Being able to estimate distances is very important. Often, in discussing an accident, you will hear remarks like "They were about six feet away when the car hit. . . ." You will, if you were a witness, no doubt be asked to estimate distances pertaining to the accident. Some people can estimate distances better than others. But with practice, one can become more adept in this technique.

At this party, the hostess beforehand will cut a clothesline into the following lengths:

1", 2", $2\frac{1}{2}$", 3", 4", 6", 8", 9", 10", 1', $1\frac{1}{2}$', $1\frac{3}{4}$', 2', $2\frac{1}{4}$', 3' or one yard, 4', 5', 6' or two yards, $16\frac{1}{2}$' or 1 rod.

She announces a rope-guessing contest. The ropes are mixed up in any order and marked so that only the hostess can tell the answer. On a sheet of paper, the guests will write their guesses when the hostess holds each different rope. She might hold up 10 different ropes to guess at. The person coming the closest on most of the guesses is declared the winner. The guests will be surprised to see how well they can really estimate distances. The best way to estimate distances is by comparing the distance with a known distance, like your height, foot, thumb, and so on.

Another method for practicing the estimation of distances would be to try such things as these:

(*a*) Put your hands 12 inches or 1 foot apart without looking at any ruled device. This would be, then, your guess of 1 foot. Have a friend take a 12-inch ruler and measure the separation between your hands. How close did you come to 1 foot?

(*b*) Without using any ruled device, draw on a piece of paper a line you believe to be 1 inch. Draw a line of these lengths: 2″, 7″, 9″, 10½″, etc. See how close you came. You should not be more than 1 inch off.

On a blackboard draw a line 3 feet long without looking at any ruler. This can be done as a contest to see who can come the closest.

(*c*) Take other objects or distances and have a guessing contest as to their length. For example:

(1) How high is the room you are in?
(2) How far is it across the street?
(3) What is the height of your house?
(4) How long is your block?

(*d*) Another good guessing game is with the use of the protractor, a device for measuring angles. At a party or group, draw an angle of any size on a piece of paper with a ruler, large enough so all can see. Have everyone write on a piece of paper his estimate of the size of this angle. Now measure the angle with the protractor. The person coming the closest is the winner.

This game could be played backwards also. Tell everyone to draw freehand on his paper an angle of a particular size announced by the host. If the hostess said to draw an angle of 57 degrees, the person whose angle measured closest to 57 would be the winner. The hostess would be the measurer and judge in all cases.

Try these at your next party.

FUN NOVELTY NO. 26

Average

Do you know the following interesting measurements:

Nautical measures

6 feet	= 1 fathom
1 land mile	= 5,280 feet
1 sea mile	= 6,080.2 feet or 1.15 land miles
1 knot	= 1 sea mile per hour

In the movies and on television, you have heard conversations which mention kilometers as distance measurements. Remember this conversion:

$$1 \text{ kilometer} = .6 \text{ mile}$$
$$20 \text{ kilometers } (\times .6) = 12 \text{ miles}$$

The weight of water and ice may be found from the following science principle:

$$1 \text{ cu. ft. water} = 62\tfrac{1}{2} \text{ pounds}$$
$$1 \text{ cu. ft. ice} = 57\tfrac{1}{2} \text{ pounds}$$

Water expands when it freezes, and a given volume is therefore 5 lbs. lighter than the same volume of water.*

Time

PUZZLES NOS. 192–199

Easy

192. (a) A clock strikes the hours only. How many times does it strike in one day, altogether?

(b) When the clock strikes 13, what time is it?

193. If a man gives his son 15 cents and his daughter 10 cents, what time would that be?

194. At what time of day was Adam created?

195. What makes you tired on April Fool's Day?

196. How fast can you answer these:

(a) How can you make 10 bushels of corn from 1 bushel of corn?

(b) What two consecutive months, besides July and August, have 31 days each?

Average

197. A man had two clocks; one did not run at all, and the other lost four minutes every day. Which clock is most often correct? Which should he keep? Explain your answer.

* See Chapter X, Geometry, for other measurements.

198. A little girl told her mother one afternoon, at 3:40, that she had been counting the number of times the clock struck or chimed. "I have heard the clock strike 34 times," she announced.

The little girl could not tell time, and the mother wanted to know what time she began counting. If the clock strikes the hours and half-hours, at what time did the little girl begin counting the chimes?

199. When Mary asked her aunt when she was born, her aunt replied, "If you write the year of my birth on a sheet of paper, then turn the paper upside down, the date will be the same." Can you figure what year Mary's aunt was born?

FUN NOVELTY NO. 27: TIME

Easy

When it is 12:00 o'clock noon in New York, the standard time in various foreign cities is:

London	5:00 P.M.	— 5 hours ahead of us
Rome	6:00 P.M.	— 6 hours ahead of us
Berlin	6:00 P.M.	— 6 hours ahead of us
Moscow	8:00 P.M.	— 8 hours ahead of us
Paris	5:00 P.M.	— 5 hours ahead of us
Tokyo	2:00 A.M.	— the next day (tomorrow)
Hawaii	7:00 A.M.	— 5 hours behind New York

In the armed services, time is reckoned by the 24-hour clock starting at midnight, or 0000, with the hours indicated by hundreds — 8:00 A.M. is 0800, 12:00 noon is 1200, 5:00 P.M. is 1700, and 10:00 P.M. is 2200. Minutes are indicated by the units and tens digits: 3:12 A.M. is 0312, 11:34 P.M. is 2334, and 6:59 P.M. is 1859.

FUN NOVELTY NO. 28

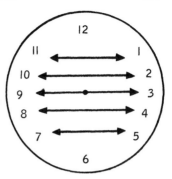

Easy

Did you know that each pair of opposite numbers on a pocket watch adds to 12?

FUN NOVELTY NO. 29: MEASUREMENT—
CALENDAR OR TIME

Average

This is one of the most fascinating procedures I have used in enriching mathematics teaching and is greatly enjoyed by my students. By this system, you can find the day of the week for any given date of the Gregorian calendar, the one we now use. This is the procedure:

First, we have certain guides to use for the months and the days. Each month has a number:

January	1	July	0
February	4	August	3
March	4	September	6
April	0	October	1
May	2	November	4
June	5	December	6

Each day has a number:

Sunday	1
Monday	2
Tuesday	3
Wednesday	4
Thursday	5
Friday	6
Saturday	0

Now, we are ready to take the steps necessary to get the day of the week.

(a) Take the last two figures of the year.

(b) Divide by 4 (omitting all fractions).

(c) Take the key number for the month.

(d) Take the day of the month or number of the date (for August 28 we would take 28).

(e) Add these four number obtained in steps (a), (b), (c), (d).

(f) Divide by 7, retaining only the remainder.

(g) This remainder gives the day of the week, as determined by the keys, or tables.

Let's try some examples. A good one would be December 25, 1959 (Christmas). What day did this fall on?

(a) 59 (last two figures of year)

(b)   14 (number you use)

$$4\overline{)59}$$
$$\underline{4}$$
$$19$$
$$\underline{16}$$
$$3 \text{ (discard the 3 — do not round off)}$$

(c) 6 (key number for December)

(d) 25 (day of the month)

(e)   59 (add the numbers obtained in steps a, b, c, d)
       14
        6
       25

      104

(f)   14   (discard; do not use)

$$7\overline{)104}$$
$$\underline{7}$$
$$34$$
$$\underline{28}$$
$$6 \text{ (remainder, the number you do use)}$$

(g) The number 6 is Friday on the chart so we know that December 25, 1959, was on Friday.

Important points to remember:

(*a*) In leap year, use 0 and 3 for key numbers of January and February, respectively.

(*b*) For years in the 1800s add 2 more
1700s add 4 more
2000s add 6 more
2100s add 4 more

(add to total arrived at in step (*e*), before dividing by 7).

The Gregorian calendar came into use in the year 1582 in most countries and supplanted the Julian calendar. So the days of years in, say, the eighteenth century would be one day according to the Julian calendar, and a different day under the Gregorian calendar. All the work here is under the Gregorian calendar.

For days under the Gregorian calendar in the early history of the United States:

in the 1600s add 2
in the 1500s add 3
in the 1400s add 4,

but remember, the day will be different from that used under the Julian calender, which, for example, was used in the year 1492. Your teacher might ask on what day did Columbus discover America (Gregorian calendar):

October 12, 1492

(*a*) 92
(*b*) 23
(*c*)   1
(*d*) 12
     4 (add for years in the 1400s)
7)132
18 with a remainder of 6

Number 6 is Friday, so Columbus discovered America on

Friday. You can determine a leap year by dividing it by 4; if the result is even with no remainder, that year is a leap year.

$$
\begin{array}{r}
373 \\
4\overline{)1492} \\
12 \\
\hline
29 \\
28 \\
\hline
12 \\
12 \\
\hline
\end{array}
$$

1492 is a leap year because it divides evenly by 4. Remember, though, this affects only the months of January and February in your key. The years 1700, 1800, and 1900 are not leap years but the year 2000 will be. Only those century years divisible by 400 are leap years:

$$
\begin{array}{r}
4 \\
400\overline{)1600}
\end{array}
$$

The year 1600 is a leap year.

Let's try another: Lincoln was shot on April 14, 1865. On what day of the week did this occur? (1865 is not a leap year.)

$$
\begin{array}{ll}
(a) & 65 \\
(b) & 16 \\
(c) & 0 \\
(d) & 14 \\
& +2 \text{ (year in 1800s)} \\
\hline
& 97
\end{array}
$$

$$
\begin{array}{r}
13 \\
7\overline{)97} \\
7 \\
\hline
27 \\
21 \\
\hline
6 \text{ (remainder)}
\end{array}
$$

Number 6 is Friday's number; therefore, Lincoln was shot on a Friday.

You will enjoy figuring the date of your next birthday, when school closes for the summer, when Christmas comes, and dates in history. This can also be computed by a formula which you will find in the Algebra section.

Distance
PUZZLES NOS. 200–205

Easy

200. What common word — one you have heard many times — is more than a mile long?

201. An electric train is traveling 100 miles an hour, against a 100-mile-an-hour headwind. Which way will its smoke blow?

202. Gene drove to his friend's home in a neighboring county in an hour and a half. The return trip took 90 minutes. On which trip did he drive faster?

Average

203. A train starts daily from San Francisco to New York, while another starts daily from New York for San Francisco; the journey lasts seven days. How many trains will a traveler meet in journeying from New York to San Francisco?

204. An explorer traveled 8 miles due south in the wilderness. He stopped to cook and eat his lunch and traveled 8 miles due west. Then he stopped for a nap; when he awoke, he set his course due north and after traveling 8 miles he was back where he started. From what place did he begin his journey?

205. A car leaving New York for Chicago travels at the rate of 40 miles an hour. At the same time, another car leaves Chicago for New York, traveling at the rate of 80 miles an hour. When the two cars meet, which one will be nearest New York?

Weight
PUZZLES NOS. 206–209

Easy

206. Which is heavier, a pound of feathers or a pound of gold?

207. What is the difference between a postage stamp and a girl?

Average

208. What is the difference between half a dozen dozen eggs and six dozen dozen eggs?

209. There are nine balls which all weigh the same amount, except for one which weighs slightly less. Using a balanced scale, and being allowed to weigh the balls only two different times, how would you find the one ball that weighs less?

Liquid Measure

PUZZLE NO. 210

Average

210. A man goes to the well with a 5-quart jar and a 3-quart jar, which is 8 quarts all together. However, he wants only 7 quarts of water. How can he get 7 quarts without using a measuring cup, using only the 5-quart and 3-quart jars?

Chapter X

GEOMETRY

Definitions

PUZZLES NOS. 211–217

Easy

211.

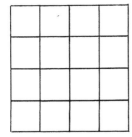

How many squares are in this figure?

212. If A's peacock laid an egg in B's yard, whose egg would it be? Think carefully.

213. What American state is round at both the beginning and the end, and high in the center?

Average

214.

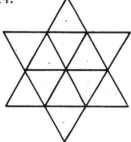

How many triangles of any size are in this star?

215. What geometrical figure represents a lost parrot?

216.

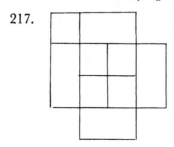

How many rectangles are in this figure? (The numbers represent the 12 small rectangles and these numbers will be used as an aid in identifying the different rectangles.)

217.

How many squares are in this figure?

FUN NOVELTY NO. 30

Easy

Take a sheet from the daily newspaper, or any big sheet of paper. I'll bet that you cannot fold this paper over more than 7 times. Why? Because after 7 folds you will have 128 thicknesses. Thus, to fold this paper 8 times would be impossible, even for Samson.

FUN NOVELTY NO. 31

Easy

Did you know that a round cloth dries faster than a square cloth?

In a square cloth, the corners hold the moisture longer and cloths usually dry from the center outwards.

FUN NOVELTY NO. 32: COMICAL DEFINITIONS OF GEOMETRY

Geome Tree (Gee, I'm a Tree!)

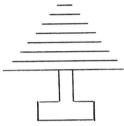

FUN PROJECT NO. 13

Average (Review, Collect, Learn)

A. Geometry Scrapbook

Do you know what the different types of triangles are? Triangles are very important in everyday life — in construction, for example. The use of triangles makes things more sturdy and rigid.

Triangles can be named by sides or angles. If named by sides:

If all three sides are equal, it is an equilateral triangle.

If two sides are equal, it is an isosceles triangle.

If all sides have different length, it is a scalene triangle.

If named by angles:

If the biggest angle is a right angle, or 90°, the triangle is a right triangle.

If the biggest angle is over 90° and under 180° (an obtuse angle), it is an obtuse triangle.

If the biggest angle is less than 90° or all three angles are under 90° (acute angles), the triangle is an acute triangle.

How are these triangles used in everyday life? Collect from newspapers and magazines pictures showing examples of each of the above triangles, and paste them in a scrapbook properly labeled. Each triangle will always be named two ways — by the side and by the angle. A triangle may be both isosceles and right, or equilateral and acute (an equilateral triangle must be an acute triangle since all angles are 60°), and so on.

Look around you in your surroundings. What kind of triangles do you see and how are they used? List these uses.

B. Symmetry

All around you, notice the many uses of symmetry. Symmetry is used in building, design, art, and can be found everywhere in nature. The definition of symmetry is "A regular, balanced arrangement on opposite sides of a line or plane, or around a center or axis." There are two kinds of symmetry, line symmetry and point symmetry. A figure that can be cut into two parts alike in size and shape has line symmetry, and a figure which is everywhere alike around a common center has point symmetry. For example:

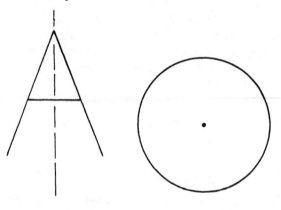

Line symmetry   Point symmetry

Cut out examples of both kinds of symmetry and label and put into a scrapbook. Again look for these in newspapers, magazines, and the like. When things are symmetrical, they are much more pleasing to the eye. Look around you and list all the different ways you see the principle of symmetry being used. There are many things in this wonderful world of ours that we completely ignore.

GAMES NOS. 16–18

Easy

16.

This is a good game for two players. There are 16 squares. The first player chooses any two neighboring squares and places an *x* in each. The second player chooses any two neighboring squares still vacant, and writes an *o* in each. The players continue in turn until one player cannot find two adjoining squares free. That player is the loser.

For example:

x	*x*		*x*	*x*		*o*	*o*	*x*	*x*	*o*	*o*		*o*	*o*	

Player A puts *x*'s in squares 4 and 5.
Player B puts *o*'s in squares 14 and 15.
Player A puts *x*'s in squares 9 and 10.
Player B puts *o*'s in squares 7 and 8.
Player A puts *x*'s in squares 1 and 2.
Player B puts *o*'s in squares 11 and 12.

Player A now cannot find two adjoining squares for his *x*'s, so he loses. Can you find a strategy that should always win? (See Answers.)

Average

17. These dots may be put on the blackboard, or on paper when playing this game. The pattern requires 15 dots in all:

```
        •   •   •
      •   •   •   •
    •   •   •   •   •   •
```

The game is played by two players who take turns erasing or crossing out the dots. A player may take any number of dots (from 1 to all) from a row. The player who has to take the last dot loses; the object of the game is to force your opponent to take the last dot. You can take dots only on one row. A player can always win if he knows the techniques to follow. Can you figure out these techniques?

Two players may play the game on a hit-or-miss basis; they may discover the winning principles. (See Answers for techniques.)

18. One person plays this game. You will need markers (coins, chips, pieces of paper, etc.), which are put over a playing board as follows:

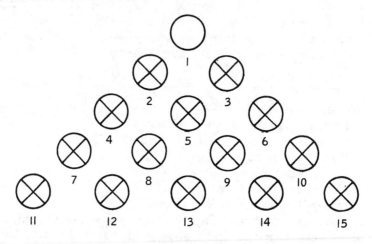

You need 14 markers in all, as space 1 is left blank. The numbers are shown for the purpose of identifying one's individual moves and for showing how one arrived at a particular solution.

The object of the game is to have as few markers left as possible, 1 being the highest score obtainable. It is a game similar to checkers: the player makes jumps over markers into an empty space, and the marker jumped is removed from the board. To start the game, there are only two jumps possible — the player may jump from space 4 into empty space 1, removing the marker on space 2 from the game; or he may jump from space 6 into space 1, removing the marker on space 3. The game continues with the player making jumps and removing all jumped men from the game. The only way to move is by jumping. You cannot move from one empty space into another without a jump. Try the game and see how close you come to having only one marker remain.

The game may be varied by leaving spaces other than space 1 open. If you record your moves, you can retrace a winning game; e.g., when you move from 6 to 1, record "6–1," etc. (Marker on space 5 is removed.) (See Answers for one possible solution.)

Geometrical Drawings

PUZZLES NOS. 218–255

Easy

218.

. . . . .

. . . . .

. . . . .

. . . . .

. . . . .

Using this pattern of 5 rows of 5 dots each, make a cross by connecting the dots with a straight and continuous line, and have 5 dots remaining inside the cross and 8 outside the cross (dots not used in the making of the cross). The cross looks like this:

219. Retrace this pattern in one continuous line, without lifting your pencil from the paper. (The numbers shown on the lines are merely for the purpose of determining the correctness of the answer, or for following a particular path described by an individual.)

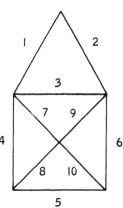

220.

        •

        •

        •

        • • •

Here are 6 coins—4 coins are in the vertical row and 3 coins are in the horizontal row. By moving only 1 coin, can you make 4 in each row, horizontally and vertically?

221. Draw 6 vertical lines:

By adding 5 more, make nine. (Note: To add to the confusion, the teacher may ask, "When does 6 and 5 more make 9?")

222. Using 8 straight lines, how can you make 4 triangles and 2 squares?

223. Can you transform the word "hole" into a building using only 2 straight lines?

h o l e

224. Using 13 cookies, how can you make 6 rows of cookies with 3 cookies on each row?

225.

There are three rectangles as shown above. How can you take away three lines and leave ten?

226.   A   B

                 a   *b*

WELL

                 c   *d*

        C   D

Families A, B, C, and D are very good friends. They draw their water from a well centrally located and equidistant from the four establishments. Four new·families, *a*, *b*, *c*, and *d* moved in between the old families and the well. A, B, C, and D took a dislike to families *a*, *b*, *c*, and *d* and decided to build a fence which would surround their homes and the well, and leave the newcomers on the outside of the fence. How did they do this?

227. Here is a picture of a house which faces to the left. Can you change this house so it faces to the right by moving only two of the lines? Tell what numbered lines you would move, and where you would place them.

House facing left   House facing right

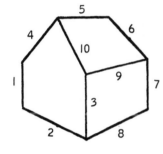
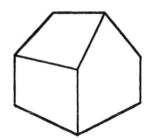

228. Can you make this drawing in one continuous line, without lifting your pencil from the paper?
(The numbers shown are merely for the purpose of determining the correctness of the answer, or for following a particular path described by an individual.)

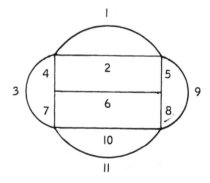

229.

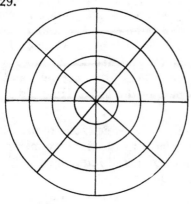

Place 8 dots on this diagram in such a way that there are 2 dots on each circle, and 2 dots on each straight line.

230. There are 10 coins. Can you rearrange these coins in reverse order (upside down) by moving only 3 coins, to look like this:

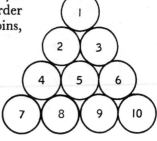

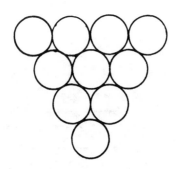

231. How can you arrange 10 apples on 5 straight lines with 4 apples on each line?

232. 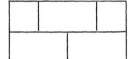 This figure contains 6 small squares. How can you remove 5 lines and leave only 3 squares?

Average

233.

Draw one continuous line, without moving the pencil from the paper in such a way as to cross all lines of the puzzle once, but no line twice. You may start anywhere. (Each break counts as a line. The top and middle lines are composed of 3 and 4 separate breaks respectively.)

234. Here is a circle with its center. How can you draw this circle with its center indicated as below, without taking your pencil from the paper — that is, make both circle and center with one continuous line?

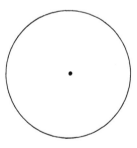

235. Using one continuous line, not lifting your pencil from the paper, cross over all of the 9 dots, using only 4 straight lines. You may not retrace over any part of your previously made line.

236.  Twelve coins are arranged in a square, with 4 coins on each side of the square. Can you rearrange the coins in a square with 5 coins on each side, but using the original 12 coins?

237. There are 12 cubes of sugar arranged 4 on a side, as shown to the right, in the shape of a square. How can you rearrange the cubes so that they will be in straight rows of 5 on a side? The new figure cannot be a square.

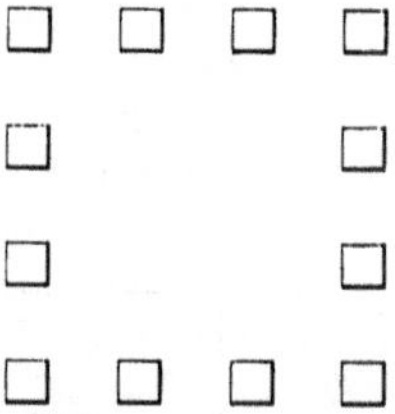

238. 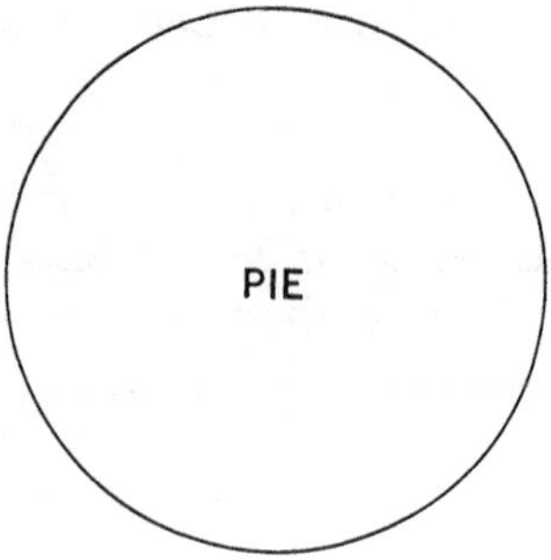 Here is an apple pie; it must be cut into 8 pieces. However, you can make only 3 cuts on the pie in dividing it. All 8 pieces must be nearly equal in surface area; otherwise those getting smaller pieces would complain, and you couldn't blame them. You cannot cut the pie into 2 halves and put the halves on top of each other. How would you get 8 nearly equal pieces by making only 3 cuts?

239.

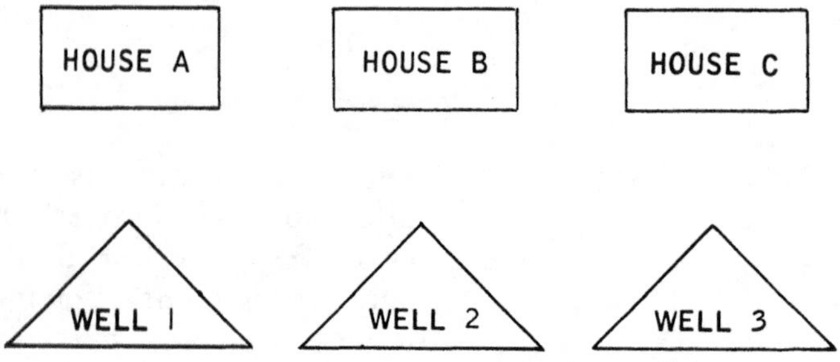

HOUSE A   HOUSE B   HOUSE C

WELL 1   WELL 2   WELL 3

Each house must have a separate path to each of the three wells; e.g., house A must have a path to well 1, to well 2, and to well 3. The same applies to houses B and C. Now, the owners of these houses are all deadly enemies and their paths cannot cross. Draw a separate path from each house to each well, but have no paths cross.

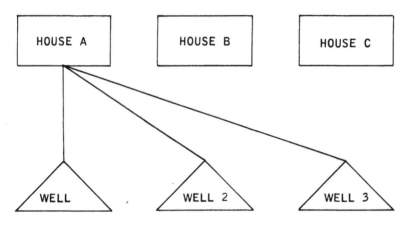

240. Make 1000 without lifting your pencil from the paper, or make 1000 in one continuous line. The answer must look like this exactly: 1000, and not like this : ⌐0̅0̅0̅
You may not erase.

241. On the following page are 4 islands and 8 bridges. Starting at B, can you cross all 8 bridges once only and go through all 4 islands as many times as you want, and yet end on land? You cannot retrace your steps; you cannot go over the same bridge twice, but you may go over an island more than once. (Use numbers and letters in your answer, so that your path may be followed.)

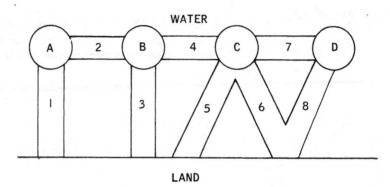

242. Using 9 straight lines of exactly equal length, can you form 5 equilateral triangles?

243. 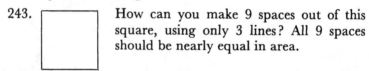 How can you make 9 spaces out of this square, using only 3 lines? All 9 spaces should be nearly equal in area.

244. How can you arrange 6 coins in such a way that you will have 2 straight rows with 4 coins on each row?

245.

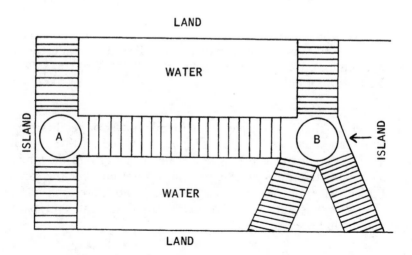

(*a*) Cross all bridges once only, beginning on land and ending on land. Do not retrace your path or cross any bridge twice.

(*b*) To make the puzzle easier, you may begin anywhere and end anywhere.

246. 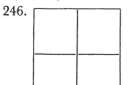 Take 4 lines away, put them back differently, but still leave 3 squares.

247. Can you draw 4 equilateral triangles, all the same size, by using only 6 straight lines? Can you figure two different solutions?

248. Arrange 9 trees to form 10 straight rows of trees with 3 trees on each row.

249. Can you form 2 squares and 4 triangles with 8 straight lines?

250.

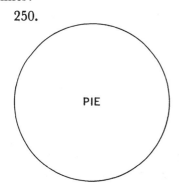

Divide this pie into 11 pieces, using 4 straight cuts or lines.

251. Using 8 straight lines, how can you make 3 squares all of different sizes?

252.

A •

     • C

       •

B

Make a triangle with points A, B, and C on the middle of the sides of the triangle, rather than the vertices of the triangle.

Difficult

253. Draw a circle and make two parallel lines perpendicular to the same line twice; draw a vertical line, then a semicircle, and end with 3 parallel lines perpendicular to the same line. What do you have?

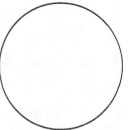

254. Can you divide this circle into four equal parts by drawing 3 curved lines of equal length?

255. Take 17 apples and arrange them in 2 straight rows with 5 apples each, and 8 straight rows with 4 apples each.

FUN NOVELTY NO. 33

Easy

A famous type of puzzle is the optical illusion drawings. Our eyes play tricks on us.

Which line is longer, A or B?

(Neither. Lines A and B are the same length!)

Are lines MR and TK parallel?

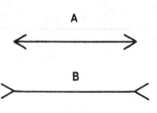

(Yes, MR and TK are parallel.)
Does line AB = line BC?

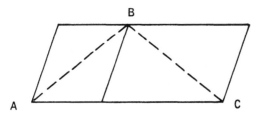

(Yes, line AB = line BC.)

FUN PROJECT NO. 14: MAP COLORING

Average

One of the oldest puzzles is the map-coloring problem. What are the most colors—no two like colors being placed adjacent to one another—needed to color any map in use today? The answer is that all maps in use today can be colored with 4 colors.

Of course, one may use 5 colors if he likes. To require the use of 5 colors, however, it has been proved one would need a map showing 36 countries. In our future discoveries about other planets, maybe such a map will be needed, but so far no need for using more than 4 colors has arisen.

For example, suppose this drawing represents 5 different countries:

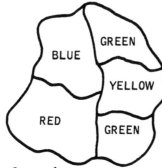

This map requires four colors.

You may have
a map which ne-
cessitates the use
of only 2 or 3
colors:

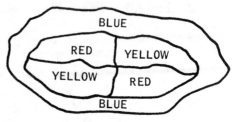

Can you make an imaginary map which requires the use of
5 colors? (Remember, if two countries have a strip of boundary
in common, each must have a different color.)

GAME NO. 19

Average

19. *Game A.* Using this game in his
classes, the author found that students
enjoyed it tremendously. The pattern is
4 rows of 5 dots in a row as shown
above.

Start at any place and connect each dot, completing as many
whole squares as possible, never taking your pencil off the
paper. You may not retrace or cross any previously made line.
When you end in a blind alley, the game is finished. For every
square completed, score 1 point. Sometimes you may have 3
sides of a square complete; this counts for 3/4 point. Two
sides count as 1/2 point, and 1 side counts as 1/4 point. To
exemplify:

7 whole squares
$\frac{3}{4}$ square
$\frac{1}{2}$
$\frac{1}{4}$
$\frac{1}{4}$
$\overline{9\frac{1}{4}}$ points

started here →

ended here

The best score in my classes was 10¾ points. Can you beat this? (See Answers to learn how 10¾ points were scored.)

Game B. This game is exactly like Game A, except that we use 5 rows of 5 dots, instead of 4 rows of 5 dots. This makes the game a bit more difficult, but gives you higher scores. Use the same scoring system as in Game A. The best score in my classes was 14 points. Can you top this? (See Answers to learn how the 14 points were scored.)

Scale Drawings and Map Work

FUN PROJECT NO. 15: WORKING WITH MAPS

Easy

Do you know how to read a road map? Can you find the distance from one city to another? Working with a road map can be fun, interesting, and educational.

Go to your neighborhood filling station, and get a map of the United States or the state in which you live. To read it you must first open it and find the scale used. This will usually appear in the upper right-hand corner or the lower right-hand corner of the map. It will show you how many miles a certain distance is, or it will give you a scale like "1 inch = 58 miles." Next locate the big cities, and notice the lines representing highways between the cities. On each highway line you will find a shield or circle with a number telling you what highway it is. These shields are also to be found on the side of the roads all along the highways so that you will know that you are on the right road in going from one place to another. On some of these maps, the lines will have numbers on them to indicate the distance from one city and another. If these are not clearly indicated, can you think of a way to find the distance from one city to another with these maps? You could not do this accurately, but you could find the airline distances between cities and add a little more onto your answer, say 20 miles, depending on the total distance. The only way to get road distances would be to cut the curved lines into straight parts as best you can and measure each little part. Airline distances, however, should be sufficient.

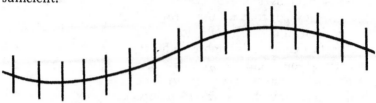

Assume the scale on the map is 1 inch = 58 miles. After measuring the distance from your city to another city, you have the distance in inches, and would have to multiply this by 58 to get the miles. Suppose the distance from St. Louis to Kansas City is 4⅜ inches:

$$4\tfrac{3}{8} \times 58 \ = \ 35/8 \times 58/1 \ = \ 253\tfrac{3}{4} \text{ or } 254 \text{ miles}$$

Find the distance in inches by measuring with a ruler from one city to another and then convert this to miles by using the scale given on the map. Try this for a number of cities. How far is it from your city to some of the other big cities?

Many other valuable pieces of information are given in these road maps.

FUN PROJECT NO. 16: MEASURING ANGLES OUTDOORS

Average

When surveyors lay out highways or locate boundaries, they measure angles. The instrument for measuring these angles is called a transit. This transit has a telescope for sighting a marker some distance away, and sits on a three-leg tripod. Naturally, these devices for measuring angles outdoors are very expensive. However, you can make a miniature transit called a field protractor very easily. With this field protractor you can measure angles at home; you will then be able to make scale drawings of your home, neighboring lots, school, and the like.

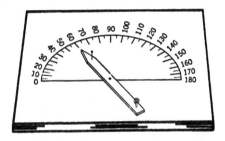

The field protractor is merely an enlarged protractor. Project the lines of the protractor onto the board. The board has a pointer fastened to it by a screw at the center of the semicircle formed by the protractor. For sights, set a very small screw eye at both ends of the pointer. The board should be level when you are measuring angles outdoors, and the pointer should move freely in a semicircle.

Now try to measure angles with your field protractor outdoors. Try using your measurements in a scale drawing.

Perimeter

PUZZLE NO. 256

Easy

256.

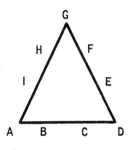

Place the digits from 1 to 9 so they equal 20 along the sides of this triangle. Replace the letters with numbers, using only 4 numbers on each side, and using each number once only.

FUN PROJECT NO. 17: MEASURING PERIMETER AND AREA

Easy

In school, you were taught to find the perimeter and area of many surfaces. For this you were given a number of formulas. In everyday life, it is also necessary to find the perimeter and area of surfaces. For example, can you find the perimeter and area of your kitchen floor? You might want to place molding around the outside, thus needing to know the perimeter. You might want to put new linoleum on the floor, and then you would need to know the surface area to be covered.

Perimeter is the distance around any flat figure. Area is the amount of surface. Most floors are rectagular or square in shape. The area of a rectangle is given by this formula:

$$\text{Area} = \text{length} \times \text{width} \qquad A = lw.$$

The perimeter is found by simply adding up the sides of the figure. For example, suppose the room is shaped like this:

Find the perimeter,
which would be:

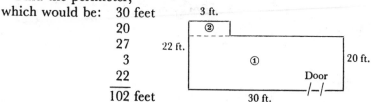

30 feet	
20	
27	
3	
22	
102 feet	

Can you find the area of this room?

$$A = lw$$
$$A_1 = 30 \times 20 = 600 \text{ square feet}$$
$$A_2 = 3 \times 2 = 6 \text{ square feet}$$
$$\text{Total area} \quad 606 \text{ square feet}$$

(1) Now find the perimeter of a room in your house, find its area also.

(2) Find the perimeter and area of the lot your house stands upon.

(3) If you are a student, find the perimeter and area of your classroom.

(4) If you can, try to figure the amount of linoleum needed in a particular room. A scale drawing will help. Linoleum comes only in certain widths, and therefore you must figure out how this linoleum can be laid in this particular room without any waste.

Circumference

PUZZLES NOS. 257, 258

Average

257. The diameter of an automobile wheel is 2½ feet. How many miles an hour is the car traveling when the wheel is turning 8 times a second? Find the answer to the nearest tenth of a mile.

258. Point *B* is the center of this circle. Line *AB*, the radius of the circle, is 2 inches long. A rectangle is boxed in by *E*, *F*, *G*, and *B*.

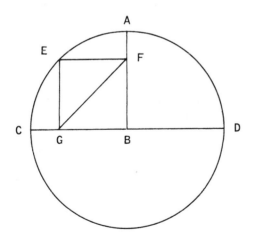

What is the length of the line *G* to *F*?

Explain how you derived your answer.

* See Linear Measurement, Chapter IX, for work on linear measurements.

Area

PUZZLES NOS. 259–270

Easy

259. Howard Jones owns 40 acres of ground, 40 sheep, 1 dog, and has 1 man to manage the farm. How many feet altogether are on his land?

260. What is the difference between a square foot and a foot square?

261. What is the area and circumference of these coins: (*a*) a quarter; (*b*) a half dollar; (*c*) a silver dollar.

Average

262. George earns his spending money by cleaning the big windows in the stores of the business district. He charges 15 cents a square yard. How much should he charge Mr. Adams to clean 2 store windows measuring 15 feet by 21 feet and 18 feet by 21 feet?

263. Mr. Simpkins' bedroom window was a yard square. He decided to board up one-half of the window because it let in too much light in the morning and prevented his sleeping late. After he boarded up one-half of the window, he was surprised to discover that the remaining half of the window was still square in shape. Not only that, it was still a yard high and a yard across. How did he board up the window?

264.

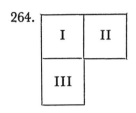

Through a mix-up in a real estate deal, 4 families claimed rights to 3 sections of land. To settle the matter, a clever agent suggested that they refund some money and then divide the 3 equal lots into 4 equal areas. This was agreeable, but all 4 families wanted the exact same area or surface and all wanted the same-shaped plot. How did they divide this ground into 4 parts equal in area and identical in shape?

265. The top of a rectangular box has an area of 120 square inches, the side an area of 96 square inches, and the end an

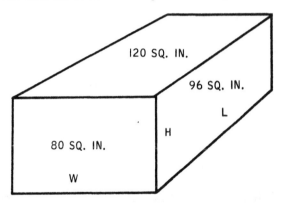

area of 80 square inches. What are the dimensions of the box (length, width, and height)? (This problem is also under Algebra.)

266. Divide into 4 equal areas or figures.

267. Here is a classical geometry problem: Prove that 64 equals 65. Draw a square 8 inches on a side, and cut this square into 4 pieces, as demonstrated by the dotted lines. Now, rearrange these pieces into a rectangle 13 inches long by 5 inches wide, as follows:

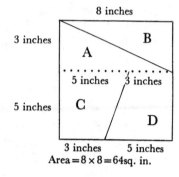

Area = 8 × 8 = 64 sq. in.

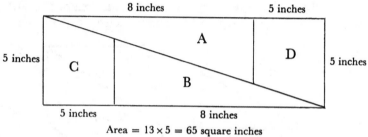

Area = 13 × 5 = 65 square inches

Hence, it is proved geometrically that 64 equals 65. Wherein lies the fallacy?

268. What is the greatest number of 5-inch by 3-inch Christmas cards you can cut out of a sheet of paper 5 feet by 3 feet, if each card has 4 pages (2 leaves)?

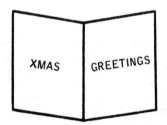

Difficult

269. When a screen is placed 10 feet from a projector, the picture occupies 10 square feet. How large will the picture be when the projector is 15 feet from the screen? (Also under Algebra.)

270. How would you find the area of a right triangle whose three sides are 4, 5, and 9 inches long, respectively?

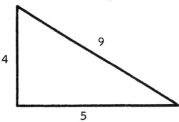

Volume

PUZZLES NOS. 271–275

Easy

271. How much dirt is there in a hole a foot long, a foot wide, and a foot deep?

272. A rectangular box has 8 corners. How many edges has it?

Average

273. (*a*) How many tons of rain fall over an acre of land when 1 inch of rain falls? What does this water weigh?

(*b*) If 1 inch of rain fell in your front yard which measures 60 feet by 40 feet, how many pounds would this water weigh? How many tons?

274. A lawn sprinkler sprayed 3 gallons of water a minute over a circular area 20 feet in diameter. How long must the sprinkler be used to give the same amount of water as a half-inch rainfall?

275. What is the greatest possible number of 1-inch cubes that can be placed into an empty box 4 inches wide by 4 inches deep by 4 inches long?

FUN PROJECT NO. 18: MEASURING VOLUMES

Average

When you find the volume of a solid, you are measuring the amount of space occupied. Can you find the volume of any three-dimensional solid? There are spheres, cylinders, cones, prisms, pyramids, rectangular solids, and so on. We usually find the volumes of these solids by formulas given in texts on the subject.

Here is another guessing-contest game. Take a big room of some sort, or maybe your living room at home. Now volume is measured by cubic units. So have your guests guess the number of cubic feet in the volume of this room. No measurements are allowed before the guess. You might show the guests how big a cubic foot is, if you can find a box near enough to this size. A cubic foot is 1 foot in all directions — length, width, height. The guests will try to estimate how many of these boxes will fit into the room. You will be surprised to see how great the range of answers will be. After all guesses are in, you will next measure the room and by multiplying find the volume in cubic feet. The person coming closest is declared the winner.

For example, in my classes, I would have my students guess the volume of the classroom, after showing them a box of the volume 1 cubic foot. We would then measure the length and width with the tape measure. Measuring the height was a problem, but this was solved by first measuring a long pole used to open windows. After finding the length of the pole, we would then hold the pole up to the ceiling. We would then measure from the bottom of the pole to the ground, and add our two answers together to get the total height.

Next we would calculate the volume using $V = lwh$. Suppose the room was 30 feet long, 20 feet wide, and 12 feet high:

$$V = 30 \times 20 \times 12 \qquad V = 7,200 \text{ cubic feet.}$$

The pupil guessing nearest to 7,200 cubic feet won.

Next, I would ask my students to ascertain how many students from the standpoint of good health should be allowed in this classroom. Authorities say that each student should have 200 cubic feet of air. I would jokingly tell a student who had his foot on the back of a neighbor's chair that he was infringing on his neighbor's 200 cubic feet of air, and that he should remove his foot.

The figuring would go like this:

$$
\begin{array}{r}
36 \\
200\,\overline{)7200} \\
600 \\
\hline
1200 \\
1200 \\
\hline
\end{array}
$$

Thirty-six students is the greatest number this room can accommodate healthfully.

I would also have the students measure the study hall, library, and other rooms to determine the volume and the number of students good health practice indicates. I would jokingly have them measure the principal's office to determine the number of students the principal may properly lecture or chastise at one time. Of course, when they were sent to the principal's office for discipline, and there were too many students in the office, I would tell my pupils to ask to leave, because it just isn't healthy! Of course, this sometimes got me into trouble with the principal.

Find the volume of the rooms in your house and determine the number of people who will for health purposes fit into these rooms.

Also for your scrapbook, you can make a collection of examples of volume as shown in newspapers and magazines. You will find advertisements showing the cubic capacity of refrigerators, freezers, trucks, cars, and so on.

FUN PROJECT NO. 19: MAKING GEOMETRIC SOLIDS

Average

It is fun to make geometric solids of all kinds. You can make cubes, prisms, pyramids, cylinders, cones, and so forth. These can be used to decorate your home. They are especially useful at Christmas time as tree ornaments in the decoration of your Christmas tree. Here are the plans for making these solids. Try them.

To make a cube:

The extra flaps are needed for pasting and the dotted lines indicate how the paper should be folded. Cardboard or heavy paper should be used.

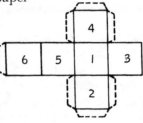

To make a triangular prism:

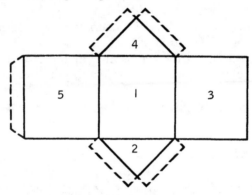

To make a cylinder:

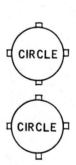

The circumference of the circles must match the length of the rectangle exactly.

To make a pyramid:

SQUARE PYRAMID:

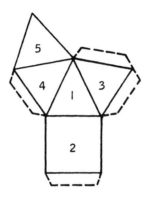

TRIANGULAR PYRAMID

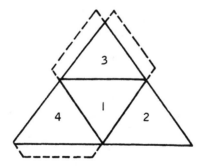

To make a cone:

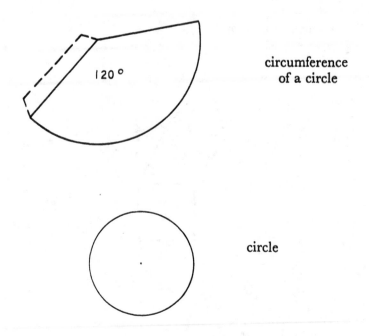

circumference
of a circle

circle

Both circumferences must match exactly.

Topology

FUN PROJECT NO. 20: MÖBIUS STRIP

Average

For really surprising results and fun, you should try these experiments. This is the famous Möbius strip puzzle. Materials needed: old newspaper, scissors, paste. Open the newspaper the longest way and cut 4-inch strips.

Trial 1. Take a strip and paste the ends together. This will make a shallow cylinder of two sides (inside and outside) and two edges. Cut the cylinder down the middle and all the way around. The result is two separate, identical cylinders, which is not surprising.

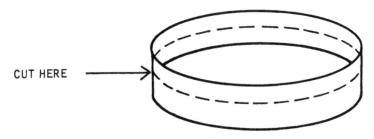

CUT HERE

Trial 2. Take another strip of paper and twist one end once before pasting the ends together. Cut the strip down the middle. Before you cut, though, what do you expect the result to be? Instead of two separate bands as in trial 1, you will have one band, but larger than the one you have started with. The band has two twists now, instead of the original one twist.

Trial 3. Take the resultant strip from trial 2 and cut down the middle of the band again. What happens? The result is two interlaced rings, joined like two links of a chain. Each link is separate from the other and, if detached, will give you the original cylinder with two twists. If you have room, you might try cutting the two interlocking chains down the middle. (Note: You might begin with a 6-inch strip instead of a 4-inch one.)

Trial 4. Start fresh with a new 4-inch strip and this time give one end two twists before pasting the ends together. Cut down the middle of the band and the result will also be two interlocking chains, with each chain or link having the original two twists. Cut each link again — you get four interlocking links!

Trial 5. This time, with a fresh 4-inch strip, give the end three twists before joining the two ends. Cut down the middle. The result now seems nebulous — all are tangled together. Do you have one chain or two interlocking chains? Take another fresh start and give the end four twists; then do one with five twists, and so on.

Trial 6. Take a fresh strip 6 inches wide and give the end one twist before pasting the ends together. Instead of cutting the band down the center, however, cut about one-third of the distance from one edge of the strip to the other and continue to cut toward the top, always one-third of the distance from the edge and parallel with it, until the end is reached. The cutting places will eventually join each other. (If you use a 6-inch strip, you may cut at 2 inches away from the edge or at 4 inches.) The result is two bands interlocked, with the bands different in size: one band is as big as the original and has one twist, whereas the other band is twice as big as the original and has two twists! Try cutting the resultant strips again. What happens?

Trial 7. Now try some of your own concoctions. There are many ways one can experiment with the Möbius strip and come up with fascinating results.

Chapter XI

GRAPHS

PUZZLE NO. 276

Easy

276.

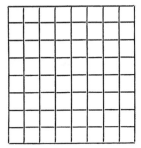

Darken in 8 squares (small squares) following the rule that no darkened square can be in a straight line with another darkened square, or on a diagonal with another darkened square.

FUN PROJECT NO. 21: GRAPHS IN EVERYDAY LIFE

Easy and Average

You will find examples of graphs in magazines, newspapers, at the foot of a hospital bed, in business news, store windows, and the like. A graph is a line or diagram showing how one quantity depends on or changes with another. It is highly important that you be able to read graphs, as graphs tell a story or facts in a concise and interesting form. In order to read graphs, you should be able to make them yourself. For a review and complete understanding of graphs, here are listed some things you can try yourself. The main types of graphs are line, bar, circle, pictograph, and the divided bar graph.

(*a*) Clip the daily temperature readings from the newspaper and make a line graph showing how the temperature varied throughout the day. The clipping will read something like this:

8 a.m.	72°
9 a.m.	75°
10 a.m.	78°
11 a.m.	80°
12 noon	83°
1 p.m.	85°
2 p.m.	89°
3 p.m.	88°
4 p.m.	80°
5 p.m.	75°

LINE GRAPH SHOWING TEMPERATURES OF A PARTICULAR DAY

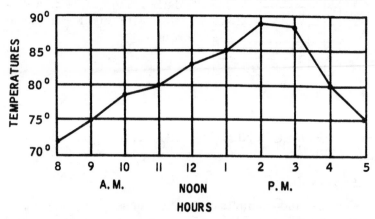

(*b*) Make a circle graph showing how you spent yesterday, or a typical 24-hour day. You might have such subdivisions as Work, School, Sleep, Eating, Recreation, Homework, House chores, and so on. Again this would be an individual matter.

For example, let's say this was the breakdown on your 24-hour day:

Work   — 8 hours
Eat   — 2 hours
Sleep   — 7 hours
Travel   — 1 hour
Housework   — 3 hours
Recreation   — 2 hours
Miscellaneous — 1 hour

Here is the circle graph:

8 hours = 8/24 or 1/3 × 360 = 120°
2 hours = 2/24 or 1/12 × 360 = 30°
7 hours = 7/24 × 360   = 105°
1 hour = 1/24 × 360   = 15°
3 hours = 3/24 or 1/8 × 360 = 45°
2 hours = 2/24 or 1/12 × 360 = 30°
1 hour = 1/24 × 360   = 15°
                   Total   = 360°

TYPICAL 24-HOUR DAY

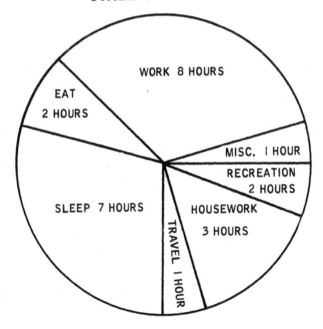

(*c*) Make a line graph showing how your weight fluctuated during the year.

(*d*) Make a circle graph to show how you spent your money for the month, using the per cents as found in a budget (see section on Budget).

(*e*) Make a line graph showing the fluctuation of a particular stock in the daily newspaper for one month (see section on Stock Market).

Here are some more ideas that a teacher or student might use in graph work:

(*a*) The teacher might fabricate a problem, using the students' names in a facetious manner — for example, make a bar graph showing the population in a state called Jonesville (if the teacher's name is Jones). Here are the populations of particular cities in Jonesville (using the last names of students and adding -burg, -ville, -town, and so on):

Smithburg	6,341	population
Brownville	5,817	
Meyerton	3,319	
Gomezburg	1,003	
Coxville	16	

The last item is for laughs — assuming Mr. Cox is a good sport.

Now make a bar graph using this information. (See diagram on opposite page.)

(*b*) Draw a bar graph or line graph showing the changes in school attendance for each month of the school year. In which month were most of the students present? Which month of the year showed the greatest amount of illness in the school?

(*c*) Make a bar graph or circle graph showing the distribution of grades on any test, or the last grading-period marks. For instance, in a class of 26:

12 — A's	5 — D's
4 — B's	2 — F's
3 — C's	

(*d*) Make a pictograph, bar graph, circle graph, or divided bar graph showing the class's preference in such items as ice cream flavors, desserts, sandwiches, and so on. How many like chocolate best? Vanilla? Strawberry? Banana? Use the class results for making a graph.

(*e*) Poll the class to ascertain what television shows they prefer. Let them elect 6 to 10 choices, then vote on their favorite programs. Make a circle graph or divided bar graph showing the class's preferences.

(*f*) Make a circle graph or divided bar graph representing the manner in which you spent last week's allowance.

These ideas are only a few of many possibilities with graphs.*

POPULATION OF THE STATE OF JONESVILLE

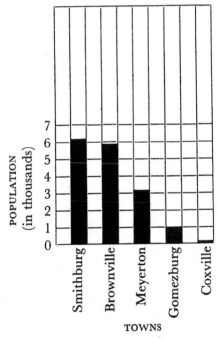

Coxville is represented by one thin line. Through this playful example, the students learn the main points and features of making a bar graph.

* For more material on line graphs, see Chapter XIV; for more material on circle graphs, see Chapter VIII, Fun Project on Budgets.

Chapter XII

INSURANCE

PUZZLE NO. 277

Average

277. Few people read the small print on their insurance policies. How much do you know about yours? Can you answer the following questions:

Life insurance

1. You want to combine insurance protection with a savings program to prepare for your child's college education, or to pay off a mortgage. Which type of policy is best?

2. What is the lowest-price-premium form of life insurance?

3. Can you get a bargain or miracle policy in life insurance?

Fire insurance

4. Your wallet, hat, or coat falls into the fireplace and burns to a crisp. Can you collect under your fire-insurance contract?

5. Are you covered against damage from fireman's use of axes, hoses, and fire extinguishers?

Automobile insurance

6. You have a blow-out, skid off the road and into a group of picnickers. Are you liable?

7. Vandals wreck your car. Can you collect?

8. You have an eight-year-old car. Do you need collision insurance?

Personal liability

9. A neighbor slips on your waxed floor, breaks her leg, sues you. Do you have to pay?

10. On a golf course, you slice the ball, shout "Fore!" but it hits a passer-by. Are you liable?

11. You have a fight with a neighbor, break his nose. Are you protected by a comprehensive-liability policy?

Losses and thefts

12. You've lost three shirts in the laundry. Do any of your insurance policies cover this loss?

13. Prowlers break into your summer cottage and steal silverware and tools. Can you make a claim under your theft policy?

14. Can you collect if your pedigreed dog is stolen?

15. Fifty dollars is stolen from your home. Can you collect?

16. On a trip to Europe your pocket is picked. Are you covered by your insurance?

17. A relative, visiting you for the summer, runs off with the family jewels. Will insurance pay for his theft?

18. Your valuable necklace has mysteriously disappeared. Does your theft policy cover the loss?

19. Burglars smash your piano. Will you be compensated?

Accident and disability

20. Can an insurance company cancel your policy after a single accident or illness?

Chapter XIII

TAXES

Average

278. Do you realize that you actually pay taxes every day of your life, not just once a year? Do you know how big your total tax bill is? Answer the following questions:

1. America's total annual tax bill is reaching (*a*) $50 billion, (*b*) $85 billion, (*c*) $100 billion.

2. Most people pay at least how many different personal taxes? (*a*) 4, (*b*) 12, (*c*), 20?

3. Hidden taxes — those you don't realize you are paying — total (*a*) 200, (*b*) 10,000, (*c*) number unknown.

4. The national average tax on a gallon of gasoline is (*a*) 3 cents, (*b*) 8.8 cents, (*c*) 12 cents.

5. If a car costs $2,000, the taxes included in the cost would be approximately (*a*) $300, (*b*) $480, (*c*) $560.

6. In a 40-hour week, an $85-a-week man works how many hours to pay for federal, state, and local taxes? (*a*) 6, (*b*) 8, (*c*) 12.

7. The number of taxes on a man's suit total (*a*) 14, (*b*) 90, (*c*) 116.

8. The number of taxes on a house come to (*a*) 40, (*b*) 150, (*c*) 600.

9. Approximately how much of your tax dollar goes for national defense? (*a*) 16 cents, (*b*) 42 cents, (*c*) 80 cents.

10. Education receives approximately how much of your tax dollar? (*a*) 1 cent, (*b*) 4 cents, (*c*) 13 cents.

11. In 1913, a married man with a net income of $5,000 a year paid an income tax of $10. Today he pays (*a*) $50, (*b*) $150, (*c*) $760.

12. When you buy one egg, how many taxes come with it? (*a*) 15, (*b*) 50, (*c*) 100.

Chapter XIV

THE STOCK MARKET

FUN PROJECT NO. 22: MAKING MONEY IN THE
STOCK MARKET

Average

Everyone wants to become rich. However, it takes money to
make money in the stock market. In this project we will use
imaginary money. We will invest $1,000 in the stock market
for a certain period of time. This can be a most interesting, as
well as educational, project. You will be able to watch your
$1,000 grow, or watch it dwindle. Putting money into the
stocks of companies is a gamble. You may gain money, but
you may also lose some of it. You may gain in two ways in
stocks. First, you gain if the stock goes up in price as quoted in
the daily newspaper; and second, you receive a dividend from
your stock every 3 months.

Look at the stock-market report in your daily newspaper
where the prices of the stocks are quoted. Study the New York
Stock Exchange quotations, as this is the biggest market for
stock investors. When you buy stock you are becoming a part
owner in a corporation, and you are lending money to this
corporation for use in its business. You buy shares of stock and
become a shareholder. You receive a stock certificate as your
proof of ownership. Most companies sell two kinds of stock,
preferred and common. We will be interested only in common
in this project.

The names of the companies are listed in the paper in alpha-
betical order and sometimes abbreviated. Go through the
whole list of stocks on the New York Stock Exchange and pick
out companies that you recognize. Many of them you will not
recognize. For each stock the dividend is given right after the
name of the stock, followed by the sales in hundreds, high price

of the day, low price of the day, closing price of the day, and the net change of the stock from yesterday's close. A plus sign means the stock has gone up, and a minus sign means the stock is down. No change is indicated by a row of dots. Explanations of the little letters behind the dividends are given at the end of the stock list. All papers, of course, have minor variations in the way the information is presented. Some editions of the newspaper are not the final one, and thus instead of having the closing prices of the stock, they will list the price as afternoon, or early, or forenoon. These prices are listed in the paper only Monday through Friday, because the stock market is closed on Saturday and Sunday. Many Sunday papers will have the week's past summary on the stocks. On the stock page you will also find Dow-Jones averages, which are merely a general picture of how all the stocks under various categories are doing. The leaders for the day are stocks which were the most active, with the most shares being traded as indicated by sales.

Brokers who are members of the Stock Exchange do the buying and selling for their customers. The customer gives his order to the broker, who in turn telegraphs the order to a New York broker who is a member of the Stock Exchange. For this service, the customer pays his broker a slight brokerage fee or commission.

In order for someone to buy a stock, someone else must sell the same stock, and vice versa. We say the stock has been traded. The stock fluctuates up and down depending on the demand for it. If there are more buyers for a stock than sellers, and the demand for the stock is high, this will force the price of the stock up. On the other hand, if many people want to sell their stock and there are few buyers, this will force the price down.

Now let's get to the project.

You will have approximately $1,000 to invest (play money, of course). You may buy from 2 to 4 stocks with this money and follow these stocks daily in the newspaper, recording the daily price and net change and following the stocks for a period of one month. At the end of the month you sell your stocks and figure your profit or loss on this business venture. You should also figure your rate of dividend on each stock, and make a line graph for each stock showing how your stocks fluctuated in value the past month (see example).

For more fun you can try this in a group such as a club, group of friends, or in a classroom or school. The person who gains the most money will win some sort of prize, maybe monetary in value. A jackpot can be set up at work for this contest. In school, the teacher can reward the student who gains the most money by adding points to his grade, such as 5 points. The person who gains the second largest amount of money on his stocks can be given a smaller prize. The person who loses the most money should be penalized in some way, perhaps by having to add to the jackpot or having a teacher deduct points from his grade in a school situation. This will teach a person that there is an element of risk involved in stocks. However, if one chooses good companies, he is safe.

Below is a sample, in more detail, of how you can do this project. Figuring of the brokerage paid has been omitted.

Stock Market Project

1. Buy stock — spend $1,000 (as nearly as possible).

Buy first day, follow for a month, and sell on the last day.

For instance, you buy 2 shares of Eastman Kodak, 5 shares of Ford and 20 shares of Canada Dry.

Eastman Kodak	2 shares at 153¾	cost	$153.75
			× 2
			$307.50
Ford	5 shares at 56	cost	$ 56.00
			× 5
			$280.00
Canada Dry	20 shares at 21	cost	$21.00
			× 20
			$420.00

Total spent $307.50
280.00
420.00
$1,007.50

(You should select the stocks, the number of shares, and combination of prices which will give you as close to $1,000 as possible; when the stock is sold, the extra $7.50 will be accounted for.)

2. Follow stocks daily:

	Date	Price	Net change
Eastman Kodak	Mar. 2	154	+1/4
	Mar. 3	153	−1/2
	Mar. 4	155	+2
	↓	↓	↓
	Mar. 30	160	+1
Ford	Mar. 2	55	−1/2
	Mar. 3	56	+1
	Mar. 4	56¼	+1/4
	↓	↓	↓
	Mar. 30	57	+1/2
Canada Dry	Mar. 2	21	- - -
	Mar. 3	21½	+1/8
	Mar. 4	20	−1⅛
	↓	↓	↓
	Mar. 30	20	−1/4

3. Sell stocks:

Eastman Kodak   2 shares at $160 $320.00 (sold for)
                         × 2   307.50 (purchased at)
                         ─────   ──────
                         $320 $ 12.50 (profit)

Ford   5 shares at $ 57 $285.00 (sold for)
                         × 5   280.00 (purchased at)
                         ─────   ──────
                         $285 $ 5.00 (profit)

Canada Dry   20 shares at $ 20 $420.00 (purchased at)
                           × 20   400.00 (sold for)
                         ──────   ──────
                          $400 $ 20.00 (loss)

Profit $12.50   Loss $20.00
           5.00   Profit   17.50
         ──────   ──────
         $17.50   Loss $ 2.50

Total loss on stock venture for the month: $2.50.

4. Find rate of dividend on each stock:

How to read stock: Eastman Kodak when purchased on March 1, read:

	Dividend	Sales	Close	Net change
EASTMAN KODAK	3	21	153¾	+ 1/4

To find the rate of dividend, divide the dividend by the price of the stock when purchased.

$$\text{Price of stock when purchased}\ \overline{)\ \text{Dividend}}$$

The rate of dividend is found only when you purchase the stock. The fluctuations of the price of the stock in no way affect or change the rate of dividend at which you bought the stock. Thus, you do not find the rate of dividend each day, but only at the time of purchase — one time. The rate of dividend is computed to nearest tenth of 1 per cent. Example:

$$
\begin{array}{r}
.0195 = .020 = 2.0\% \\
153.75\overline{)3.000000} \\
1\ 5375 \\
\hline
1\ 46250 \\
1\ 38375 \\
\hline
78750 \\
76875 \\
\hline
1875
\end{array}
$$

(Caution: In computing the dividend, be sure to take into consideration the little letters sometimes appearing behind the number for the dividend. Example: EASTMAN KODAK .75e. The "e" might mean that this $.75 is paid quarterly rather than annually. Thus, 4 × $.75 = $3.00 annually.)

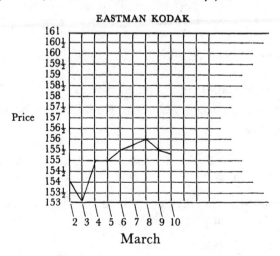

EASTMAN KODAK

March

This project may start you on your way to becoming a financial genius.

Chapter XV

POWERS AND ROOTS

Powers
PUZZLES NOS. 279–283

Easy

279. Write 24 with 3 equal figures, none of them 8, and using exponents. Remember, in this puzzle exponents must be used. Example: $4^4 + 4 = 260$
$$256 + 4 = 260$$
However, in this puzzle, the answer must be 24.

Average

280. Being asked for his home address, Jimmy replied, "I cannot remember the number, but I know the number is a perfect square and that if I turn the number upside down, this number would also be a perfect square." Can you help Jimmy? What is his address?

281. Using five 2's, make 7.
$$2 \quad 2 \quad 2 \quad 2 \quad 2 = 7$$
You may use any of the operational signs: $+$, $-$, $\times$, or $\div$.

Difficult

282. What is the largest number that can be indicated with three digits?

283. Write 31, using only the digit 3 five times.
$$3 \quad 3 \quad 3 \quad 3 \quad 3 = 31$$

FUN NOVELTY NO. 34

Average

You probably know that $3^2 + 4^2 = 5^2$
$$9 + 16 = 25$$
$$25 = 25$$

but do you also know that $3^3 + 4^3 + 5^3 = 6^3$
$$27 + 64 + 125 = 216$$

Square Root and Cube Root

PUZZLES NOS. 284, 285

Average

284. I/VII is 1/7, as VII is 7 in Roman numerals. Now, can can you make I/VII equal to I by merely changing the position of one of the straight lines in I/VII?

Make   I/VII = I

285. Using four straight lines, write three numerical equations, all giving a result of 1. (Example: II − I = I).

Four straight lines are used in the left side of the equation in this example. Write two more examples.

Also, can you write an equation equal to 1 using only three straight lines?

FUN PROJECT NO. 23: SQUARE ROOT AND CUBE ROOT

Average and Difficult

Do you remember how to find the square root and cube root of numbers? Few people do. Those who learned it usually forget how it is done. Many others never learn these procedures, as they are usually not taught in elementary mathematics courses, though they could well be taught in eighth-grade mathematics or ninth-grade algebra. A complete explanation of these important techniques, therefore, will be presented here with examples. See if you can learn how to do square root and cube root the long way.

Cube root is much harder than square root. When you are finding the square root of a number, you are finding out what number multiplied by itself will produce this original number. For example, the square root of 49 is 7 because $7 \times 7 = 49$, and the square root of 64 is 8 because $8 \times 8 = 64$. These numbers — 49 and 64 — are called perfect squares, but most numbers, such as 61 or 24, are not perfect squares. The square roots of numbers can be found by using a table, but a table only goes so high. The method described below will find the square root of any number.

The cube root of a number is that number which multiplied by itself three times will give you the original number. For example, the cube root of 27 is 3 because $3 \times 3 \times 3 = 27$, and the cube root of 64 is 4 because $4 \times 4 \times 4 = 64$. But how to find the cube root of any number will be explained below.

Square Root

(*a*) Beginning at the right, separate the given number into periods of two figures each, beginning at the decimal point and working to the left:

$$\sqrt{8\ 91} \qquad \sqrt{16\ 84} \qquad \sqrt{3\ 84\ 31}$$

(2 periods)   (2 periods)   (3 periods)

In the answer one number goes over each period; numbers are always brought down by periods (by two's), and two 0's are added at one time. Let's take $\sqrt{891}$ and follow this example through all the steps.

(*b*) Find the greatest square that is smaller than the first left-hand period; write the square root of this as the first figure of the required root.

$$\begin{array}{r} 2 \\ \sqrt{8\ 91} \\ 4 \\ \hline \end{array}$$

Four is the largest square that can be subtracted from 8. The square root of 4 is 2, which goes into the answer.

(*c*) Subtract the square of this root from the first left-hand period of two numbers to form a new dividend:

$$\begin{array}{r} 2 \\ \sqrt{8\ 91} \\ 4 \\ \hline 4\ 91 \end{array}$$

(*d*) The number we divide by is different each time, and we call this the "trial divisor." We try to divide by this number to ascertain how many times it will go. To get the trial divisor, we use two steps:

(1) Double the root already found.
(2) Add a 0 to this.

Now, divide by this trial divisor to get the next figure of the root, or answer.

$$
\begin{array}{r}
2 \\
\sqrt{8\ 91} \\
4 \\
\hline
40\,)\overline{4\ 91}
\end{array}
$$

It looks as if the divisor would go 10 times; however, this is impossible, so we use a 9.

(*e*) Add to the trial divisor the number of times the trial divisor went into the present dividend, to get the complete divisor, or the number you are dividing by. Also, put the number of times it goes into the root. Multiply this complete divisor by the last number written in the root; subtract the product from the dividend and bring down the next period to form another new dividend.

$$
\begin{array}{r}
2\quad 9. \\
\sqrt{8\ 91.} \\
4 \\
\hline
40\,\overline{)491} \\
\text{(goes 9 times)}—\quad 9\,\overline{)441}\quad (9 \times 49) \\
\hline
49\quad 50
\end{array}
$$

Note that the remainder is larger than the divisor; this sometimes happens and is not necessarily wrong.

(*f*) Continue the process until all periods have been used or the desired decimal place is attained. The result will be the required square root.

Example: Find to the nearest tenth:

$$\begin{array}{r} 2\ \ 9.\ \ 8\ \ 4 = 29.8 \\ \sqrt{8\ 91.\ 00\ 00} \\ 4 \\ \hline 40\overline{)4\ 91} \\ 9\overline{)4\ 41} \\ \hline 49 \end{array}$$

(29 doubled = 58; add   )   50 00
one 0)   580
                   8) 47 04
                  ─────
                  588
(9 is too big)   5960   2 96 00
                   4
                 ─────
                 5964)   2 38 56
                         57 44

Now, try some of your own problems.

Cube Root

This is much more difficult and is based upon the Binomial theorem in algebra as was the square root. You who have had work with the binomial theorem will quickly understand the why's and how's of the mechanics of these procedures. Here we will find the cube root of 12,812,904:

$$\sqrt[3]{12,812,904}$$

(*a*) Beginning at the right, separate the given numbers into periods of three figures each:

$$\sqrt[3]{12\ 812\ 904}$$

(*b*) Find the greatest cube that is smaller than the first left-hand period; write the cube root of this as the first figure of the required root:

$$\begin{array}{l} \phantom{\sqrt[3]{12\ }}2 \\ \sqrt[3]{12\ 812\ 904} \\ \phantom{\sqrt[3]{1}}8 \end{array}$$

(c) Subtract the cube of this root from the first left-hand period and bring down the next period to form a new dividend:

$$\begin{array}{r} 2 \\ \sqrt[3]{12\ 812\ 904} \\ 8 \\ \hline 4\ 812 \end{array}$$

(d) Consider the root already found as having a 0 added, and write down three times the square of this as a trial divisor:

$$\begin{array}{r} 2 \\ \sqrt[3]{12\ 812\ 904} \\ 8 \\ \hline \end{array}$$

(3×20^2) $1200\overline{)\ 4\ 812}$

(e) Determine by trial division what the next figure in the root will be, and write it in its place in the root:

$$\begin{array}{r} 2 \quad 3 \\ \sqrt[3]{12\ 812\ 904} \\ 8 \\ \hline \end{array}$$

$1200\overline{)\ 4\ 812}$

Since 4 will not work, as you can see if you continue, try 3.

(f) Add to the trial divisor three times the product of the first part of the root (considered as tens) by the second part of the root, and also the square of the second part of the root. This sum will be the complete divisor:

$$\begin{array}{r} 2 \quad 3 \\ \sqrt[3]{12\ 812\ 904} \\ 8 \\ \hline \end{array}$$

	1200 4 812
$(3 \times 20) \times 3 =$	180
$3^2 =$	9
	1389

(*g*) Multiply the complete divisor by the second part of the root and subtract:

$$
\begin{array}{r}
2 \quad 3 \\
\sqrt[3]{12\ 812\ 904} \\
8 \\
\hline
\end{array}
$$

$$
\begin{array}{rr}
1200 & 4\ 812 \\
180 & 4\ 167 \qquad (3 \times 1389) \\
\underline{9} & \overline{645\ 904} \\
\overline{1389} &
\end{array}
$$

(*h*) Continue this process until all the figures of the root have been found and complete the example:

$$
\begin{array}{r}
2 \quad 3 \quad 4 \\
\sqrt[3]{12\ 812\ 904} \\
8 \\
\hline
\end{array}
$$

$$
\begin{array}{rr}
1200 & 4\ 812 \\
180 & \\
\underline{9} & \\
\overline{1389} & 4\ 167 \\
 & \overline{645\ 904}
\end{array}
$$

$$
\begin{array}{rr}
(3 \times 230^2) & = 158\ 700 \\
(3 \times 230) \times 4 & = \quad 2\ 760 \\
4^2 & = \qquad 16 \\
\hline
 & 161\ 476
\end{array}
$$

$$
645\ 904
$$

Try this with simpler examples, but you must follow these steps exactly.

Chapter XVI

LOGIC OR MATHEMATICAL REASONING

PUZZLES NOS. 286–296

Easy

286. How can a cat go into a cellar with four feet and come out with eight feet?

287. George came to a bridge marked "Total weight 200 pounds." Now George weighed 190 pounds, but he had three pineapples, each weighing 5 pounds. He couldn't toss them across the river because the pineapples would break. How did George cross the bridge?

288. Two children are born of one mother at the same time and place, but are not twins. How do you explain this?

289. While walking down the street, I dropped a nickel and a dime. The nickel rolled down a nearby sewer and was lost, but the dime did not. Why?

290. A beggar's brother died. But the man who died had no brother! How is this possible?

291. How can you make one word out of NEW DOOR?

Average

292. Here is one of the oldest puzzles known. John has to ferry a fox, a goose, and a bag of grain across the river in his boat. His boat is so small that only one of the three can fit in with himself. How can he manage so the fox will have no opportunity to kill the goose, or the goose no opportunity to eat the grain? It is assumed, of course, that neither fox nor goose will run off while left alone, and that the fox will not eat the grain. How can John accomplish this?

293. How smart are you? Can you answer these questions:

(a) How fast does a snail travel?

(b) How large a part of the animal kingdom do insects comprise?

(c) If you are 16 years old on earth, how old would you be on the planet Mars?

(d) What fractional part of an iceberg or ice cube is submerged under the water?

294. Are you a good detective? This crime depends upon mathematics for solution.

Judge Watkins left a $1,000 bill on his desk, absent-mindedly. Later, when he remembered and came back for it, the money had disappeared. Only two people were in the house who could have had access to the money — the butler and the maid.

The maid said, "I saw the note and for safety folded it and placed it under the red book on your desk." The Judge looked but saw no $1,000 bill.

The butler said, "Yes, sir. I found the note under the red book and thinking it might get lost, I placed it inside the book between pages 133 and 134." Judge Watkins opened the book and again found no money.

Who stole the $1,000 bill? What was the evidence of guilt?

295. Some people love to make bets. If one of them approaches you, try one of the following bets on which you will be sure to win — provided you know the answers.

(a) Bet that he cannot answer four questions wrong.

(b) Bet that you can tell the score of the next school basketball game — before it starts.

Difficult

296. Three men, traveling with their wives, came to a river which they had to cross. There was but one boat and only two could cross at one time. Since the husbands were jealous, no woman could be left with a man unless her husband was present. How did they get across that river?

FUN NOVELTY NO. 35

Easy

Mary tells her friends that she can prove life is not worth two cents. She says, "*Life* is a magazine. Through the mail, a magazine is cent. One cent is not worth two cents. Therefore, life is not worth two cents." This is most effective if given orally.

FUN PROJECT NO. 24: THINKING LOGICALLY (MATHEMATICAL LOGIC)

Average and Difficult (Read and Learn)

In elementary mathematics through the tenth or eleventh grades, logic pertaining to numbers is very rarely taught. Simple mathematical logic could be taught in the eighth grade or lower. This logic is simple and easy to understand, plus being the basis for our number operations in simple mathematics. Thus, most of you reading this section have not had any work with mathematical logic at all. Here is a brief synopsis of mathematical logic. See by reading this section if you can get a clearer picture of what logic is.

We shall use the letters a, b, and c to represent any numbers. There are certain laws by which our number systems are governed. These are called:

> *law of closure*
> *commutative law*
> *associative law*
> *distributive law*

They pertain particularly to addition and multiplication of numbers. Although these laws might seem very simple and obvious, they are important and basic to higher algebra and mathematical theory. Here are some of the laws with numerical examples to exemplify their meanings.

Addition

I. *Law of closure for addition.* For every pair of numbers a and b, there is a third number denoted by $a + b$, called the sum of a and b:

$$a + b = c$$
$$2 + 3 = 5$$

II. *Commutative law for addition*

$$a + b = b + a$$
$$2 + 3 = 3 + 2$$
$$5 = 5$$

The commutative law for addition does not hold for subtraction. In addition, the order in which you add numbers makes no difference. However, in subtraction, the order in which you subtract makes a big difference:

$$2 - 3 \text{ is not equal to } 3 - 2$$
$$2 - 3 = -1$$
$$3 - 2 = 1$$

III. *Associative law for addition*

$$(a + b) + c = a + (b + c)$$
$$(2 + 3) + 4 = 2 + (3 + 4)$$
$$5 + 4 = 2 + 7$$
$$9 = 9$$

In addition, the order in which we add numbers makes no difference. The commutative and associative laws are used when we add a column of numbers, either up or down the columns:

$$
\begin{array}{r}
6 \\
9 \\
2 \\
\hline
17
\end{array}
$$

Adding the column down: $(6 + 9) + 2 = 15 + 2 = 17$; adding the column up: $(2 + 9) + 6 = 11 + 6 = 17$. In addition, we add two numbers together, and then add this sum to the third number, and so on, right down the column.

Multiplication

I. *Laws of closure for multiplication.* For every pair of numbers *a* and *b*, there is a third number denoted by *ab* or $a \times b$, called the product of *a* and *b*:

$$a \times b = c$$
$$2 \times 3 = 6$$

II. *Commutative law for multiplication*

$$a \times b = b \times a$$
$$2 \times 3 = 3 \times 2$$
$$6 = 6$$

In multiplication, the order in which you multiply by the different factors makes no difference. This law does not hold in division:

$$2 \div 3 \text{ is not equal to } 3 \div 2$$
$$2 \div 3 = 2/3$$
$$3 \div 2 = 1\tfrac{1}{2}$$

III. *Associative law for multiplication*

$$(a \times b) \times c = a \times (b \times c)$$
$$(2 \times 3) \times 4 = 2 \times (3 \times 4)$$
$$6 \times 4 = 2 \times 12$$
$$24 = 24$$

You could even have $(a \times c) \times b$ or $(2 \times 4) \times 3 = 8 \times 3 = 24$.

Addition and Multiplication: distributive law

$$a \times (b + c) = ab + ac$$
$$2 \times (3 + 4) = 2 \times 3 + 2 \times 4$$
$$= 6 + 8$$
$$= 14$$

This problem might also have been done:

$$2 \times (3 + 4) = 2 \times 7 = 14$$

The work within the parentheses must be done first. However, you are taught in algebra if no parentheses appear in the problem, the value of any expression containing a series of operations is found by first performing all multiplications and divisions in the order in which they occur, and next combining all the terms connected by addition and subtraction signs. For example, the above without parentheses:

$$2 \times (3+4) \text{ would be } 2 \times 3 + 4$$

The multiplication must be done first and then the addition:

$$2 \times 3 + 4 = 6 + 4 = 10 \text{ which is a different answer.}$$

For example:

$$2 \times 3 + 6 \div 2 + 3 \times 1 + 7 - 3 =$$
$$6 \ + \ 3 \ + \ 3 \ + 7 - 3$$

Doing the multiplications and divisions first, thinking:

$$(2 \times 3) + (6 \div 2) + (3 \times 1) + 7 - 3 =$$
$$6 \ + \ 3 \ + \ 3 \ + 7 - 3 = 16$$

However, if the problem contains parentheses, this work must be done first:

$$2 \times (3+6) + 3 \times (6-3) =$$
$$2 \times \quad 9 \ + 3 \times \quad 3 \quad =$$
$$18 + 9 = 27$$

There are other fundamental laws, a few of which we shall briefly state.

I. *Law of identity* $a = a$
$$2 = 2$$

II.   If $a = b$
$$b = a$$
$$\text{If } 2 = 3$$
$$3 = 2$$

(obviously not true)

III. If $a = b$, and $b = c$, then $a = c$, because things equal to the same thing are equal to each other.

$$\text{If } 1 = 2$$
$$2 = 3$$
$$1 = 3$$

IV. If equals are added to, subtracted from, multiplied by, and divided by equals, the results are equal.

If $a = b$ and you add c to both, then $a+c = b+c$. Similarly, $a-c = b-c$; $a \times c = b \times c$; and $a \div c = b \div c$.

Suppose $\quad a = 4, b = 4, c = 2$
$$4 = 4$$
$$4+2 = 4+2$$
$$4-2 = 4-2$$
$$4 \times 2 = 4 \times 2$$
$$4 \div 2 = 4 \div 2$$

The law stated in III ($a = b$, $b = c$, thus $a = c$) is the basis for deductive reasoning in logic, which can be found on many standardized tests given by schools and colleges to test how well a student can reason or draw conclusions from the given hypothesis or supposition. Example:

Hypothesis: All dogs are animals.
      All animals eat meat.

Conclusion: Therefore, all dogs eat meat.

If A stands for dogs, B for animals, and C for meat, then this follows the relationship:

	Show by sketch:
If $A = B$	All A's are equal to B.
If $B = C$	All B's are equal to C.
Then $A = C$	Thus all A's are equal to C.

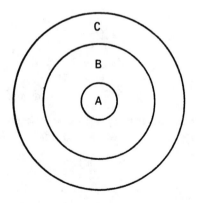

Another example:

> All Dallas people live in Texas.
> All Texas people live in the United States.

> Therefore, all Dallas people live in the United States.
This is shown by a sketch:

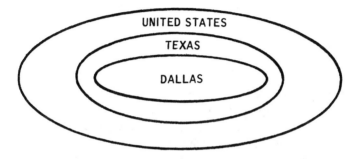

You can see that all Dallas people live in the United States.

Chapter XVII

SIGN NUMBERS

FUN PROJECT NO. 25

Average (Read, Review, and Learn)

Many people who go no further than the eighth grade have little understanding of the operations involved in working with sign numbers. In fact, when I tell my students that there are numbers below 0, they are surprised. I will say subtract 8 from 5, and my students will clamor that you can't do that. But $5 - 8 = -3$, I tell them. I tell them to think of a thermometer. If the temperature was 5 above zero, and the thermometer dropped 8 degrees as it got colder, the temperature would be 3 degrees below 0, or -3. So I tell my students there are numbers below 0 or negative numbers. Being able to operate with sign numbers is very important in higher mathematics. Sign numbers are usually taught in algebra. When we work with quantities that are opposite in kind and direction, we use sign numbers. Numbers above 0 are considered positive $(+)$, and numbers below 0 are considered negative $(-)$. Zero is the dividing point. The purpose of this section is to give a new and novel as well as clear explanation of sign numbers, so that all can understand. The principles are explained with examples based on everyday living. To review sign numbers, or learn about sign numbers for the first time, read this section and then try some problems of your own.

A. *Addition of Sign Numbers*

In doing additions of sign numbers, think of a thermometer. Addition of sign numbers is done by going up or down the scale.

Scale

```
+10
 +9
 +8
 +7
 +6
 +5
 +4
 +3
 +2
 +1
  0
 -1
 -2
 -3
 -4
 -5
 -6
 -7
 -8
 -9
-10
```

Numbers having no sign before them are considered +. To add +3 begin at +3° on the scale and go down 2

$$\frac{-2}{}$$

degrees to +1°. A minus sign means to go down the scale. The answer is +1 or 1.

Add +5

$$\frac{-8}{}$$

Start with 5 degrees above 0 and go down 8 degrees. When you have gone down 5 degrees, you are at 0 and must continue 3 more degrees to take away 8 degrees; you will arrive at the answer: −3°.

Add −5°

$$\frac{-4°}{}$$

Start at 5 degrees below 0, and go down 4 more degrees and you will stop at −9° below zero.

These problems may also be done by rules and are usually done more quickly by this method, which is the common one normally used in schools. The rules are:

(a) If the signs are alike, you add and use the common sign.

(b) If the signs are unlike, you subtract and use the sign of the larger number.

Let's try these examples by the rules:

+3   The signs are unlike, so you subtract, which gives
−2   1. The larger number is 3 and it has a plus sign in
___   front of it, so you use plus in the answer.
+1

+5   The signs are unlike, so you subtract the 5 from
−8   the 8 to get 3, and use a minus sign in the answer
___   because the larger number, 8, has a minus sign in
−3   front of it.

−5   The signs are alike, so you add to get 9 and use the
−4   minus sign in the answer because the signs are alike.
___
−9

A third method, not as good as the first two, is just to look at the problem. Example: +3 Think of the pluses as boys and
                                              −2

the minuses as girls. You have 3 boys and 2 girls. How many more boys than girls do you have? You have one more boy, so the answer is 1. In the example $+5$ you have 5 boys and 8
$\quad\quad\quad\quad\quad\quad\quad\quad\quad\quad\quad\quad\quad\quad -8$
girls. There are three more girls than boys, or -3. In the last example, there are 5 girls and 4 more girls, which makes 9 girls in all.

To add a large column of sign numbers like:

$$-6$$
$$+8$$
$$-3$$
$$-7$$
$$+1$$
$$+3$$
$$-8$$
$$+3$$

you may use either method. The thermometer may be used, starting at 6° below 0:

Start at   6° below 0°
Go up   8° to $+2°$
Go down 3° to $-1°$
Go down 7° to $-8°$
Go up   1° to $-7°$
Go up   3° to $-4°$
Go down 8° to $-12°$
Go up   3° to $-9°$

and the answer is -9.

Another method is to separate the pluses in one column and the minuses in another, and use the rules for addition of sign numbers. Of course, one could go straight down the column of numbers, using the rules.

$+8$	-6	$+15$
$+1$	-3	-24
$+3$	-7	-9
$+3$	-8	
$+15$	-24	

Adding all the pluses gives $+15$; adding all the minuses gives -24; then, add $+15$ and -24 to get -9 as in the answer.

B. *Subtraction of sign numbers*

Many folks think subtraction is merely taking one number from another. Actually, subtraction is the difference between two numbers in relationship to their position on our number scale. Again, the thermometer should be used for clearer understanding of subtraction of sign numbers.

To subtract $+3$ you are asking what is the difference be-
$$\underline{-2}$$
tween 3 degrees above 0 and 2 degrees below 0. The answer is 5 degrees. Shall we use a plus or a minus in the answer? Look at the scale:

$$
\begin{array}{l}
+3 \\
+2 \\
+1 \\
0 \\
-1 \\
-2
\end{array}
\qquad 5 \text{ degrees}
$$

You are taking -2 from $+3$, which is in the up or plus direction, and the answer is $+5$.

In the example $+5$ if we subtract by looking at the scale
$$\underline{-8}$$

$$
\begin{array}{l}
+5 \\
+4 \\
+3 \\
+2 \\
+1 \\
0 \\
-1 \\
-2 \\
-3 \\
-4 \\
-5 \\
-6 \\
-7 \\
-8
\end{array}
$$

the difference is $13°$ and we are taking -8 from $+5$, which is the up direction. The answer is $+13$.

To subtract: -5
$$\underline{-4}$$

$$-0$$
$$-1$$
$$-2$$
$$-3$$
$$-4$$
$$-5$$

(down direction)

the difference is 1°, and to subtract -4 from -5 we go in the down direction; thus, the answer is -1.

Notice that sign numbers do not violate what you have already learned about whole numbers. For instance, to subtract 6 from 8:

$$8$$
$$7$$
$$6$$
$$5$$
$$4$$
$$3$$
$$2$$
$$1$$
$$0$$

(difference: 2 in up direction)

The answer is 2.

Subtraction of sign numbers can also be done by the following rules: Change the sign of the bottom number and use the rules for addition of sign numbers.

In the examples we previously used:

$+3$	$+5$	-5	$+8$
$\underline{-2}$	$\underline{-8}$	$\underline{-4}$	$\underline{+6}$

Change the bottom numbers to $+2$, $+8$, $+4$, and -6, respectively, and add:

$+3$	$+5$	-5	$+8$
-2	-8	-4	$+6$
$\oplus$	$\oplus$	$\oplus$	$\ominus$
$+5$	$+13$	-1	$+2$

The circled signs are the changed signs and the ones we use to add. Do not erase the old sign.

C. *Multiplication and division of sign numbers*

Both multiplication and division of sign numbers are similar, so we will consider them together. The best way to multiply and divide sign numbers is by the rules.

Multiply and divide as normally, but to determine what sign to use in your answer, follow these rules:

> If the signs are alike, use a plus in your answer.
> If the signs are unlike, use a minus in your answer.

Example:

$$-8 \times +3 = -24 \qquad \text{signs unlike}$$
$$+8 \times +3 = +24 \qquad \text{signs alike}$$
$$-8 \times -3 = +24 \qquad \text{signs alike}$$
$$+8 \times -3 = -24 \qquad \text{signs unlike}$$

$$-24 \div -4 = +6 \qquad \text{signs alike}$$
$$+24 \div +4 = +6 \qquad \text{signs alike}$$
$$+24 \div -4 = -6 \qquad \text{signs unlike}$$
$$-24 \div +4 = -6 \qquad \text{signs unlike}$$

The best way to illustrate why you get these answers under multiplication of signs numbers is to consider a bank problem:

$$+8 \times +3 = +24$$

Tom puts $8 in the bank each month; thus, his savings account increases $8 each month, an increase which is here considered as $+8$. In three months ($+3$), his account will be increased by $24, or $+24$.

$$-8 \times 3 = -24$$

Tom takes out $8 a month from his savings account and this decrease is represented by -8. In three months at this rate, his savings account will have decreased by $24, or -24.

$$+8 \times -3 = -24$$

Tom puts $8 in the bank every month, thus his savings account increases $8 a month. Three months ago (-3) his account was $24 less than it is now, or -24 because he had not put any money into it at that time.

$$-8 \times -3 = +24$$

Tom takes $8 out of the bank each month and his savings decreases $8 a month. Three months ago (-3) his account was $24 more than it is now, or $+24$ since the money had not been drawn out of the bank.

Originate your own problems on sign numbers, and practice the rules and procedures given in this section.

Chapter XVIII

ALGEBRA*

Formulas

PUZZLES NOS. 297, 298

Average and Difficult

297. In algebra and geometry, we have many formulae or formulas. Each formula stands for an important mathematical rule. Here are a few which stand for nothing important in mathematics, as far as working problems is concerned; however, these letters stand for words which, when combined in one sentence, will give a student good general guides to follow in his classroom work. They deal with a mathematics classroom in particular. What does each formula stand for? See if you can help the student decipher them.

(a) $NH = 1 RF.$

(b) $\dfrac{TLM}{TOW} = GCC + DPOP$

(c) $MR = \dfrac{NFB}{IYW}$

Try making up some formulas yourself, or general rules.

298. What does the following formula mean?

$$YYUR + YYUB = ICURYY4ME$$

FUN NOVELTY NO. 36

Average

Under Arithmetic, it was explained how one determines the day of the week corresponding to the day of the month in any

* Except for the problems appearing under Formulas, all the problems in this section should be worked by algebraic methods.

given year. Review that section before continuing here (Fun Novelty No. 29).

Now, we use a formula to find the day of the week for any given year. The following formula gives the day under the Gregorian calendar:

$$S = Y + D + \frac{Y-1}{4} - \frac{Y-1}{100} + \frac{Y-1}{400}$$

S = sum or total
Y = year
D = day of the year beginning with January 1

Divide S by 7 and take the remainder, which will give you the day of the week by the following scale:

> 0 — Saturday
> 1 — Sunday
> 2 — Monday
> 3 — Tuesday
> 4 — Wednesday
> 5 — Thursday
> 6 — Friday

Let's try an example. What day does July 4, 1916, fall on? In the formula, Y = 1916, and D = 186 because 1916 is a leap year.

$$\begin{array}{r} 479 \\ 4\overline{)1916} \\ 16 \\ \hline 31 \\ 28 \\ \hline 36 \\ 36 \\ \hline \end{array}$$

Thus, January   31 days
        February   29 (leap year)
        March   31
        April   30
        May   31
        June   30
        July   4
                186 days

$$\frac{Y-1}{4} = \frac{1916-1}{4} = \frac{1915}{4} = 478 \text{ (ignore remainder)}$$

$$\frac{Y-1}{100} = \frac{1915}{100} = 19 \qquad \text{(ignore remainder)}$$

$$\frac{Y-1}{400} = \frac{1915}{400} = 4 \qquad \text{(ignore remainder)}$$

Now, substitute in the formula

$$S = Y + D + \frac{Y-1}{4} - \frac{Y-1}{100} + \frac{Y-1}{400}$$

and you get:

$$S = 1916 + 186 + 478 - 19 + 4$$
$$S = 2565$$

```
          366    (forget — don't use)
    7)2565
       21
       ──
       46
       42
       ──
       45
       42
       ──
        3    (remainder — use in answer)
```

The remainder, 3, is Tuesday — so July 4, 1916, falls on a Tuesday.

Try other examples — like today's date.

To find the day of a date way back in the 1400's, before the Gregorian calendar came into use (for Julian calendar only — before 1500)*:

$$S = Y + D + \frac{Y-1}{4} - 2$$

* See Chapter IX, Fun Novelty No. 29.

FUN NOVELTY NO. 37

$$T = C_4 + 37$$

This is called the "cricket formula"; it will give you the outdoor temperature of a hot summer night in degrees Fahrenheit.

T = outdoor temperature
C_4 = the number of times a cricket chirps in 1/4 minute (15 seconds)
C = chirps
4 = 1/4 minute

Add 37 to the number of chirps in a quarter of a minute (15 seconds) and you will have the outdoor temperature, Fahrenheit.*

Simple Equation

PUZZLES NOS. 299–314

Average

299. A sly old fox ate 100 grapes in five days, each day eating 6 more than on the day before. How many did he eat on each of the five days?

300. A bottle and a cork together cost $1.10. The bottle costs $1.00 more than the cork. How much does the cork cost? How much does the bottle cost?

301. Farmer Alexander was asked how many cows he had. He answered, "If 1/4, 1/5, and 1/6 of the herd were added together, they would make 37." How many cows does he have?

302. Find four consecutive odd numbers which, when added together, total 80.

303. Farmer Knutson told Dave and Rusty they could take apples off his tree, provided neither took more than 20 apples. After a minute Rusty asked Dave, "Have you picked your limit yet?" Dave replied, "Not yet — but if I had twice as

---

* For work on sign numbers, see Chaper XVII.

many as I have now, plus half as many as I have now, I would have my limit." How many did he have?

304. Solve this equation: $\dfrac{x}{.3} = \dfrac{5}{.6}$

305. How high is a tree which is 15 feet shorter than a pole three times as tall as the tree?

306. If 1/4 of 20 is not 5 but 4, 1/3 of 10 should be what?

307. A brick weighs 6 pounds plus half of its total weight. What is the total weight of the brick?

308. An important citizen needed his lawn cut for a big party he was having that evening, and it was a very big lawn. He called the Ace Employment Agency, who sent three men out. The first man claimed he could cut the whole lawn in 6 hours; the second said he could do it in 4 hours; and the third man said he could cut the grass in 3 hours.

It was midafternoon, and time was short, so the important citizen said, "I will hire all three of you."

Assuming the men can work as fast as they claim, can they finish the job in time if they all work together? How long would the job take?

309. Albert Einstein was once asked how many students he had. He replied, "One-half of them study mathematics, 1/3 of them study geometry, 1/7 study chemistry — and there are 20 who don't study at all." How many students did he have?

310. A water tank has 3 drains. If No. 1 drain is open, the water drains in 15 minutes. If No. 2 drain is open, the water drains in 30 minutes. If No. 3 drain is open, the water drains in 45 minutes. How long will it take to drain the water out of the big tank if all three drains are opened at the same time?

311. When a screen is placed 10 feet from a projector, the picture occupies 10 square feet. How large will the picture be when the projector is 15 feet from the screen?

312. Solve by algebra: George is 4 years older than John, who is 4 years older than Jim, who is four years older than Sam, who is 1/2 the age of George. How old is each boy?

313. Can you solve these problems:

(*a*) If 3 = 5, what does 4 equal?

(*b*) If 1/2 of 5 = 3, what is 1/3 of 10?

314. The village miller took 1/10 of the meal or flour he ground, for his fee. How much did he grind if a customer had exactly one bushel after the fee had been subtracted?

FUN PROJECT NO. 26: FORMULAS AND ALGEBRA IN EVERYDAY LIFE

Average (Read, Review, and Learn)

Why do we learn algebra? Many people ask what value this has in everyday living. Of course algebra is a prerequisite for higher mathematics work and scientific work. To learn chemistry, one must be able to manipulate formulas by algebra. But this is not the only reason for learning algebra. Algebra also helps in doing arithmetic. Algebra makes arithmetic more systematic. The following section on percentages done with the help of algebra will serve to illustrate this point. Percentage has always been a difficult topic for many of you. There are three different percentage cases requiring three separate operations by arithmetic. Knowing which of the three operations is needed to solve a particular problem in arithmetic is very confusing at times. By algebra, we use systematic procedures which require only one formula to solve all three cases. In the next section, it is shown how algebra can be used in cooking and scale drawing. Algebra may also be used in other formulas such as those of area, volume, interest, and the like, to find any missing fact. By arithmetic, one must sometimes multiply numbers to get the missing fact. The next time, however, one must multiply and then divide to get the missing fact. Knowing which technique to use can be very confusing. By algebra, this confusion is limited after one learns how to operate with the four simple equations.

A. Percentages

Here is presented a different way to do percentages, one which combines the methods of algebra with those of arithmetic. As I said above, each percentage problem consists of three parts, and any one of these parts can be missing. Also, being able to distinguish between the three can be quite confusing. Now, by algebra and the per cent formula $P = BR$, the problem becomes not three problems, but one — that of solving an algebraic equation. Before this can be done, you must be able to recognize and tell which number represents the base, which represents the rate, and which represents the percentage. Here are some simple rules to help you remember the three parts of a percentage problem.

(*a*) First find *base* or *whole* — the number coming after the word "of."

(*b*) Second, find *rate* — always the per cent (%).

(*c*) Third, find *percentage* or *part* — the other number, the number left over, the one you compare to the base.

Example:
$$6 \text{ is } 50\% \text{ of } 12$$

12 is the "base" (after the word "of")
50% is the "rate" (%)
6 is the "percentage" (other number left over)

$$\begin{array}{ccc} R & B & P \\ \end{array}$$
$$30\% \text{ of } 10 \text{ is } 3$$

You may abbreviate by putting a B over the base, R over the rate, and P over the percentage, as we did above.

Now, to solve percentages by algebra, let's take three examples, one of each type.

$$\begin{array}{ccc} P & R & B \\ \end{array}$$
$$6 \text{ is } 20\% \text{ of } \underline{\hspace{2em}}$$

Put in your B, R, and P. The base is missing, as you see. Write down the per cent formula and substitute as follows:

$$P = BR$$
$$6 = B \times .20$$
$$6 = .20B \quad \text{(put number before letter)}$$
$$.20B = 6 \quad \text{(turn around)}$$
$$\frac{.20B}{.20} = \frac{6}{.20} \quad \text{(divide both sides by .20 to solve for B)}$$
$$B = 30$$

$$.20\overline{)6.00}_{\wedge}^{\,30.}$$

The base is 30 or a whole number. In algebra, we always solve for the missing letter, wherever it might be.

The problem could have been done:

$$6 = B\,1/5 \quad \text{(use 1/5 for 20 per cent)}$$
$$1/5\,B = 6$$
$$5 \cdot 1/5\,B = 6 \cdot 5 \quad \text{(multiply both sides by 5)}$$
$$B = 30$$

This time, the rate is missing:

$$\begin{array}{ccc} P & R & B \\ \end{array}$$
$$6 \text{ is } \underline{\quad}\% \text{ of } 11$$

(write the same formula, always) $P = BR$

$$6 = 11R \quad \text{(substitute)}$$
$$11R = 6$$
$$\frac{11R}{11} = \frac{6}{11} \quad \text{(divide both sides by 11)}$$
$$R = 55\% \qquad \begin{array}{r} .545 = .55 = 55\% \\ 11\,\overline{)6.000} \end{array}$$

The rate is 55 per cent. Remember, R stands for rate and must be a per cent answer.

Now, assume the percentage is missing:

$$\begin{array}{ccc} R & B & P \\ \end{array}$$
$$16\% \text{ of } \$12 \text{ is } \underline{\quad}$$
$$P = BR$$
$$P = (\$12)(.16) \quad \text{substitute}$$
$$P = \$1.92$$

$$\begin{array}{r} \$12 \\ .16 \\ \hline 72 \\ 12 \\ \hline \$1.92 \end{array}$$

When two numbers are written side by side in a formula, this indicates multiplication. Thus, the percentage or part is $1.92.

With algebra, you do not actually need to know what is missing, or what type of per cent problem you have. You merely solve for the missing letter. Thus, algebra reduces per cent from three problems to one. Any per cent problem can be solved by using $P = BR$, the per cent formula and algebra.

B. Other formulas

In geometry, we come upon many formulas in finding the perimeter, area, and volume. Take the formula:

$$C = \pi d$$

which gives the circumference of a circle. In arithmetic, the textbooks give the diameter and you are asked to figure by simple substitution and calculation the circumference of the circle. Thus, you merely multiply π and the diameter to get the answer.

Assume that we have a big tree, and want to know its thickness or diameter. We can measure around the tree (its circumference), but we cannot measure the diameter. With algebra, we can solve the problem and find the diameter:

$$
\begin{aligned}
\text{Circumference} &= 9 \text{ feet} \quad \text{(around the trunk)} \\
C &= \pi d \qquad \pi = 3\tfrac{1}{7} \\
9 &= 22/7\ d \\
22/7\ d &= 9 \qquad \text{Solve for } d \\
7 \cdot 22/7\ d &= 9 \cdot 7 \quad \text{(multiply both sides by 7)} \\
22/22\ d &= 63/22 \quad \text{(divide both sides by 22)} \\
d &= 2\tfrac{19}{22} \text{ or } 2.9 \text{ feet (approx.)}
\end{aligned}
$$

A classroom has a cubic volume of 7,200 feet. Its width is 20 feet, its length is 30 feet. What is its height?

$$
\begin{aligned}
V &= lwh \\
7200 &= 30 \cdot 20\ h \quad \text{(substitute)} \\
7200 &= 600\ h \\
600h &= 7200 \qquad \text{(divide by 600)} \\
\overline{600} &= \overline{600} \\
h &= 12 \text{ feet high}
\end{aligned}
$$

The area of a square is given by a formula:

$$
\begin{aligned}
A &= s^2 \\
81 &= s^2 \\
s^2 &= 81 \quad \text{(take the square root of both sides)} \\
s &= 9
\end{aligned}
$$

You can easily devise many examples of area and volume formulas of your own, but solve for different letters rather than solving for the dependent variables.

The simple interest formula may also be used at this point: $I = PRT$. Sometimes the amount of interest is given, but the principal, rate of interest, or time might be unknown.

Example: How long would you have to lend a savings and loan company, paying 5 per cent interest, $600 to earn $10 interest:

$$I = PRT$$
$$\$10 = \$600 \cdot 5/100 \cdot T \quad \text{(substitute; time is missing)}$$
$$10 = 30\ T$$
$$\frac{30T}{30} = \frac{10}{30} \quad\quad\quad\quad \text{(divide by 30)}$$

$$T = 1/3 \text{ year or 4 months}$$

Rate is usually based upon a year, so an answer of 1/3 for time means 1/3 of a year or 4 months. If R is missing, a per cent answer would be expected.

Use other formulas, such as $d = rt$, the distance formula; or $SP = C+E+P$, the selling price formula; $c^2 = a^2+b^2$, the Pythagorean formula; and so on. Any missing variable can be found by the use of algebra. Try problems of your own.

FUN PROJECT NO. 27: USING ALGEBRA IN COOKING AND SCALE DRAWING

Average (Read and Learn)

As I said in the last section, algebra is very useful in everyday life and makes arithmetic more systematic. In this section, you will learn how algebra can be used in figuring the amount of each ingredient needed for any number of people in a cookbook recipe, other than the normal serving called for in the recipe. Also, you will learn how to use algebra in changing easily from one scale to another. In order to do this work, an understanding of ratio and proportion is necessary. When two numbers are compared by division, the result is called their ratio. When you compare two numbers like 4 and 8, you may say that they have the ratio of 4 to 8 and may be written as 4/8, which is reduced to 1/2, 4 ÷ 8, or 4:8. In 4:8, the ratio sign (:) indicates division and is read "divided by" or "to." The ratio of 8:4 is 8/4 = 2.

A proportion is a statement that two ratios are equal. For example, 2/10 = 3/15 or 2:10 = 3:15 means that 2 compares with 10 the same way that 3 compares with 15. You also know that both reduce to 1/5. However, in any proportion, the cross products are equal, and this is the important fact that we use in solving proportions by algebra. For example, in 2/10 = 3/15, 2 × 15 = 10 × 3:

$$\frac{2}{10} \diagup\!\!\!\diagdown \frac{3}{15}$$

$$3/4 = 9/12 \quad \text{because } 3 \times 12 = 4 \times 9$$

However, does 2/5 = 3/8? No, because 2 × 8 is not equal to 3 × 5.

In algebra, we can find any missing part of a proportion. For example:

$$x/20 = 7/50$$

$$\frac{x}{20} \diagup\!\!\!\diagdown \frac{7}{50}$$

Multiplying crossways we get:

$$50x = 140$$

Dividing both sides of the equation by 50 we get:

$$x = 2\tfrac{4}{5} \qquad \text{as our answer.}$$

The problem could have been stated also like this:

$$x:20 = 7:50$$

The problem is solved the same way by merely rewriting into the above form x/20 = 7/50.

With this brief explanation, we are ready to go ahead with the discussion of how to use algebra in cooking.

A. *Uses of algebra in cooking*

Here is a recipe for barbecued frankfurters from a standard cookbook. Servings: 4 people. Ingredients:

Sauté 1/4 cup chopped onion
in   2 tablespoons salad oil

Add, and simmer for 15 minutes:

2 teaspoons sugar
3/4 teaspoon dry mustard
1/4 teaspoon salt
1/8 teaspoon pepper
3/4 teaspoon paprika
6 tablespoons catsup
6 tablespoons water
3 tablespoons vinegar
2 teaspoons Worcestershire sauce
2 drops Tabasco sauce

Split and place in a baking dish:

8 frankfurters

Pour the sauce over them and bake in a moderate oven (375°) for 1/2 hour. Baste several times during baking.

Now this recipe serves four people. Suppose you wanted to serve only three people. How much of each ingredient would you use? Use a ratio and proportion here. The recipe calls for 2 teaspoons sugar for 4 persons. How many teaspoons sugar are required for 3 persons?

$$2 \quad : \quad 4 \quad = \quad x \quad : \quad 3$$
$$\text{tsps.} \qquad \text{persons} \qquad \text{tsp.} \qquad \text{persons}$$

$$2/4 = x/3$$
solving this proportion: $4x = 6$
Dividing by 4: $4x/4 = 6/4$
$$x = 1\tfrac{1}{2} \text{ teaspoons needed}$$

The recipe calls for 3/4 teaspoon dry mustard. For 3 servings you would need:

$$\begin{array}{ccccccc} 3/4 & : & 4 & = & x & : & 3 \\ \text{tsp.} & & \text{persons} & & \text{tsp.} & & \text{persons} \end{array}$$

$$\frac{3/4}{4} = \frac{x}{3}$$

$$4x = 9/4$$

Dividing by 4: $\qquad\qquad x = 9/16$ of a teaspoon

Most measuring spoons are 1 teaspoon, 1/2 teaspoon and 1/4 teaspoon. Thus, 9/16 teaspoon would be just a tiny bit over 1/2 teaspoon, which is 8/16. The rest of the ingredients are figured similarly. Can you do this?

But suppose you wanted to feed a whole school of, say, 220 boys and girls. The problem of a caterer or chef is a little different from that of the homemaker but the setting of a proportion will still solve the problem.

In the recipe given, 8 frankfurters are called for. How many would you need for 220 boys and girls?

$$\begin{array}{ccccccc} 8 & : & 4 & = & x & : & 220 \\ \text{franks} & & \text{servings} & & \text{franks} & & \text{servings} \end{array}$$

$$8/4 = x/220$$
$$4x = 1760$$
$$x = 440 \text{ frankfurters}$$

1/8 teaspoon of pepper is needed for 4 servings — how much is needed for 220 servings?

$$1/8 : 4 = x : 220$$

$$\frac{1/8}{4} = \frac{x}{220}$$

$$4x = 27\tfrac{1}{2} \text{ or } 55/2$$
$$x = 55/8 \text{ or } 6\tfrac{7}{8} \text{ teaspoons of pepper,}$$

but no doubt $6\tfrac{7}{8}$ would be considered 7 teaspoons of pepper.

Take any cookbook and make problems for serving your own family, yourself, and so forth, by changing the amount of ingredients needed for a particular recipe, depending upon the number of people to be served.

B. Scale drawing

On scale drawings, proportions are used by draftsmen, carpenters, architects, and so forth. For instance, on a scale drawing for a house, the architect uses a scale of 1/8 inch = 3 feet. How long is a bedroom which measures 3/4 inches on the drawing?

$$1/8 \quad : \quad 3 \quad = \quad 3/4 \quad : \quad x$$
$$\text{inch} \qquad \text{feet} \quad \text{inch} \qquad \text{feet}$$

$$\frac{1/8}{3} = \frac{3/4}{x}$$

$$1/8 \; x = 9/4$$

Multiply by 8

$$x = 18 \text{ feet long}$$

This example goes from the scale drawing to the actual size. Often, the reverse is true. The architect wants to make a scale drawing from certain facts. The scale is 1/8 inch = 3 feet. The kitchen is to be 13 feet wide. How many inches will he use to represent this on the scale drawing?

Scale		Real	Scale		Real
1/8 inch	:	3 feet	= x inches	:	13 feet

$$\frac{1/8}{3} = \frac{x}{13}$$

$$3x = 13/8$$

$$x = 13/24 \text{ inch}$$

This brings up the question: how can you measure 13/24 of an inch on a ruler graduated into sixteenths of an inch? We solve this problem by setting up another proportion

$$13/24 = x/16 \quad \text{(13/24 equals how many sixteenths?)}$$
$$24x = 208$$
$$x = 8\tfrac{2}{3} \quad \text{marks}$$

This means that 13/24 of an inch is closest to $\dfrac{8\frac{2}{3}}{16}$ inches, or 9/16 of an inch. A hairbreadth under 9/16 of an inch will give the desired length to represent 13 feet on the scale drawing. Measure $8\frac{2}{3}$ marks from 0 on a rule graduated into sixteenths, or between 0 inches and 1 inch.

Make up uneven problems of your own with the ruler, like 3/5 of an inch = ?/16 of an inch. How can this be measured on a ruler?

$$3/5 = x/16$$
$$5x = 48$$
$$x = 9\tfrac{3}{5} \text{ marks, or } \dfrac{9\frac{3}{5}}{16} \text{ of an inch,}$$

or about halfway between 9/16 and 10/16 of an inch.

Parentheses and the Simple Equation

PUZZLES NOS. 315–317

Average

315. A wise guy goes into a dry goods store and says, "Give me as much money as I have with me now, and I will spend $10 in your store." The proprietor agrees, and the man spends the money.

He goes into a second store and says, "Give me as much money as I have with me now and I will spend $10 in your store." The same thing happens.

In a third store, he repeats his proposition, after which he has no money left.

How much money did this man have to begin with?

316. Simplify or solve:

$$6 \times 8 \div 12 + 3 \times 24 - 12 \div 6 + 8 = ?$$

317. Show, by algebra, why this numerical computation which gives your telephone number, works:

(*a*) Take 60.

(*b*) Divide by 2.

(*c*) Add your telephone number digits.

(*d*) Subtract 25.

(*e*) Multiply by 3.

(*f*) Subtract 15.

(*g*) Multiply by 2.

(*h*) Divide by 6.

(*i*) The answer is your telephone number.

To solve by algebra, let x = your telephone number.

Simplification

PUZZLES NOS. 318–320

Average

318. Show by algebra why this numerical game works. The calculation gives you your house number and your age.

(*a*) Take your house number and double it.

(*b*) Add 5.

(*c*) Multiply by 50.

(*d*) Add your age.

(*e*) Add 365 for the number of days in a year.

(*f*) Subtract 615.

(*g*) Point off for dollars and cents, or put in a decimal point.

(*h*) The dollars will be your house number and the cents your age.

To solve by algebra, let x = your house number

y = your age

319. Give the algebraic explanation for this trick:

(*a*) Take any two digit number with different figures, like 87. You may use like numbers also, except 99.

(*b*) Double the number.

(*c*) Add 4.

(d) Multiply by 5.

(e) Add 12.

(f) Multiply by 10.

(g) Subtract 320.

(h) Cross out the 0's in your answer.

(i) The number left should be the number you started with — if you made no errors.

This will also work with three-figure numbers, four-figure numbers, etc.*

320. $\dfrac{STOP}{CUTS} = C$ (C is greater than 2)

What numbers do STOP and CUTS represent? None of the letters stands for 0. All C's represent the same number, as do the S's and T's. All different letters must be represented by different numbers.

GAME NO. 20

Average

20. (a) Take a number.

(b) Multiply by 2.

(c) Add 8.

(d) Divide by 2.

(e) Subtract the number you started with.

(f) Your answer is 4.

Assuming your first number was

$$
\begin{array}{r}
16 \\
\times 2 \\
\hline
32 \\
+8 \\
\hline
2\overline{)40} \\
\hline
20 \\
-16 \\
\hline
4
\end{array}
$$

If you know the trick to this puzzle, you can always give the answer beforehand. It is governed by step C, in which you add

* See further examples under Games, in Arithmetic section.

8. To determine the final answer, merely take 1/2 of the number you tell them to add in step C. In this case, it was 4.

Example 2:

(a) Take a number.
(b) ×2.
(c) +22.
(d) ÷2
(e) − number started with.
(f) = 11.

In step *c* you added 22; 1/2 of 22 is 11, which is the answer.

Take the number 89:

$$
\begin{array}{r}
89 \\
\times 2 \\
\hline
178 \\
+22 \\
\hline
2\,)\,\overline{200} \\
\hline
100 \\
-89 \\
\hline
11
\end{array}
$$

One-half of *c* is always the answer. Algebra helps explain why this trick works:

Example 1: Let x = number

$$\text{Simplify} \quad \frac{2x+8}{2} - x$$

$$= x + 4 - x$$

$$= 4$$

Example 2:

$$\text{Simplify} \quad \frac{2x+22}{2} - x$$

$$= x + 11 - x$$

$$= 11$$

Factoring

PUZZLES NOS. 321–323

Difficult

321. Prove $1 = 2$

Let $r = s$

Multiply by r	$r^2 = rs$
Subtract s^2 from both sides	$r^2 - s^2 = rs - s^2$
Factor	$(r-s)(r+s) = s(r-s)$
Divide by $(r-s)$	$r+s = s$
However,	$r = s$
therefore	$r+r = s$
	$2r = s$
or	$2r = r$
Divide by r	$2 = 1$
or	$1 = 2$

Obviously, something is amiss. Where is the fallacy in these steps?

322. Prove $0 \div 0 = 10$ or, $10 = 0$

$$25 - 25 = 0$$
$$5 - 5 = 0$$

Divide $(25-25)$ by $(5-5)$, thus $\dfrac{25-25}{5-5} = 0$

Factor $\dfrac{(5-5)\ (5+5)}{5-5} = 0$

Cancel $5+5 = 0$

$$10 = 0$$

Where is the fallacy here?

323. Prove $4 = 5$.

Now $16 - 36 = 25 - 45$ (since $-20 = -20$)

Add $81/4$ to each side $16 - 36 + 81/4 = 25 - 45 + 81/4$

Factor $(4 - 9/2)^2 = (5 - 9/2)^2$

Take the square root of both sides $4 - 9/2 = 5 - 9/2$

Add $9/2$ to each side $4 = 5$

Where is the fallacy here?

Equations in Two Unknowns
PUZZLES NOS. 324–329

Difficult

324. Farmer Blackwell and Farmer Meyer were taking their sheep to the market. Blackwell said, "Give me one of your sheep and I'll have as many as you." Meyer said, "Yes, but if you give me one of your sheep, I'll have twice as many as you have." How many sheep did each farmer start out with?

325. To make sure that Mark did good work in arithmetic, his father told him he would give him 8 cents for every problem correct on his homework, and deduct 5 cents for every problem he missed. The homework assignment consisted of 26 problems.

The next evening when Mr. Twine came home he asked Mark how much he owed him. Mark said, "You owe me nothing, Pop — we're even." How many problems did Mark do correctly? How many did he miss? (Solve by algebra.)

326. The top of a rectangular box has an area of 120 square inches; the area of the side is 96 square inches and of the end, 80 square inches. What are the dimensions of the box — length, width, and height? (See drawing, puzzle 265.)

327. Jimmy caught a big fish — its head was 5 inches long. Now, the tail is as long as the head plus half its body. Its body is as long as its head plus its tail. How long is the fish Jimmy caught?

328. Mrs. Burke is selling chicken eggs, duck eggs, and turkey eggs. Mr. Samson wants to buy 22 eggs and has 22 cents to spend. Chicken eggs cost 1/2 cent each; duck eggs cost 2 cents each, and turkey eggs cost 3 cents each. How many of each kind can Mr. Samson buy?

329. Explain how and why this mathematical game can be played by algebra:

(a) Think of any three numbers less than 10.
(b) Multiply the first number by 2.

(c) Add 5 to the product.
(d) Multiply this sum by 5.
(e) Add the second number.
(f) Multiply this last result by 10.
(g) Add the third number.
(h) What is your answer?

To get the number chosen in the beginning, merely subtract 250 from the result in Step h. The remainder is always the first three numbers thought of, and in the order in which you thought of them.

Now, show why this trick works with algebra. (This game is also included in the Arithmetic section.)

Quadratic Equations

PUZZLES NOS. 330–334

Average

330. Can you find the base of a right triangle whose altitude is 1/2 of its base, and whose hypotenuse is 10 inches long? (Find to the nearest tenth.)

331. A rope is tied to the top of pole *AD* which is 50 feet high, to the top of pole *BC* which is 20 feet high. The poles are 16 feet apart. How long is the rope from *D* to *C*?

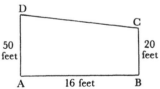

332.

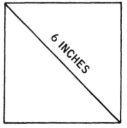

If the diagonal of a square is 6 inches long, what is the length of the side of the square, to the nearest tenth?

Difficult

333. Sammy jumped onto one end of a piece of tree trunk lying on top of a hill. The log was exactly 13 feet long (unlucky for the boy), and the impact caused the log to begin rolling downhill. As it rolled, Sammy managed to keep upright and slowly walked across the log to the other end, which he reached just as the log came to rest at the bottom of the hill, 84 feet from where it began to roll.

The log was 2 feet in diameter. How far did Sammy actually travel? How far would he have traveled had the log been 3 feet in diameter?

334. The difference between the square of two numbers is 16. One number is exactly 3/5 of the other. What are the two numbers?

ANSWERS TO PUZZLES

I. Introduction and History of Mathematics

1. Though scholars say the superstition came later, many still believe it originated from the number present at the Last Supper — 13.

2. Odd numbers were believed to be divine or heavenly, while even numbers were considered human and earthly.

II. Whole Numbers

READING AND WRITING WHOLE NUMBERS

3. The letter B (13 = 4) or N (IV), the Roman numeral for 4.

4. H O B O .

5. IVY (pronounced *i v*, the Roman numeral for 4).

ADDITION OF WHOLE NUMBERS

6. Both are wrong. Correct: "Seven and five *are* 12, not 13."

7. Here are three possible solutions:

6	1	8
7	5	3
2	9	4

2	7	6
9	5	1
4	3	8

8	1	6
3	5	7
4	9	2

8. Here are the five more, making ten: T E N .

9. Strike out the first figure of the top row, the whole of the second row, and the first two figures of the last row. The sum will stand:

$$\begin{array}{r} .11 \\ \cdots \\ ..9 \\ \hline 20 \end{array}$$

10. 2| (21)

11.

The sum, in all
directions, is 18.

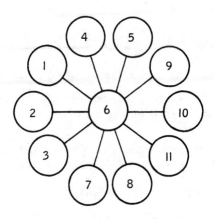

12. When you put them all together, this is only one hay-
stack.

13.   888
        88
         8
         8
         8
      ─────
      1,000

14. 18

15. (a)   44   (b)   444
           44   444
            4   44
            4   44
            4   4
          ─────   4
           100   4
                              4
                              4
                              4
                              4
                           ─────
                           1,000

16. From 11 A.M. to 1 P.M.

17.

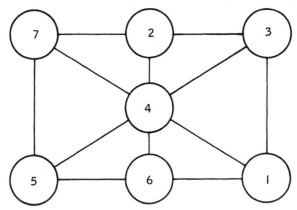

(adds to 12 in all directions)

18. What happened to the eleventh man? The second and the eleventh men are counted as the same man in this problem.

19.

20	1	12
3	11	19
10	21	2

(adds to 33 in all directions)

20. $22 + 2 = 24$

21. (a)
```
   5
   5
 +5
 ──
  15
```

(b) Two solutions
```
23    or    05
23          05
23          05
23          05
──          ──
92          20
```

(c)
```
89
 9
──
98
```

(d)
```
 999
   1
─────
1,000
```

22. 3 soldiers

23. To get the answer, merely add the figures in each upper left-hand corner of the squares in which the number appears. The sum will equal the age.

In the example of 30 given, the numbers in the upper left-hand corners are:

Square II	4
Square III	8
Square IV	2
Square V	16
Sum	30

Try other examples. Suppose you select the number 49:

Square I	1
Square V	16
Square VI	32
Sum	49

24. Begin the problem here:

```
       (S)  E  N  D
       (M)  O  R  E
      ─────────────
      (MO)  N  E  Y
```

      S
Now +M   cannot add to more than 19, so there is 1 to carry. Thus, M must be 1.

```
      S  E  N  D
      1  O  R  E
     ──────────
   1  O  N  E  Y
```

S must be 9 to give 10, and the letter O must be zero.

```
      9  E  N  D
      1  0  R  E
     ──────────
   1  0  N  E  Y
```

By continued experimentation, the final result is:

```
      9  5  6  7
      1  0  8  5
     ──────────
   1  0  6  5  2
```

25. 9 8 7 6 5
       1 2 3 4
     ─────────
     9 9 9 9 9

26. This problem is fairly easy to solve; the trick is that you do not have to use all these numbers to make 100. Just use those you wish to use.

$$
\begin{array}{lcr}
\text{Use two 16's} & = & 32 \\
\text{Use four 17's} & = & 68 \\
\hline
\text{Sum} & & 100
\end{array}
$$

27. Move 9 from Column III to Column I

$$
\begin{array}{ccc}
\text{I} & \text{II} & \text{III} \\
1 & 4 & 7 \\
2 & 5 & 8 \\
3 & 6 & \overline{15} \\
9 & \overline{15} & \\
\overline{15} & &
\end{array}
$$

All columns now total 15.

28. The same as a previous puzzle:

$$
\begin{array}{r}
888 \\
88 \\
8 \\
8 \\
8 \\
\hline
1,000
\end{array}
$$

29. The number of rows of grains on a normal ear of corn is always an even, never an odd number. Sweet corn usually has 8, 10, 12, or 14 rows. Field corn usually has 14, 16, 18, or 20 rows.

30. Here are three solutions:

1	15	14	4
12	6	7	9
8	10	11	5
13	3	2	16

1	14	15	4
8	11	10	5
12	7	6	9
13	2	3	16

1	12	13	8
15	6	3	10
4	9	16	5
14	7	2	11

31. 13 (counts as two odd numbers)
    3
    3
    1
    ――
    20

32. Here are four solutions:

859	364	765	849
743	725	324	357
1,602	1,089	1,089	1,206

33. 15
     36
     47
      2
    ――
    100

34. The first night, the men rearranged the remainder thus:

10	7	10
7		7
10	7	10

Total: 68 (4 are gone)

They took 2 men from each middle cell (8 men) and replaced one man in each of the four corners (4 men), allowing four to escape. The same procedure was continued for four nights. The arrangements for the second, third and fourth nights are:

Second night			*Third night*			*Fourth night*		
11	5	11	12	3	12	13	1	13
5		5	3		3	1		1
11	5	11	12	3	12	13	1	13
Total: 64			Total: 60			Total: 56		

Note that the total is still 27 on all four sides. This formula or technique will run out after four nights when 16 men have escaped, leaving 56 men still in jail.

35. 3915 (There are other
      15   possible solutions.)
    4826
    ――――
    8756

36. First day   8
    Second day   14
    Third day   20
    Fourth day   26
    Fifth day   32
                 ――――
                  100

37. 173	85	38. 17
4	92	19
177	177	21
		23
		80

SUBTRACTION OF WHOLE NUMBERS

39. Remove the "s" from "seven," and you have "even."

40. Only once, because later subtractions would not be from 190 but from a smaller resultant number.

41. 5809
2649
3160

42. (*a*) The catch in this problem is "three hundred and won." The answer is 536, not 537. Most people think you mean "one" (1).

Correct	Incorrect
236	236
300	301
536	537

(*b*) 19. There were twenty sick sheep, not twenty-six sheep.

43. TELEPHONE. Take away TELEPH and ONE is left.

44. The problem is wrongly stated. The men did not actually pay $27 for the room, but $25. If the problem is stated this way, the amount will total $30. The cost of the room ($25 + $3 rebate + $2 the bellboy kept) is $30.

Another way to state the problem is that the room costs $30, less a $3 rebate, leaving $27. Now, here is the fallacy of the originally stated problem. The $2 the bellboy got is not added to $27 to get $29, but should be subtracted from the $27 to get $25. The hotel clerk rebated $5 − $3 the men got back, but the $2 was kept by the bellboy. The total is $30.

45. L O V E. Take away L, O, and E, and V remains (Roman numeral for 5).

46. Use Roman numerals: XIX = 19. Take I away = XX or 20.

47. 16 days. At the end of 15 days, the frog has climbed 15 feet; on the sixteenth day, he climbs 5 feet more and is out of the well, so he does not fall back 4 feet on that day.

48. Take three groups:

	11	7	6
Move 1. Take 7 from 11 and add it to the 7 group:	4	14	6
Move 2. Take 6 from the 14 group and add it to the 6 group:	4	8	12
Move 3. Take 4 from the 12 group, add to the 4 group, which gives you the desired result.	8	8	8

49. $9+8+7+6+5+4+3+2+1 = 45$
$\underline{-1+2+3+4+5+6+7+8+9 = 45}$
$8+6+4+1+9+7+5+3+2 = 45$

50. D O Z E N S. Subtract "S" and DOZEN remains = 12.

51. II = IIII − II

52. (*a*) 70,839   (*b*) 24,794   or   36,156
　　　　6,458　　　　　16,452　　　　28,693
　　　　64,381　　　　　8,342　　　　　7,463

53. 5 sheep and 7 sheep

54. $98 - 76 + 54 + 3 + 21 = 100$

MULTIPLICATION OF WHOLE NUMBERS

55. 31 and 1 (31 × 1 = 31)

56. 0

57. Twice ten is 20 and 2 times 11 is twenty-two (too).

58. 496 pages. The pages between "the first and last book" are only 2 books, or $248 \times 2 = 496$ pages.

59. Jim is carrying empty bags.

60. 4 brothers and 3 sisters.

61. Three different answers: $6 \times 6 - 6 = 30$
$$5 \times 5 + 5 = 30$$
$$33 - 3 = 30$$

62. (a)
$$\begin{array}{r} 8009 \\ \times\ \ 58 \\ \hline 64072 \\ 40045 \\ \hline 464522 \end{array}$$

(b)
$$\begin{array}{r} 384 \\ \times 26 \\ \hline 2304 \\ 768 \\ \hline 9984 \end{array}$$

63. The same three cats!

64. (a) 3,628,800 different ways. This would require a period of over 9,935 years ($10 \times 9 \times 8 \times 7 \times 6 \times 5 \times 4 \times 3 \times 2 \times 1$).

(b) 120 ways ($5 \times 4 \times 3 \times 2 \times 1 = 120$).

65. Problem:
$$\begin{array}{r} ..3 \\ \times\ \ 2.. \\ \hline .1.7 \\ .7. \\ .14. \\ \hline .25..7 \end{array}$$

Solution:
$$\begin{array}{r} 573 \text{ (multiplicand)} \\ \times\ 219 \text{ (multiplier)} \\ \hline 5157 \\ 573 \\ 1146 \\ \hline 125487 \end{array}$$

How to get this answer:

(1) The units digit of the multiplier must be 9 because only $3 \times 9 = 27$.

(2) Two in the hundreds digit of the multiplier times 3 in the units digit of the multiplicand is 6 ($3 \times 2 = 6$).

(3) The third partial product consists of four digits, thus the hundreds multiplicand digit must be over 4 so that there will be at least one to carry ($4 \times 2 = 8$ only); ($5 \times 2 = 10$). Thus the tens digit of the multiplier must be a 1; otherwise the middle partial product would be greater than the three digits (middle partial product is .7.).

$$\begin{array}{r} \text{(must be over 4)} \rightarrow (.)\ .\ 3 \\ 2\ (.)\ . \\ \hline /\text{(must be 1)} \end{array}$$

Say
$$\begin{array}{r} (5)\ .\ 3 \\ 2\ (2). \\ \hline 2\ \ .\ 5 \end{array} = (10, \text{ which is 1 to carry}), \text{ thus you would have}$$

..7. for the middle partial product which is too large. The only way to get .7. is for the tens digit to be 1. So far, then, we have

$$
\begin{array}{r}
..3 \\
219 \\
\hline
.1.7 \\
.73 \\
.146 \\
\hline
.25..7
\end{array}
$$
  (multiply by 7 whenever you can)

(4) To get the 4 in the third partial product, the tens digit in the multiplicand must be a 2 or 7 since $2 \times 2 = 4$ and $2 \times 7 = 14$. However, there must be 1 to carry because the third digit in this third partial product is a 1, and 2 times anything always equals an even number. Therefore, to get an odd number there must be 1 to carry. Thus, $2 \times 7 = 14$ is the only possible choice. So the tens digit in the multiplicand is a 7.

The problem now looks like this:

$$
\begin{array}{r}
.73 \\
219 \\
\hline
.157 \\
.73 \\
.146 \\
\hline
.25487
\end{array}
$$
  (multiply by 7 wherever you can)

(5) There are several ways to get the hundreds digit in the multiplicand. Take the first partial product — $9 \times 7 = 63 + 2 = 65$ — or there is 6 to carry to the final multiplication which has a 1 as its end digit. The answer can only be 11, 21, 31, 41, etc., after you multiply by 9 and carry 6.

We said earlier that this digit must be 5 or more. Take trial multiplications to determine correctness.

Try 5 $9 \times 5 = 45 + 6 = 51$ (okay)

,, 6 $9 \times 6 = 54 + 6 = 60$ (no)

,, 7 $9 \times 7 = 63 + 6 = 69$ (no)

,, 8 $9 \times 8 = 72 + 6 = 78$ (no)

,, 9 $9 \times 9 = 81 + 6 = 87$ (no)

Thus 5 is the only number which works.

Another method is to take the third partial digit. Here the answer must also end in 1 — there is 1 to carry from $2 \times 7 = 14$.

Try 5 $2 \times 5 = 10 + 1 = 11$ (okay)

„   6 $2 \times 6 = 12 + 1 = 13$ (no)

    etc.

Again 5 is the only number that works. Thus, putting in the 5, we get the final answer:

$$
\begin{array}{r}
573 \\
219 \\
\hline
5157 \\
573 \\
1146 \\
\hline
125487
\end{array}
$$

66.
$$
\begin{array}{r}
117 \\
319 \\
\hline
1053 \\
117 \\
351 \\
\hline
37323
\end{array}
$$

67. Two solutions are possible:

$$
\begin{array}{rcr}
1253 & \text{or} & 3759 \\
69 & & 23 \\
\hline
11277 & & 11277 \\
7518 & & 7518 \\
\hline
86457 & & 86457
\end{array}
$$

68. Since there are 36 heads (36 creatures) in all, if all had been birds they would have 72 feet; if all were beasts, they would have 144 feet. It is clear, therefore, that we had some of each and, assuming there was an equal number of each, we would have:

18 birds	36 feet
18 beasts	72 feet
36 heads	108 feet

But 108 feet is 8 too many. Each bird added takes away 2 feet and gives us 1 fewer beasts. Since an equal division gives us 8 too many feet, we must deduct 4 beasts and add 4 birds and thus we get:

(add 4 birds)	22 birds	44 feet
(deduct 4 beasts)	14 beasts	56 feet
	36 heads	100 feet

69. $6 - 5 + 7 \times 4 - 3 = 26$

70. There are three possible answers. From what we are given:

$$
\begin{array}{r}
..3 \\
..3 \\
\hline
3.. \\
.3. \\
..3 \\
\hline
.....
\end{array}
$$

you can readily see some of the other digits:

$$
\begin{array}{r}
1.3 \\
1.3 \\
\hline
3.9 \\
.3. \\
1.3 \\
\hline
....9
\end{array}
$$

The second digit in the second partial product is 3. To get this you would have to multiply 1×3 or 2×6 and have 1 to carry. Here are two possible answers:

$$
\begin{array}{r}
123 \\
163 \\
\hline
369 \\
738 \\
123 \\
\hline
20049
\end{array}
\qquad
\begin{array}{r}
113 \\
133 \\
\hline
339 \\
339 \\
113 \\
\hline
15029
\end{array}
$$

71. 357
      43
    ‾‾‾‾
    1071
    1428
    ‾‾‾‾‾
    15351

72. 1475
      677
    ‾‾‾‾‾
    10325
    10325
    8850
    ‾‾‾‾‾‾
    998575

DIVISION OF WHOLE NUMBERS

73. The catch in this problem is the word "ears." If he carries two ears (his own) on his head and one ear of corn each day, it will take him six days. Corny, eh?

74. Serve mashed potatoes.

75. 9 minutes — the tenth piece will require no cutting.

76. 3 socks. If you take out a green one the first time, a red one the next, the third has to be red or green.

77. $\dfrac{8888 - 888}{8} = 1{,}000$

78.
```
       38
  50)1900
     150
     ‾‾‾
     400
     400
     ‾‾‾
```

79.

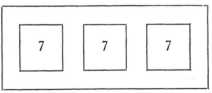

Put 7 pigs in each of three small pens, then put a fourth pen around all of them in case they escape the smaller pens. There is then an odd number in each of the 4 pens, with 21 in the large pen.

80. Use Roman numerals: XII = 12.

Take half ✗✗✗ and get VII (7).

81. $7\overline{)364}$ Take 9 of the 349, turn it upside down to make a 6, move it between the 3 and 4 to get 364. The division comes out even with an answer of 52.

82. 420 days   83. 301

84. $1+2+3+4 \div 5+6-7+8 = 9$. (This problem must be done in the order in which it is written and not by rules of algebra.)

85.
$$
\begin{array}{r}
173 \\
215\overline{)37195} \\
215 \\
\hline
1569 \\
1505 \\
\hline
645 \\
645 \\
\hline
\end{array}
$$

Here's how you get this answer:

(1) The first quotient figure is 1, which makes the first product 215

$$
\begin{array}{r}
1xx \\
215\overline{)xxxxx} \\
215 \\
\hline
x5x9 \\
x5x5 \\
\hline
x4x \\
x4x \\
\hline
\end{array}
$$

(2) The last product has but 3 digits, thus in x times 215, the x cannot be over 4 because $5 \times 215 = 1075$, or a 4-digit number. Also, 3×215 is the only number which gives 4 as the middle digit.

$$
\begin{array}{r}
215 \\
\times 3 \\
\hline
645
\end{array}
$$

Now, we have

$$
\begin{array}{r}
1x3 \\
215\overline{)xxxxx} \\
215 \\
\hline
x5x9 \\
x5x5 \\
\hline
645 \\
645 \\
\hline
\end{array}
$$

(3) To get the middle-quotient digit, one sees this number x times 215 must give $x5x5$. What digit in the quotient will give a 5 as the units digit and a 5 as the hundreds digit? Also, when you multiply, the product must be a 4-digit answer. We know that 1×215 and 3×215 do not give 4 digits; 2, 4, 6, and 8 will not work as they give a result of 0 in the units digit.

Try 5 $215 \times 5 = 1075$ (no, because hundreds digit is 0)

„   7 $215 \times 7 = 1505$ (correct)

„   9 $215 \times 9 = 1935$ (no)

The number 7 is the only number which yields a 5 in the units and hundreds digits.

(4) Put the 7 in its place and complete the problem, but first multiply to get the dividend:

$$\begin{array}{r} 215 \\ \times\ 173 \\ \hline 645 \\ 1505 \\ 215 \\ \hline 37195 \end{array}$$

Now,

$$\begin{array}{r} 173 \\ 215\overline{)37195} \\ 215 \\ \hline 1569 \\ 1505 \\ \hline 645 \\ 645 \\ \hline \end{array}$$

86. $\dfrac{3527}{7\overline{)24689}}$

87. It would take a total of 20,349 weeks, or more than 390 years, for all different combinations of 5 friends to eat together. I don't think they'll complete the plan. This problem may be worked by algebra.

Answer: $\dfrac{21 \times 20 \times 19 \times 18 \times 17}{5 \times 4 \times 3 \times 2 \times 1} = 20,349$

88. $\begin{array}{r} 82 \\ -11 \\ \hline 71 \end{array}$ were then members

       left

Five countries were permanent, so no election was held. Six were left and 3 new ones were elected each year.

$$\dfrac{23\tfrac{2}{3}\ \text{or 24 years}}{3\overline{)71}}$$

89. $(6 \times 8 \div 12) + (3 \times 24) - (12 \div 6) + 8 =$
$\qquad 4 \qquad + 72 \qquad - \quad 2 \qquad + 8 =$
$\qquad\qquad\qquad 76 \qquad - \quad 2 \qquad + 8 =$
$\qquad\qquad\qquad\qquad 84 - 2 =$

Answer: 82

90.
```
        90809
  12)1089708
     108
     ───
      97
      96
      ───
      108
      108
      ───
```

AVERAGES

91. There are several ways to work this problem; the important thing is to recognize that the 3-mile check carries more weight than the $1\frac{1}{2}$-mile check — actually twice as much. A simple way to work this problem is to do it by halves:

$3 = 6$ halves $\qquad$ 140 mph for each half
$1\frac{1}{2} = 3$ halves $\qquad$ 168 mph for each half

In the last $1\frac{1}{2}$ are 3 halves — 210 mph for each half:

```
  140      168      210      840
  × 6      × 3      × 3      504
  ───      ───      ───      630
  840      504      630     ────
                           1974
```

How many halves are there in 6 miles? 12; thus,

```
        164½
  12)1974
     12
     ──
     77
     72
     ──
      54
      48
     ──
       6
```

The average is $164\frac{1}{2}$, or 164.5 mph.

Another method: Count the three-mile count twice:

$$
\begin{array}{r}
140 \\
140 \\
168 \\
210 \\
\hline
4\,)\overline{658} \\
\hline
164\frac{1}{2} \text{ mph}
\end{array}
$$

92. The scores on the other papers were both 49. Carl probably wanted to forget the "flunking" grades and tore up the paper. We arrive at 49 by the following steps:

(1) Add the four grades given.

$$
\begin{array}{r}
100 \\
84 \\
72 \\
60 \\
\hline
316
\end{array}
$$

(2) The average of the six papers is 69.

$$
\begin{array}{r}
69 \\
\times\,6 \\
\hline
414
\end{array}
$$

(3) 414 should be the sum of the grades on the six papers.

$$
\begin{array}{r}
414 \\
-316 \\
\hline
98 \text{ difference}
\end{array}
$$

(4) 98 points are missing from the total sum necessary.

$$
\begin{array}{r}
49 \\
2\,)\overline{98}
\end{array}
$$

Carl got the same scores on the missing tests, or 49. Notice all four processes are utilized in this problem.

MAKING CHANGE

93. The puzzle said, "One coin is not a 50-cent piece." However, the other coin *is* a 50-cent piece — the one that is not is a nickel — a matter of listening carefully!

94. He used a $50 bill, a $5 bill, and four $2 bills:

$$\begin{array}{r} \$50 \\ 5 \\ \underline{8} \quad (4 \times \$2) \\ \hline \$63 \end{array}$$

95. (*a*) 21 coins:

1 half dollar	$0.50		2 quarters	$0.50		7 dimes	$0.70
2 dimes	.20		3 dimes	.30		4 nickels	.20
3 nickels	.15		1 nickel	.05		10 pennies	.10
15 pennies	.15		15 pennies	.15			
21 coins	$1.00		21 coins	$1.00		21 coins	$1.00

(*b*) 50 coins:

40 pennies	$0.40
8 nickels	.40
2 dimes	.20
50 coins	$1.00

96.

5	1	25	10
10	25	1	5
1	5	10	25
25	10	5	1

97. It is possible to change a dollar in 292 different ways. There are 40 combinations without pennies, 40 combinations without nickels, 74 without dimes, 158 without quarters, and 242 without half-dollars!

98. The coins were 2 pennies, 3 dimes, 1 quarter, and 1 half dollar. They could not change a dollar. They could not change 50 cents because:

$0.25
.20 (2 dimes)
.02 (2 pennies)
―――――
$0.47

They could not change a quarter because:

$0.20 (2 dimes)
.02· (2 pennies)
―――――
$0.22

They could not change a dime because all they had was 2 pennies — and they couldn't change a nickel, either!

III. Fractions

REDUCING FRACTIONS

99. 6/9.
100. (a) 76/95 = 4/5 (reduce by 19)
    (b) 85/102 = 5/6 (reduce by 17).

ADDITION OF FRACTIONS

101. (a) $99\frac{99}{99}$ (b) $99\frac{9}{9}$.
102. The teacher said she would give the student a quarter. She did not say the quarter was a coin; she gave the student a quarter of the torn paper! One of the four pieces is a quarter of a whole sheet.

103. He cut his horse into halves and two halves make a whole (hole). Now he can get out through the hole.

104. If you say $2\frac{1}{4}$ inches, you are with the majority; however, you are wrong. The worm travelled 1/4 inch.

When two volumes stand together on a bookshelf, Volumes I and II respectively, the first page of Volume I and the last page of Volume II are separated only by two covers. Try it yourself and you'll believe it. Each cover is 1/8 inch thick; thus two covers are 2/8 or 1/4 inch thick, and the worm ate its way through the two covers or 1/4-inch thickness.

Vol.	Vol.
I	II

page 1 of book ↗ ↖ last page of book

105. The man simply laid down one of his boards across the corners of the land and, placing the other board on top of that, was able to span the intervening distance and walk safely over to the castle.

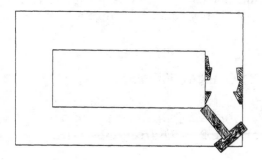

106. The first man could do the whole job in 6 hours or 1/6 of the job in 1 hour; the second could do 1/4 of the job in 1 hour (4 hours by himself); the third could do 1/3 of the job in 1 hour (3 hours by himself). If all men work for an hour, together they will do:

$$1/6 = 2/12$$
$$1/4 = 3/12$$
$$1/3 = 4/12$$
$$\overline{9/12 \text{ or } 3/4 \text{ of the job}}$$

They can do 3/4 of the job in 1 hour:

$$3/4 = 1 \text{ hour}$$
$$1/4 = 1/3 \text{ hour}$$
$$4/4 = 4/3 \text{ or } 1\tfrac{1}{3} \text{ hours}$$

The whole lawn can be cut in $1\frac{1}{3}$ hours, or an hour and 20 minutes, and therefore the men can finish cutting the lawn before dinner time if they all work together.

107.

$1\frac{3}{6} + 98\frac{27}{54} + 0$	$= 100$	15
$80\frac{27}{54} + 19\frac{3}{6}$	$= 100$	36
$70 + 24\frac{9}{18} + 5\frac{3}{6}$	$= 100$	47
$87 + 9\frac{4}{5} + 3\frac{12}{60}$	$= 100$	$\overline{98}$
		$+2$
		$\overline{100}$

$$9 \times 8 + 7 + 6 + 5 + 4 + 3 + 2 + 1 = 100$$

108. 60 cows

109. $9 + 99/99 = 9 + 1 = 10$

110. $79 + 5\frac{1}{3} = 84 + 2/6$

111. There is a trick to this problem: "1/2 of them study mathematics, 1/3 of them study geometry . . ." Geometry is a part of mathematics (included in the general field of mathematics), this 1/3 is included in the 1/2 listed for mathematics. There are really only two fractions used — one for mathematics and one for chemistry.

(a) $\quad 1/2 = 7/14 \quad$ (14/14 represents the whole class, thus
$\quad +1/7 = 2/14 \quad$ 5/14 do not study, period.)
$\qquad \overline{9/14}$

$$5/14 = 20$$
$$1/14 = 4$$
$$14/14 = 56 \text{ students}$$

If you forget the tricky statement and use the fractions listed in the problem the solution is:

(b) $\quad 1/2 = 21/42$
$\quad 1/3 = 14/42$
$\quad 1/7 = \underline{\quad 6/42}$
$\qquad 41/42$ of a possible 42/42, thus
$\quad 1/42 = 20$
$\quad 42/42 = 840$ students — and that is too many students.

Since (*a*) makes sense, that is probably correct, but you may use either solution.

112. Once you see the pattern, a thousand or more answers can be given. These fractions both add and multiply to the same result:

$$3 \text{ and } 1\tfrac{1}{2} \begin{cases} 3 + 1\tfrac{1}{2} = 4\tfrac{1}{2} \\ 3 \times 3/2 = 4\tfrac{1}{2} \end{cases}$$

$$4 \text{ and } 1\tfrac{1}{3} \begin{cases} 4 + 1\tfrac{1}{3} = 5\tfrac{1}{3} \\ 4 \times 4/3 = 5\tfrac{1}{3} \end{cases}$$

$$5 \text{ and } 1\tfrac{1}{4} \begin{cases} 5 + 1\tfrac{1}{4} = 6\tfrac{1}{4} \\ 5 \times 5/4 = 6\tfrac{1}{4} \end{cases}$$

$$6 \text{ and } 1\tfrac{1}{5} \begin{cases} 6 + 1\tfrac{1}{5} = 7\tfrac{1}{5} \\ 6 \times 6/5 = 7\tfrac{1}{5} \end{cases}$$

$$7 \text{ and } 1\tfrac{1}{6} \begin{cases} 7 + 1\tfrac{1}{6} = 8\tfrac{1}{6} \\ 7 \times 7/6 = 8\tfrac{1}{6}, \text{ etc.} \end{cases}$$

The denominator of the fraction is always one number smaller than the whole number. This pattern may be continued indefinitely.

113. The father died at 84, the son at 42 when his father was 80. The father's life: childhood, 14 years; youth, 7 years; bachelorhood, 12 years; married at 33; the son was born when his father was 38. This problem may be worked by addition of fractions:

$$\begin{aligned} 1/6 &= 14/84 \\ 1/12 &= 7/84 \\ 1/7 &= \underline{12/84} \\ & \ 33/84 \end{aligned}$$

He must have died at 84 since the denominators of the fractions, 6, 12, and 7, have 84 as their least common denominator. He was married at 33 because 33/84 of his life came before his marriage. His son came 5 years later when the father was 38, and died at 42, half the age of his father when he died. The father was 80 years old at the time of the problem.

114. $35/70 + 148/296 = 1$
  $1/2 + 1/2 = 1$

115. In making his will, the man must have had in mind that his wife inherit twice as much as a daughter, but only half as much as a son. (If a son were born, he would get 2/3 of the estate and the wife 1/3; if a daughter were born, she would get 1/3 of the estate and his wife 2/3). This plan could be fulfilled by giving the daughter 1/7 of the estate, the wife 2/7, and the son 4/7.

Daughter: 1/7, which is 1/2 of 2/7
Wife: 2/7
Son: 4/7, which is twice 2/7

116. $98\frac{27}{54} + 1\frac{3}{6} = 100$

SUBTRACTION OF FRACTIONS

117. $8 - 8/8 = 7$

118. The other half of the apple.

119. One method is to make three subtraction problems:

$$25\tfrac{3}{7} - 16\tfrac{3}{8} - 3\tfrac{1}{9} - 2\tfrac{3}{10} = \ ?$$

$$25\tfrac{3}{7} = 25\tfrac{24}{56}$$
$$16\tfrac{3}{8} = 16\tfrac{21}{56}$$
$$\overline{\quad 9\tfrac{3}{56}\quad}$$

$$9\tfrac{3}{56} = 9\tfrac{27}{504} = 8\tfrac{531}{504}$$
$$-3\tfrac{1}{9} = 3\tfrac{56}{504} = 3\tfrac{56}{504}$$
$$\overline{\quad 5\tfrac{475}{504}\quad}$$

$$5\tfrac{475}{504} = 5\tfrac{2375}{2520}$$
$$2\tfrac{3}{10} = 2\tfrac{756}{2520}$$
$$\text{Answer:}\quad 3\tfrac{1619}{2520}$$

Another method would be to add $16\tfrac{3}{8}$, $3\tfrac{1}{9}$, and $2\tfrac{3}{10}$; then subtract this result from $25\tfrac{3}{7}$.

MULTIPLICATION OF FRACTIONS

120. $8 - 8 - \dfrac{0}{0}$ (0 or nothing is left top and bottom.)

Also, zero; $\frac{1}{2}(\frac{1}{2} - \frac{1}{2} = 0)$.

121. (a) 2/3 of SIX is IX or 9
    (b) 1/2 of FIVE is IV or 4
    (c) 1/2 of XI is XI or VI = 6

122. $1\frac{1}{2}$ days

123. Y, which is 1/4 of the word YARD which equals 36 inches; thus, 1/4 of 36 = 9 and Y = 9 inches.

124. Spell out 12 and 7:

$$1/3 \text{ of T W } \underline{\text{E L}} \text{ V E} = \underline{\text{EL}}$$
$$+4/5 \text{ of S } \underline{\text{E V E N}} = \underline{\text{EVEN}}$$
$$\text{ELEVEN}$$
$$\text{EL} + \text{EVEN} = \text{ELEVEN}$$

125. There are only 3 women, not 4. They were grandmother, mother, and daughter. Two were mothers: grandmother and mother. Two were daughters: mother and daughter. (1/3 of $18 = $6.) They spent $6.

126. The fractions 1/2, 1/3, and 1/9 do not add to unity or a whole.

$$
\begin{array}{rl}
1/2 &= 9/18 \\
1/3 &= 6/18 \\
1/9 &= 2/18 \\
\hline
&17/18
\end{array}
$$

Evidently this farmer was not a good arithmetician; he did not divide all of his horses so that the whole amount would have been the total result. By adding another horse to make 18, the division of the horses is possible but the total result is 17 since 17/18 of 18 = 17.

127. 79 applenuts

First man: $79 \div 3 = 26 + 1$ left over for dog

$$
\begin{array}{r}
79 \\
-27 \\
\hline
52 \text{ left}
\end{array}
$$

Second man: $52 \div 3 = 17 + 1$ left over for dog

$$52$$
$$-18$$
$$\overline{34} \text{ left}$$

Third man: $34 \div 3 = 11 + 1$ left over for dog

$$34$$
$$-12$$
$$\overline{22} \text{ left}$$

Morning division: $22 \div 3 = 7 + 1$ for dog.

128. $\dfrac{1/3 \times 6}{4/6 \times 12/2} + 3/4 = \dfrac{2}{2/3 \times 6} + 3/4$

$= 2/4 + 3/4 = 5/4 = 1\frac{1}{4}$ (answer)

129. "And" means plus ($+$) and "of" means times ($\times$). The rule in algebra is that all multiplications must be done before the additions. The wording is most important.

(a) $1/3 + (1/2 \times 1/3) + (1/2 \times 10/1) = 1/3 + 1/6 + 5 = 5\frac{1}{2}$

(b) Here, the word "and" was changed to "of"; also, the comma is important — it does not appear in (c).

$(1/3 + 1/2 \times 1/3) \times (1/2 \times 10/1)$
$= (1/3 + 1/6) \times 5$
$= 1/2 \times 5 = 2\frac{1}{2}$

(c) When the comma is taken away, you have a completely different problem:

$1/3 + 1/2 \times 1/3 \times 1/2 \times 10/1$
$= 1/3 + 10/12$
$= 1/3 + 5/6 = 1\frac{1}{6}$

130. $2\frac{2}{3}$, found as follows:

Since 5 is 4 and 1/3 of $10 = 3\frac{1}{3}$,

the correct answer is only 4/5 of what it should be, thus:

$4/5 \times 3\frac{1}{3} = 4/5 \times 10/3 = 8/3 = 2\frac{2}{3}$

131. The watermelon weighs 2 pounds.

1 watermelon = 2/3 lb. + 2/3 watermelon,
thus, 1/3 watermelon = 2/3 lb.
3/3 watermelon = 2/3 × 3/1 = 2 lbs.

Easy by algebra:

Let x = number of pounds of the watermelon
x = 2/3 lb. + 2/3 x
1/3 x = 2/3
x = 2 lbs.

132. He had 8 apples. Twice as many would be 16, half as many would be 4; the total is 20.

133. Joan's father is 25 years old. Joan is 4 years and 2 months old, or $4\frac{1}{6}$ years.

DIVISION OF FRACTIONS

134. $\dfrac{3/7}{1/2}$ = 3/7 ÷ 1/2 = 3/7 × 2/1 = 6/7 (answer)

135. $\dfrac{3/8 - 1/12}{6/5 + 3/10} = \dfrac{9/24 - 2/24}{12/10 + 3/10} = \dfrac{7/24}{15/10}$

= 7/24 ÷ 15/10 = 7/24 × 10/15 = 7/36

136. Four ways to show that 6 ÷ 1/2 = 12:

(a) Regular method — Inversion

6 × 2/1 = 12

(b) Take 6 pies and cut them into halves:

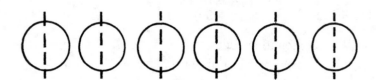

you get 12 halves. The number of halves in 6 pies is 12.

(c) Use subtraction of fractions and keep taking halves away until 0 remains:

$$
\begin{array}{r}
6 \\
-\frac{1}{2} \\
\hline
5\frac{1}{2} \\
-\frac{1}{2} \\
\hline
5 \\
-\frac{1}{2} \\
\hline
4\frac{1}{2} \\
-\frac{1}{2} \\
\hline
4 \\
-\frac{1}{2} \\
\hline
3\frac{1}{2} \\
-\frac{1}{2} \\
\hline
3 \\
-\frac{1}{2} \\
\hline
2\frac{1}{2} \\
-\frac{1}{2} \\
\hline
2 \\
-\frac{1}{2} \\
\hline
1\frac{1}{2} \\
-\frac{1}{2} \\
\hline
1 \\
-\frac{1}{2} \\
\hline
\frac{1}{2} \\
-\frac{1}{2} \\
\hline
0
\end{array}
$$

The number of 1/2's subtracted is 12; thus, you can take only 12 halves away from 6.

(d) Change both fractions to the same denominator:

$$6 \div 1/2 = 12/2 \div 1/2$$

Now, you may divide the first numerator by the second numerator:

$$12 \div 1 = 12$$

137. Add 31/42 = 31/42

$$+3/7 = 18/42$$

$$49/42 = 1\tfrac{7}{42} = 1\tfrac{1}{6}$$

The overlap is 1/6; thus, the window which is 8 feet high is 1/6 of the height of the whole house.

1/6 of the house = 8 feet

6/6 of the house = 48 feet

The house is 48 feet high.

138.

$$= 4\overline{)3\,\overline{)6/8}} \qquad + 3\,\overline{)3/16 + 3}$$

$$= 4\overline{)6/8 \div 3/1} + 3\,\overline{)3\tfrac{3}{16}}$$

$$= 4\overline{)6/8 \div 3/1} + 3\,\overline{)3\tfrac{3}{16}}$$

$$= 4\overline{)3/4 \times 1/3} + 3\,\overline{)51/16}$$

$$= 4\overline{)1/4} \qquad + 3\,\overline{)51/16}$$

$$= 1/4 \div 4/1 \quad + 51/16 \div 3/1$$

$$= 1/4 \times 1/4 + 51/16 \times 1/3$$

$$= 1/16 + 17/16$$

$$= 18/16 = 1\tfrac{2}{16}$$

$$= 1\tfrac{1}{8} \text{ (answer)}$$

139. $\dfrac{5/3 - 3/7}{1/2 + 1/11} = \dfrac{35/21 - 9/21}{11/22 + 2/22} = \dfrac{26/21}{13/22} = 26/21 \div 13/22$

$$= 26/21 \times 22/13 = 44/21$$

$$= 2\tfrac{2}{21} \text{ (answer)}$$

140. Solve by division of fractions.

(a) If 3 = 5, then 4 = ?

3 out of 5 = 3/5

4 ÷ 3/5

4 × 5/3 = 20/3 = $6\tfrac{2}{3}$ (answer)

(*b*) 1/2 of 5 = $2\frac{1}{2}$
  1/3 of 10 = $3\frac{1}{3}$
  If $2\frac{1}{2}$ = 3, then $3\frac{1}{3}$ = ?
  $2\frac{1}{2} \div 3$
  $5/2 \times 1/3 = 5/6$

  $3\frac{1}{3} \div 5/6$ $\dfrac{\overset{2}{\cancel{10}}}{\underset{1}{\cancel{3}}} \times \dfrac{\overset{2}{\cancel{6}}}{\underset{1}{\cancel{5}}}$ = 4 (answer).

141. $5 \div 5 \div 5 \div 5 \div 5 \div 1/5 \div 1/5 \div 1/5$ = 1 (answer)
  $= 1 \div 5 \div 5 \div 5 \div 1/5 \div 1/5 \div 1/5$
  $= 1/5 \times 1/5 \div 5 \div 1/5 \div 1/5 \div 1/5$
  $= 1/25 \times 1/5 \div 1/5 \div 1/5 \div 1/5$
  $= 1/125 \times 5 \div 1/5 \div 1/5$
  $= 1/25 \times 5 \div 1/5$
  $= 1/5 \div 1/5$
  $= 1/5 \times 5/1$
  $= 1$

142. The brick weighed 12 pounds. The weight of each of the halves would have to be equal; since 1/2 of the weight is 6 pounds, the other half must also be 6 pounds.

143. $1\frac{1}{9}$ bushels
  $10/9 \times 1/10 = 1/9$ and $1\frac{1}{9} - 1/9$ = 1 bushel left
  or $9/10$ = 1 bushel
   $1/10 = 1/9$ bushel
   $10/10 = 10/9$ or $1\frac{1}{9}$ bushels

IV. Decimals

ADDITION OF DECIMALS

144. $11,000   eleven thousand
     1 100   eleven hundred
      .11   and eleven
   ─────────
   $12,100.11   (answer)

So you write eleven thousand, eleven hundred, and eleven as $12,100.11.

145. Jim is an elevator operator in the Empire State Building in New York. He makes two trips every 4 minutes to the eightieth floor and back — a distance of 2,000 feet. During a 6-hour day, this totals 180,000 feet, or 34.58 miles.

146. The letter is "A" or "a." The letter "a" does not appear when you spell out the numbers from 1 to 999:

    27   twenty-seven
    342   three hundred forty-two
    981   nine hundred eighty-one (no *a*'s)

The letter "a" does appear in the word "thousand," and all numbers from 1,000 to 1,000,000 will have an "a" in them.

    1932   one thous*a*nd nine hundred thirty-two

The letter "a" also appears in mixed decimals:

    23.68   twenty-three *a*nd sixty-eight hundredths
    1.7   one *a*nd seven tenths

SUBTRACTION OF DECIMALS

147. $6\frac{3}{8} - 4.175 =$

(*a*) $6.375 - 4.175 = 2.2$

(*b*) $6\frac{3}{8} - 4\frac{7}{40} = 6\frac{15}{40} - 4\frac{7}{40} = 2\frac{8}{40} = 2\frac{1}{5}$

The answer is 2.2 or $2\frac{1}{5}$.

148. The amount started with was $8.75.

First store	$ 8.75	$17.50
	$+8.75$	-10.00
	$17.50	$ 7.50 left
Second store	$ 7.50	$15.00
	$+7.50$	-10.00
	$15.00	$ 5.00 left
Third store	$ 5.00	$10.00
	$+5.00$	-10.00
	$10.00	$ 0.00 left

149. The cork cost $0.05; the bottle cost $1.05.

150. $5 + 5 - 5 + .5 + .5 = 6$.

MULTIPLICATION OF DECIMALS

151. .00072

152. 1.25 or $1\frac{1}{4}$ ($1.25 \times 4 = 5$)

153. The fallacy is that the multiplication of fractions was not done correctly. Improper rules were used.

The quantity $16\frac{1}{2}$ means $16 + 1/2$ and $12\frac{1}{2}$ means $12 + 1/2$. Thus, the multiplication must be done like this:

$$
\begin{array}{ll}
16\frac{1}{2} & \\
12\frac{1}{2} & \\
\hline
8 & (1/2 \times 16) \\
6 & (1/2 \times 12) \\
\frac{1}{4} & (1/2 \times 1/2) \\
32 & (16 \times 2) \\
16 & (16 \times 1) \\
\hline
206\frac{1}{4} & \text{(answer)}
\end{array}
$$

You get 206.25 through multiplication of decimals.

154. The man suggested cutting up one of the 5 separate pieces he brought in. He suggested cutting all 3 links on one (1) chain into 3 separate links and using these links to join the remaining 4 separate pieces into one complete chain.

Take one separate piece

CUT   CUT   CUT

Put it back

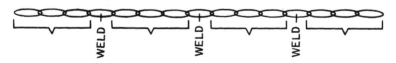

WELD   WELD   WELD

(only 4 separate pieces remain)

The cost is:

	3 cuts	3 cents
	3 welds	6 cents
	total	9 cents

The machinist used the customer's own links to weld the broken chain.

155. 10 right and 16 wrong

10	16	$0.80
.08	.05	−.80
$0.80	$0.80	0

156.

14 sheets of paper	$0.07
8 pens	.08
2 pencils	.05
1 eraser	.05
25 articles	$0.25

157. 16 chicken eggs
   4 duck eggs
   2 turkey eggs

$$\frac{16}{.005} = \$0.08$$

$$\frac{4}{.02} = .08$$

$$\frac{2}{.03} = \frac{.06}{\$0.22}$$

DIVISION OF DECIMALS

158.

$$.67/3.2 = 3.2_\wedge)\overline{.6_\wedge700} \quad .209 = .21 \text{ (answer)}$$

$$\begin{array}{r} 6\ 4 \\ \hline 300 \\ 288 \\ \hline 12 \end{array}$$

159. $\dfrac{7+7}{.7} = 20$

160. $\dfrac{6.314 + 7\frac{3}{4}}{6\frac{1}{2} - 3.615} \div \dfrac{1.89}{3.42}$

$= \dfrac{6.314 + 7.75}{6.5 - 3.615} \div \dfrac{1.89}{3.42}$

$= \dfrac{14.064}{2.885} \div \dfrac{1.89}{3.42}$

$= \dfrac{14.064}{2.885} \times \dfrac{3.42}{1.89}$

$= \dfrac{48.09888 \rightarrow (14.064 \times 3.42)}{5.45265 \rightarrow (2.885 \times 1.89)}$

$8.82 = 8.8 \text{ (answer)}$

$= 5.45265_{\wedge} \overline{)48.09888_{\wedge}8}$

161. He knew that 35/247 of all the fish he caught were tagged on the second trapping. He tagged 135 fish to begin with, so

35/247 of all the fish $= 135$
1/247 of all the fish $= 135 \div 35 = 3.86$ approx.
247/247 of all the fish $= 247 \times 3.86 = 953$,,

Answer: approximately 950 fish.

162. The reciprocal of 7 or 1/7

$\begin{array}{r} .142857 \\ 7\overline{)1.000000} \end{array}$

$\begin{array}{r} .142857 \\ +.142857 \\ \hline .285714 \\ +.142857 \\ \hline .428571 \\ +.142857 \\ \hline .571428 \\ +.142857 \\ \hline .714285 \\ +.142857 \\ \hline .857142 \\ +.142857 \\ \hline .999999 \end{array}$

Now if .142857 is added to itself, you will get a sum in which the same digits appear but differently arranged. All the subtotals contain the same digits as the number you began with, and after the sixth addition, your answer is all 9's.

163. $7/.7 \times 7/.7 = 10 \times 10 = 100$

164. $\dfrac{7.293}{14.586} = 1/2$

V. Percentages

PERCENTAGE MISSING

165. $1.00, found as follows:

$$
\begin{array}{r}
10000\% = 100 \\
\$0.01 \\
\times 100 \\
\hline
\$1.00
\end{array}
$$

RATE OF PER CENT MISSING

166. $66\frac{2}{3}\%$ or 2/3 pure. Pure gold is 24 carats, thus 16 carats is 2/3 or $66\frac{2}{3}\%$ pure.

167. 48% are girls and 52% are boys.

25% or 1/4 of all the girls went to the game.

50% or 1/2 of all the boys went to the game.

$1/4 \times 48\% = \underline{12\%}$ of the girls went to the game.

$1/2 \times 52\% = \underline{26\%}$ of all the boys went to the game.

Answer: $\overline{38\%}$ of all the students went to the game.

168.   1/3 is ———% of 1/2

      2/6 is ———% of 3/6

2 out of 3 is 2/3 and the answer is $66\frac{2}{3}\%$.

169. He gained the nearest to 20,000 per cent by the return of the dollar. After returning the $5, he was broke, with $0. The return of the dollar was a sheer gift on the part of his friend. John was left with nothing at all, and it is upon that "nothing" that the percentage of gain must be figured. The

per cent of gain from 0 to $1 is the same as computing what per cent 1 is of 0.

Now, $1 \div 0$ is not defined — it is impossible to divide by 0 and get an exact answer. However, when you divide by 0, you get a huge answer, so large that it is unimaginable — it is usually called infinity or ∞. Consequently, the largest per cent listed is 20,000 per cent gain. This is the nearest to a correct answer, even though the answer would be much larger.

Note that a gain from 0 to $2, 0 to $10, 0 to $50, etc., would all give the same answer of ∞ or a tremendously large per cent.

BASE MISSING

170. 30% of 50 is 6% of————.

$$30\% \text{ of } 50 = \begin{array}{r} 50 \\ .30 \\ \hline 15.00 \end{array}$$

Thus, 15 is 6% of————.

$$6\% = 15$$
$$1\% = 2.5$$
$$100\% = 250 \text{ (answer)}$$

171. 1,200 feet long

(1) $\begin{array}{r} 20\% \\ + 16\frac{2}{3}\% \\ \hline \end{array}$

$36\frac{2}{3}\%$ of the bridge not over the river
$63\frac{1}{3}\%$ of the bridge does span the river

thus, $63\frac{1}{3}\% = 760$ feet

$$1\% = 760 \div 63\frac{1}{3}$$
$$= 760 \div 190/3$$
$$= 7\overset{4}{6}\cancel{0} \times 3/\underset{1}{\cancel{190}}$$
$$1\% = 12$$
$$100\% = 1,200 \text{ feet}$$

(2) This problem may also be solved with fractions:

$$20\% = 1/5 = 6/30$$
$$16\tfrac{2}{3}\% = 1/6 = 5/30$$
$$\overline{\phantom{16\tfrac{2}{3}\% = 1/6 = }11/30}$$

$$19/30 = 760$$
$$1/30 = 40$$
$$30/30 = 1{,}200 \text{ feet}$$

VI. Business Mathematics

DISCOUNT

172. 20% "off" means he paid 80% of the original price.

$$80\% = \$34$$
$$1\% = \$.425$$
$$100\% = \$42.50$$

```
        .425
80)34.000
   32 0
   ----
    2 00
    1 60
    ----
      400
      400
```

The original price was $42.50.

173. He will sell the dress for $27.26.

.12 = 12% discount, first reduction

40 to $35.20   40)4.80

```
$35.20              $35.20
  .12                4.22
 -----              ------
 70 40              $30.98    after second reduc-
352 0                3.72     tion
-------             ------
$4.2240            $27.26     (answer)

$ 30.98
    .12
 ------
  61 96
 309 8
 ------
$3.7176 = $3.72
```

COMMISSIONS

174. $5,368,709.12 would be your earnings on the thirtieth day. The problem is actually 2^{30} and the doubling amounts to:

Day			Day		
1	$0.01		11	$	10.24
2	.02		12		20.48
3	.04		13		40.96
4	.08		14		81.92
5	.16		15		163.84
6	.32		16		327.68
7	.64		17		655.36
8	1.28		18		1,310.72
9	2.56		19		2,621.44
10	5.12		20		5,242.88

Day		
21	$	10,485.76
22		20,971.52
23		41,943.04
24		83,886.08
25		167,772.16
26		335,544.32
27		671,088.64
28		1,342,177.28
29		2,684,354.56
30		5,368,709.12

175. His salary is $55 and he earned $80, which is $25 over his salary. He also earns 1 per cent of everything over $800 in sales, thus:

$$1\% = \$25$$
$$100\% = \$2,500$$
$$\$2,500$$
$$+800$$
$$\overline{\$3,300} \text{ (answer) sold in one week}$$

176. There are two possible solutions:

(*a*) They originally sold them at the rate of 7 for 2 cents each. The oldest sold 14 cents' worth and had 1 left.

$$7 \text{ at 2 cents each} = 14 \text{ cents}$$

$$
\begin{array}{r}
7\,\overline{)50} \\
49 \\
\hline
1
\end{array}
$$

The second sold 8 cents' worth and had 2 left.

$$
\begin{array}{r}
4 \\
7\,\overline{)30} \\
28 \\
\hline
2
\end{array}
$$

The third sold 2 cents' worth and had 3 left.

$$
\begin{array}{r}
1 \\
7\,\overline{)10} \\
7 \\
\hline
3
\end{array}
$$

The watermelons left over were the choicest, so they sold for a higher price of 6 cents each:

First	14¢ + 6¢	= 20¢
Second	8¢ + 12¢	= 20¢
Third	2¢ + 18¢	= 20¢

and each one brought home 20 cents.

(*b*) Standard rate: 10 cents a dozen, 5 cents for any leftovers.

First   sold 4 dozen = 48 + 2 left = 50 watermelons
$$40¢ + 10¢ = 50¢$$
Second   sold 2 dozen = 24 + 6 left = 30 watermelons
$$20¢ + 30¢ = 50¢$$
Third   sold 10 watermelons at 5¢ = 50¢

Each brought home 50 cents.

SELLING PRICE

177. $20. When he sold the horse for $90, it had no effect upon the answer because we do not know how much he paid for the horse in the first place. He bought the horse back for $80 and resold him for $100; the gain on this transaction (his profit) is $20.

178. He lost $ 5 on the hat
              15 in bills
              ─────
              $20 total loss

or, he lost $15 and the hat.

179. (a) Selling price = 100% (SP = cost + expenses + profit).

Cost	= 3/5 of 100%	60%
Profit	= 1/6 of 60%	10%
Expenses	= 3 × 10%	30%
Check		100%

(b)

Cost	Expense	Profit
$ 20	$ 20	$ 20
.60	.30	.10
$12.00	$ 6.00	$ 2.00

VII. Banking and Interest

BANKING

180. 25 ones.

181. A cent or penny.

182. There is no reason to expect the sum of the two columns to be equal. Experiments with other withdrawals and balances will clarify any erroneous thinking associated with this puzzle, which is exceptional in that the sum of the withdrawals is arranged to result to within $1 of the sum of the bank balance.

183. The largest bill made by the United States Government is the $10,000 bill. The sum of one each of all U.S. currency is:

$$
\begin{aligned}
&\$10,000 \\
&5,000 \\
&1,000 \\
&500 \\
&100 \\
&50 \\
&20 \\
&10 \\
&5 \\
&2 \\
&1 \\
&1 \text{ silver dollar} \\
&.50 \\
&.25 \\
&.10 \\
&.05 \\
&.01 \\
\hline
&\$16,689.91
\end{aligned}
$$

184. (a) False. It is not sensible, since the amount can easily be altered; but it is legal.

(b) False. You simply endorse the check twice, first as it is spelled on the payee's line, then as you correctly spell it.

(c) True. But if the banker thinks the check is "stale" — old — he may refuse to honor the check.

(d) True. Banks can plead a disclaimer if the check was originally too carelessly written, inviting alteration.

(e) False. The law in most states provides that checks must be presented for payment "within a reasonable time" — usually three months to a year.

(f) False. In most states, the bank usually pays the amount written in words, unless a serious discrepancy makes it advisable to get in touch with the depositor.

(g) False. If funds on deposit are insufficient to cover the full amount of your check, the bank is not required to pay any part of it.

(h) True. Perfectly good checks have been written for amounts ranging from $00.00 to $7,500,000,000.00. A check for $00.00 was sent to the Collector of Internal Revenue by a taxpayer who wanted to impress upon the Collector that he owed nothing. The $7,500,000,000 check was written by the Treasury Department in the process of transferring funds.

(i) True. "Counter checks" are provided by the banks for depositors who wish to draw from their accounts. They are not generally negotiable.

(j) True. A "certified" check guarantees that sufficient funds from the depositor's account have been set aside to honor the check when it is presented.

(k) True. Since your bank cannot know who made the change or erasure, it does not have to honor an altered check.

(l) False. State laws against doing business on Sunday chiefly concern the making of contracts. A check is not a contract, but an order on your bank.

(m) True. Endorsement with merely a signature (a "blank endorsement") transfers ownership of a check to the bearer.

(n) True. This is known as a "restrictive endorsement" and means that the check can be used for no purpose other than a deposit to your account.

(o) True. A restrictive endorsement which reads "Pay to John McCarthy only" means that no one else can cash the check — and neither can he endorse it to a third party.

(p) True. A bank will often stop payment via a telephone call, but only out of courtesy and as a temporary measure to accommodate the depositor until he can make it official in writing — a letter will probably not reach the bank for another day.

(q) False. A recent court ruling held that only the person who signs the check can issue a stop-payment order on it.

185. The check was $123 (or $132, $231, $213, $312, or $321).

$$1 \times 2 \times 3 = 6$$
$$1 + 2 + 3 = 6$$
$$\overline{\text{Difference } 0}$$

INTEREST

186. Carl paid nothing for borrowing a quarter for a week because:

$$I = PRT$$
$$I = 25/100 \times 4/100 \times 7/360$$

(25 cents = 25/100 and 7 days is 7/360 of a year, using 360 days to the year)

$$I = 7/36,000 = 36,000\overline{)7.0000}^{\;.00019 \,=\, .0002}$$

The interest is $.0002.

Now, to earn 1 cent interest on a quarter:

$$1/100 = 25/100 \times 4/100 \times T$$
$$1/100 = 1/100\,T$$
$$T = 1 \text{ year}$$

It would take 1 year exactly for Jim's quarter to earn 1 cent interest at the rate of 4 per cent.

To earn 1 cent interest on a nickel:

$$1/100 = 5/100 \times 4/100 \times T$$
$$1/100 = 5/100\,T$$
$$T = 5 \text{ years}$$

It would take 5 years exactly for Jim's nickel to earn 1 cent interest at the rate of 4 per cent.

IX. Measurement

LINEAR MEASUREMENT

187. Go to bed in the daytime.

188. Carpet.

189. A yardstick.

190. The three pieces would be

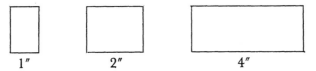

1"   2"   4"

after making two cuts. He would then pay as follows:

First night   1-inch piece (total 1 inch)

Second night 2-inch piece and took back 1-inch piece (total 2 inches)

Third night   gave back 1 inch (total 3 inches)

Fourth night gave 4-inch piece and took back 1-inch and 2-inch pieces in exchange (total 4 inches)

Fifth night   gave back 1-inch piece (total 5 inches)

Sixth night   gave back 2-inch piece and took back 1-inch piece (total 6 inches)

Seventh night gave 1-inch piece (total 7 inches)

Chart of pieces each has after each night

Night	Employer	Employee
1	4" 2"	1"
2	4" 1"	2"
3	4"	1" 2"
4	1" 2"	4"
5	2"	1" 4"
6	1"	2" 4"
7	0"	1" 2" 4"

191. Make a drawing to facilitate the answer:

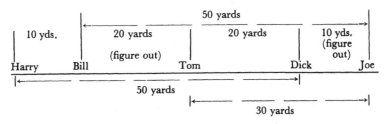

The drawing will give you the complete information. Two distances are easily figured, as indicated by the other information given.

Joe is in first,   10 yards ahead of Dick.
Dick is second,   20 yards ahead of Tom.
Tom is third,   20 yards ahead of Bill.
Bill is fourth,   10 yards ahead of Harry.
Harry is fifth   — ahead of nobody.

TIME

192. (a) 156 times in a 24-hour day:

$$
\begin{array}{r}
1 \\
2 \\
3 \\
4 \\
5 \\
6 \\
7 \\
8 \\
9 \\
10 \\
11 \\
12 \\
\hline
78 \\
\times 2 \\
\hline
156 \text{ times}
\end{array}
$$

(b) Time to get the clock repaired.

193. A quarter to two.

194. A little before Eve.

195. The march (March) you've just had of 31 days.

196. (a) Pop it (or plant it).
    (b) December–January.

197. The clock which doesn't run at all is correct twice a day; the other is correct only twice a year. If a clock loses 4

minutes every day, and makes one complete revolution every 12 hours, it will take 180 days before the hands coincide again.

$$
\begin{array}{rl}
24 & \text{hours} \\
60 & \text{minutes} \\
\hline
1440 & \text{minutes in 24 hours} \\
\hline
360 & \text{times}
\end{array}
$$

$$4\,\overline{)1440}$$

The clock needs to turn 360 times before the hands will coincide, or 180 days since the hour hand goes around twice in one day.

198. She started counting at 11:00 in the morning — 34 chimes in all. Going backwards:

3:30	1 chime
3:00	3 chimes for the hour
2:30	1 chime
2:00	2 chimes
1:30	1
1:00	1
12:30	1
12:00	12
11:30	1
11:00	11
	34 chimes

199. The year 1881.

DISTANCE

200. SMILES — there is a MILE between the first and last letters.

201. No way. An electric train should not produce smoke.

202. He drove the same average speed. An hour and a half is 90 minutes.

203. 15 trains. Every day a train starts from each end, and seven trains are en route to begin with. The traveler meets another train as he leaves, which makes 15.

204. North Pole.

205. Neither. Wherever the cars meet, they will be the same distance from New York at that moment.

WEIGHTS

206. A pound of feathers. This is true because feathers are weighed by the avoirdupois pound which contains 7,000 grains, while gold is weighed by the troy pound which contains only 5,760 grains:

$$\text{avoirdupois pound} = 16 \text{ ounces}$$
$$\text{troy pound} \qquad = 12 \text{ ounces}$$

207. One is mail fee and the other is female.

208.
$$\text{Half-dozen dozen eggs} = 6 \text{ dozen eggs}$$
$$\text{six dozen dozen eggs} \quad = 72 \text{ dozen eggs}$$
$$72 \text{ dozen} - 6 \text{ dozen} \quad = 66 \text{ dozen eggs}$$
Answer: 66 dozen or 792 eggs.

209. Divide the balls into three groups of three balls each. Place two of the three groups on opposite ends of the scale. This will determine the group that is the lightest, if the lightest ball is contained in one of these groups of three. If the groups balance on the scale, then the lightest ball is in the group of three not being weighed.

Now take this group of three that contains the lightest ball and make your second test on the scales. Place one ball on each side of the balanced scale. If the scale does not balance, the side containing the lighter ball will rise. If the scale balances, the ball not being weighed is the one that weighs the least.

LIQUID MEASURE

210. Fill the 5-quart jar and from that fill the 3-quart jar. This leaves 2 quarts in the 5-quart jar. Now, pour the contents of the 3-quart jar into the stream and pour the 2 quarts remaining in the 5-quart jar into the 3-quart jar. Fill the 5-quart jar again and then the 5 quarts and the 2 quarts will add to 7 quarts.

X. Geometry

DEFINITIONS

211. 30 squares.

212. Neither — peacocks do not lay eggs, the peahens lay the eggs.

213. O-*HI*-O — round at both ends and high (HI) in the middle.

214. Twenty triangles.

215. Polygon (Polly gone).

216. Fifty-one rectangles. They are:

1	2-4-6	5-6-12
2	4-6-8	6-12
3	4-6	1-2-3-4
4	6-8	1-2-3-4-5-6
5	1-3	3-4-5-6
6	1-3-5	3-4-5-6-7-8
7	3-5	5-6-7-8
8	3-5-7	9-10-3-5
9	5-7	9-10-3-5-4-6
10	9-3	3-5-4-6-11-12
11	9-3-4	4-6-11-12
12	3-4	1-2
1-2-3-4-5-6-7-8	3-4-11	7-8
1-3-5-7	4-11	9-10
2-4-6-8	10-5	11-12
9-3-4-11	10-5-6	
10-5-6-12	5-6	
9-3-4-11-10-5-6-12		
2-4		

Total: 51

217. Eleven squares.

GEOMETRICAL DRAWINGS

218.

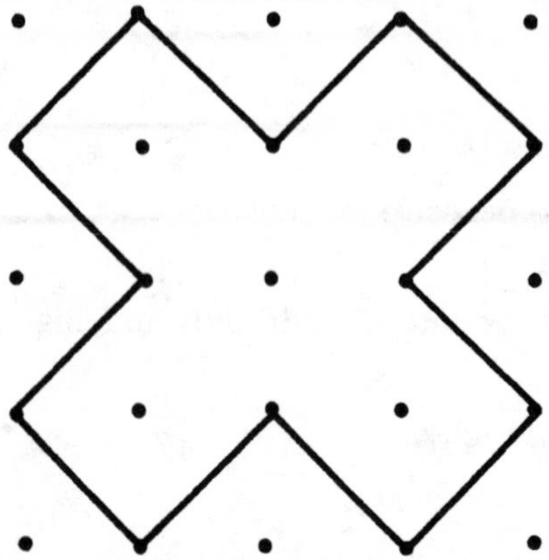

5 dots are inside and 8 dots remain outside.

219. One possible solution: Follow the numbers: start at 4-3-2-1-7-10-6-9-8-5.

220.

(move this one to the corner)

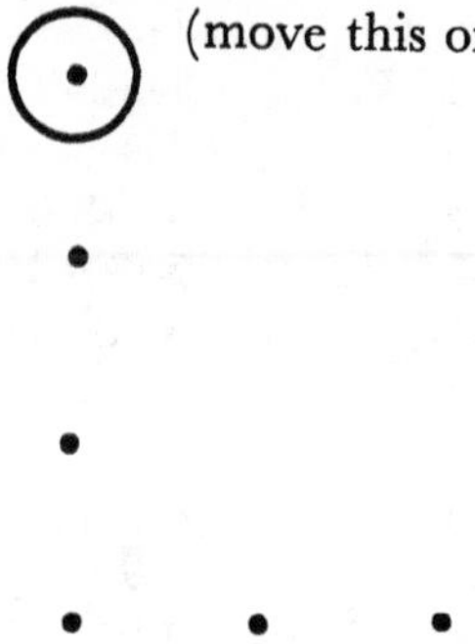

Put this coin on top of the other coin, giving 4 coins in each row.

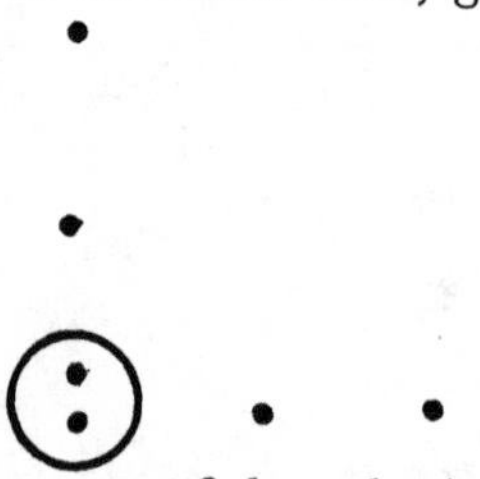

(on top of the other)

221. N I N ☰   (add 5 lines to get NINE)

222.

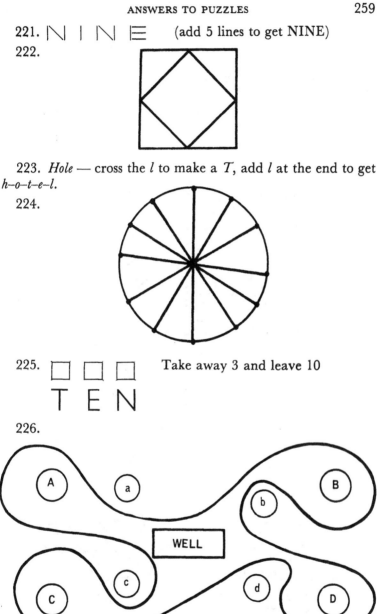

223. *Hole* — cross the *l* to make a *T*, add *l* at the end to get *h–o–t–e–l*.

224.

225. ▢ ▢ ▢   Take away 3 and leave 10

T E N

226.

227. Move number 9 line, and place it on top of lines 1 and 3. Move number 10 line and place it between lines 5 and 6.

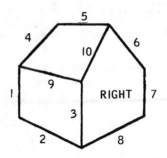

228. Start at line 5 and follow this path: 5, 2, 4, 6, 8, 10, 11, 9, 1, 3, 7. One can also start at line 7.

229. One solution:

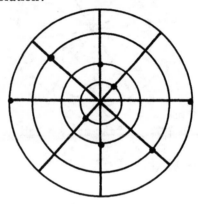

230. Move coins numbered 1, 7, 10.

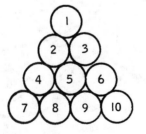

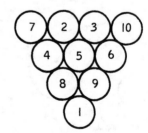

231.

(Using 10 apples and 5 lines with 4 apples in each line.)

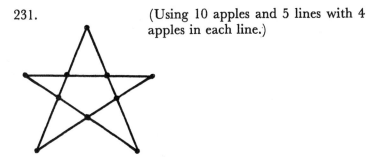

232.

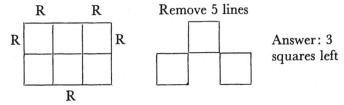

R = remove

233. The trick here is to go up a line of the puzzle:

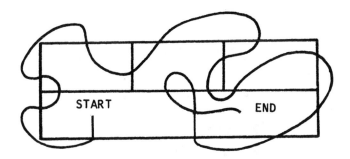

Nothing was stated against going up a line of the puzzle. Also, in the end you crossed a line of the puzzle which had not yet been crossed, and not really your own line; however, nothing was said in the original problem about crossing your own line of the puzzle. Therefore, this is a valid solution.

234. To make this in one continuous line requires a kind of trick.

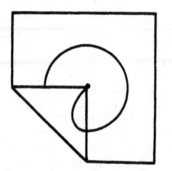
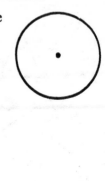

Use the edge of a piece of paper and fold this edge as indicated above. Put the dot for the center of the circle on the nonfolded part of the paper, right next to the vertex of the folded part. Draw the line from the dot down onto the folded edge and then go off the side of the folded edge to begin your circle as shown. Continue the circle and complete it by unfolding your paper to its original condition.

235.

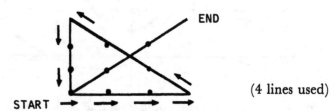

(4 lines used)

The trick is to go beyond the dots until you are in a straight line with other dots you need to cross.

236. The trick is to place one coin on top of another at each of the corners of the square.

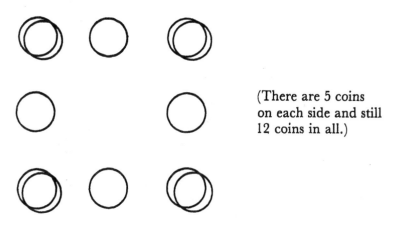

(There are 5 coins on each side and still 12 coins in all.)

237. The cubes should be arranged in the form of a triangle:

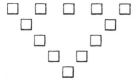

238. Make one round cut and two straight cuts (8 pieces in all). If correctly cut, the inner sector of the circle should be nearly equal in area to the outer portion.

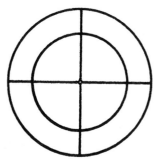

239.

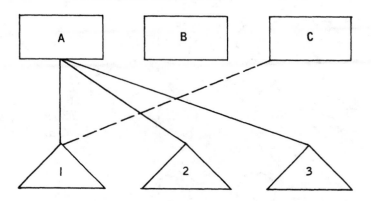

There will always be one path that must cross another, so the answer is that owner C digs a tunnel underground to well 1, which he cannot reach otherwise — that or a pipe line.

240. The trick here is to fold or crease an edge of a piece of paper once, then draw "1000": "1000" will appear all alone when the edge is placed back in position.

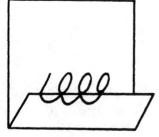

241. Start at island B, cross bridge 3 to the land. Path: B-3-land-5-c-6-land-8-D-7-C-4-B-2-A-1-land.

242.

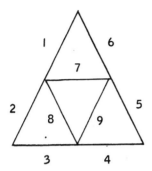

(9 lines of equal length, as indicated, and 5 equilateral triangles.)

243. The catch is that one line is not a straight line. The puzzle stated that only 3 lines must be used, but straight lines were not specified. The answer: two straight lines and one curved line, making 9 spaces.

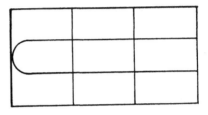

244. The trick, again, is to place one coin on top of another:

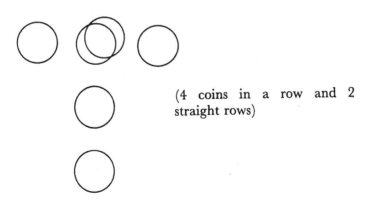

(4 coins in a row and 2 straight rows)

245. (a) This is impossible — you cannot start on land and end on land.

(*b*) This is possible if you are allowed to start anywhere:

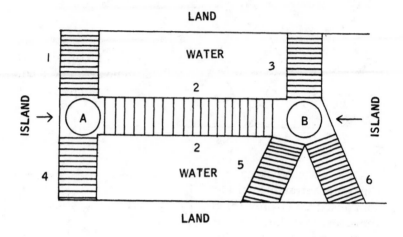

Follow this path: Start on land at bridge 5, proceed to island B, bridge 3, land, bridge 1, island A, bridge 2, island B, bridge 6, land, bridge 4 to island A — you end at island A.

246.

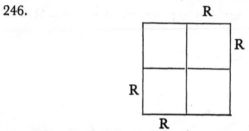

R = remove these lines (4) and replace like this:

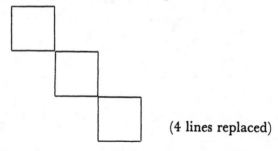

(4 lines replaced)

247. *Solution* (*a*): 4 equilateral triangles of the same size:

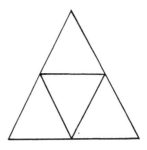

Solution (*b*): This is supposed to be a pyramid. All 4 triangles of the pyramid are equilateral and 6 lines are used.

248. Arrange the trees like this: (10 rows with 3 trees on each row, using 9 trees)

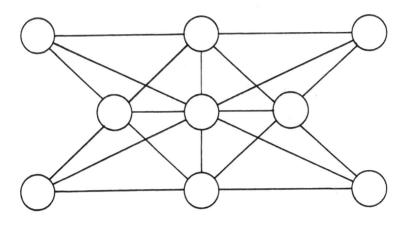

249.   (4 triangles, 2 squares, using 8 straight lines)

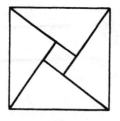 or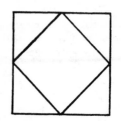

250. 11 pieces with 4 slices. (However, some of the pieces are very small.)

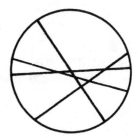

251.

(8 lines giving 3 squares all of different sizes)

252. The final result will look like this:

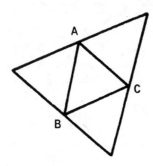

Connect A, B, and C to make a triangle, then draw a line parallel to a side of the triangle through each vertex or the opposite vertex. Through A, draw a line parallel to BC. Through B draw a line parallel to AC. Through C, draw a line parallel to AB. The resulting figure is a triangle with points A, B, and C on the middle of the sides.

253. You have the word O F F I C E.

254. Draw a diameter and divide it into 4 equal parts. Draw a semicircle on the top and bottom of each segment of the diameter as shown.

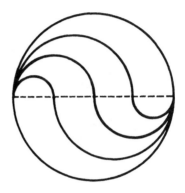

255. (2 rows of 5 apples and 8 rows with 4 apples, using 17 apples)

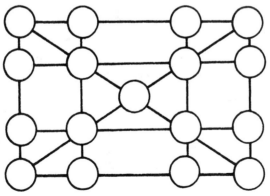

PERIMETER

256.
(Each side of the triangle adds up to 20.)

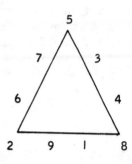

CIRCUMFERENCE

257. $D = 2\frac{1}{2}$ feet
$C = \pi D$
$C = 22/7 \times 5/2 = 110/14 = 7\frac{6}{7}$ feet
$7\frac{6}{7} \times 8 = 55/7 \times 8/1 = 440/7 = 62\frac{6}{7}$ feet per second

How many seconds in an hour?

$$3{,}600 \text{ seconds} = 1 \text{ hour}$$
$$\times 62\frac{6}{7}$$
$$7\overline{)21{,}600}$$
$$3\,085\frac{5}{7}$$
$$7\,200$$
$$216\,00$$
$$\overline{226{,}285\frac{5}{7}} \text{ feet per hour}$$

5,280 feet = 1 mile

$$42.85 = 42.9 \text{ miles per hour}$$
$$5280\overline{)226{,}286.00}$$
$$211\,20$$
$$\overline{15{,}086}$$
$$10\,560$$
$$\overline{4\,5260}$$
$$4\,2240$$
$$\overline{30200}$$
$$26400$$
$$\overline{3800}$$

The answer is 42.9 miles per hour.

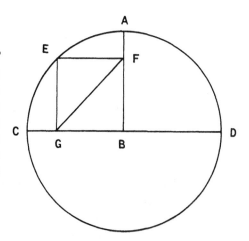

258. The line *GF* is 2 inches long. Proof: *B* is the center of the circle. *AB*, a radius, is 2 inches. Now, a line from *B* to *E*, or *BE*, is also 2 inches, because all radii of the same circle are equal.

BE is a diagonal of the rectangle, *EFGB*, and so is *GF*. Now, all diagonals of the same rectangle are equal, which means that

$$BE = GF$$
$$BE = 2 \text{ inches, therefore}$$
$$GF = 2 \text{ inches.}$$

AREA

259. Only 2 feet (the man's). The 40 acres is in square feet; sheep have hooves, not feet; dogs have paws, not feet.

260. A foot square is a square measuring 1 foot in length on each of its four sides. A square foot can be of any shape, so long as its area is 1 square foot. For example, take a triangle whose base is 2 feet and whose height is 1 foot,

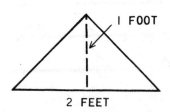

$A = 1/2 \, bh$
$A = 1/2 \times 2 \times 1$
$A = 1$ square foot
This triangle has an area of 1 square foot. A square foot is merely a unit of measure, used for measuring surfaces.

261. The circumference and area of coins are:

(*a*) Quarter:

    $D = 31/32$ inch approx. or .97 inch approx.
    $r = .485$ inch approx.
    $A = \pi r^2$
    $A = 3.14 \times .485 \times .485$
    $A = .74$ square inch, approx.
    $C = \pi d$
    $C = 3.14 \times .97$
    $C = 3.05$ inches or 3 inches, approx.

(*b*) Half dollar:

    $D = 1\frac{7}{32}$ or 1.2 inches, approx.
    $r = .6$ inch approx.
    $A = \pi r^2$
    $A = 3.14 \times .6 \times .6$
    $A = 1.13$ square inches, approx.
    $C = \pi d$
    $C = 3.14 \times 1.2$
    $C = 3.77$ or 3.8 inches, approx.

(*c*) Silver dollar:

    $D = 1\frac{1}{2}$ inches or 1.5 inches, approx.
    $r = .75$ inch approx.
    $A = \pi r^2$
    $A = 3.14 \times .75 \times .75$
    $A = 1.77$ square inches, approx.
    $C = \pi d$
    $C = 3.14 \times 1.5$
    $C = 4.71$ or 4.7 inches, approx.

262. $23.10. There is a trick to this problem. All store windows have 2 sides, not 1.

First window   15 ft. × 21 ft. = 5 yds. × 7 yds. = 35 sq. yds.
Second window   18 ft. × 21 ft. = 6 yds. × 7 yds. = 42 sq. yds.
                                                    ─────────
                                                    77 sq. yds.

          77 sq. yds.
         × 2 (2 sides to the window)
         ───
         154 sq. yds.
         .15 a square yard
         ───
         770
         154
         ─────
         $23.10

263. He boarded up the window like this:

We said the remaining half of the window was still a square in shape. Not only that, but "it" was still a yard high and a yard across. "It" refers to the unboarded window, not the square, as the drawing shows. The window is 1 yard high and 1 yard across.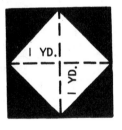

264. Divide into four equal parts:

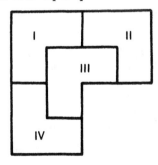

265. Length = 12 inches
     Width = 10 inches
     Height = 8 inches
(Also solved by algebra, in that section.)

266. Divides into four
equal trapezoids:

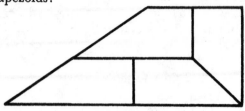

267. The explanation is that the diagonal line in the rectangle is really not a straight line, and when you piece the parts
together to make the rectangle, a small gap is left, amounting
to 1 square inch. The four figures almost make a perfect
rectangle, but miss by 1 square inch. (When you cut this
square out and try to make a rectangle, you will see for
yourself.)

268. Area of small card = 5 in. × 3 in. = 15 sq. inches
Area of large card = 60 in. × 36 in. = 2,160 sq. inches

$$15\overline{)2160} \quad \frac{144}{}$$

Two leaves to a card = 72 cards. Thus, you can make 72
Christmas cards out of this paper.

269. You cannot compare linear feet with square feet. The
screen is 10 feet from the projector with the picture occupying
10 square feet. To compare 10 feet, you must change it to
square feet:

$$10^2 = 100 \text{ square feet}$$

To compare 15 feet, you must change it to square feet:

$$15^2 = 225 \text{ square feet}$$

Now: $225/100 \times 10 = 2250/100 = 22\frac{1}{2}$ square feet (answer).
(This is also solved in the Algebra section.)

270. This is impossible. You cannot find the area of a triangle whose sides are 4, 5, and 9 inches long, because no

triangle can have such lengths. In all triangles, the sum of any two of the sides must be greater than the remaining third side.

VOLUME

271. There is no dirt in a hole.

272. 12 edges.

273. (a) $113\frac{7}{16}$ tons

$V = Ah$ (volume of any prism)
$V = 43,560$ sq. ft. $\times 1/12 = 3,630$ cu. ft.

(An acre of land contains 43,560 square feet and 1 inch — 1/12 of a foot.)

1 cubic foot of water weighs $62\frac{1}{2}$ pounds

$$
\begin{array}{r}
3630 \\
62\frac{1}{2} \\
\hline
1815 \\
7260 \\
21780 \\
\hline
226875
\end{array}
$$
lbs. — change pounds to tons:

$$
\begin{array}{r}
113\frac{7}{16} \text{ tons} \\
2,000\,\overline{)226,875}
\end{array}
$$

(b) $6\frac{1}{4}$ tons

Use the same formula: $V = Ah$
$V = 2400 \times 1/12$
$V = 200$ cu. ft.

$$
\begin{array}{r}
200 \\
62\frac{1}{2} \\
\hline
100 \\
400 \\
1200 \\
\hline
12500
\end{array}
$$
lbs.

$$
\begin{array}{r}
6\frac{1}{4} \text{ tons} \\
2,000\,\overline{)12,500}
\end{array}
$$

274. First find the volume of the imaginary cylinder formed by $\frac{1}{2}$ or .5 inch of rainfall:

$$V = \pi r^2 h \qquad d = 20 \text{ feet}$$
$$V = 22/7 \times 10/1 \times 10/1 \times 5/120$$
$$5/10 \text{ of an inch} = 5/120 \text{ of a foot}$$
$$V = 13\tfrac{2}{21} \text{ cu. ft.}$$
$$1 \text{ cubic foot} = 7\tfrac{1}{2} \text{ gal.}$$
$$13\tfrac{2}{21} \times 7\tfrac{1}{2} = 273/21 \times 15/2 = 97\tfrac{1}{2} \text{ gal.}$$

The sprinkler sprayed 3 gallons of water a minute over the same area.

$$97\tfrac{1}{2} \div 3 = 195/2 \times 1/3 = 195/6 = 32\tfrac{1}{2} \text{ minutes}$$

It would take 32.5 minutes for the sprinkler to water the lawn.

275. Only 1. After that, the box isn't empty.

XI. Graphs

276.

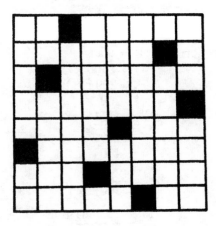

XII. Insurance

277. 1. An endowment policy.

2. Term insurance; it is "pure protection" against death.

3. No; all contracts are mathematically equal — you get what you pay for.

4. No. This is a "friendly" fire; your insurance covers only "hostile" fires and smoke rising from them, as well as lightning. A "friendly" fire is where it should be, doing what it should be doing — a log burning in the fireplace, or an oven broiling a steak. A "hostile" fire is an unplanned fire.

5. Yes, if the damage arises directly from the fire.

6. Yes. You are guilty of not keeping your car in safe shape.

7. Only if you have comprehensive automobile insurance.

8. No. It's not worth the expense unless you have a particularly big, beautiful, or new car.

9. Yes. This was negligence, not merely good housekeeping; you created a safety menace.

10. Yes. You cannot stop negligence which has already begun.

11. No. The insurance company cannot be expected to sponsor your personal antagonisms.

12. No, unless the loss was caused by theft.

13. No. Summer houses, except by special endorsement, are covered only when actually occupied.

14. No.

15. Yes — up to $100 for money, to $500 for securities.

16. Yes, in the Western Hemisphere.

17. No. Losses caused by a relative who lives with you for an extended period are excluded.

18. Yes.

19. Yes. "Theft damage" is covered by your policy.

20. Yes, if the policy has a "cancellable" clause.

XIII. Taxes

278. 1 (c). For the first time in history, the nation's tax bill is approaching the $100-billion mark. This equals more than $600 for every man, woman, and child.

2 (a). The different kinds of levies are personal income tax, social security tax, property taxes, and certain direct excise taxes.

3 (c). There are so many hidden taxes that no one knows the whole number. They include transportation levies, license and inspection fees, unemployment compensation taxes, and import taxes. Frequently, these taxes are built into the price of the products you buy and passed along to you — the taxes the manufacturer, wholesaler, and retailer have to pay Federal, state, or local governments.

4 (b). Federal tax is 3 cents; the average state tax is 5.8 cents.

5 (c). This figure represents direct and hidden taxes. It includes $158 in estimated taxes on materials, parts, their transportation before delivery to the auto manufacturer, plus $146 in Federal excise taxes on the car, radio, and heater.

6 (c). He spends $1\frac{1}{2}$ days out of 5 earning money for his governments.

7 (c). These include 16 Federal and state taxes paid by the New York manufacturer and retailer, and 15 taxes paid by the Georgia cotton manufacturer who made the pocketing for the suit.

8 (c). This isn't too bad, considering that there are 150 taxes on a woman's hat and 151 on a loaf of bread.

9 (b). National defense comes first in the amount taken from your total tax dollar.

10 (c). Education is second.

11 (c).

12 (c). The farmer whose chicken laid an egg paid at least 10 Federal, state, and local taxes. The egg wholesaler paid 17 taxes. The trucker who brought the eggs to the grocer was assessed 20 taxes. The grocer's taxes totaled 14 (Federal, state, and local). You might add to these the feed-store owner who

sold the farmer poultry feed and paid 14 taxes, the railroad which brought the feed and paid 11 taxes, and the corporation which milled the feed to the tune of 14 taxes. The only one who didn't pay a tax was the hen.

XV. Powers and Roots

POWERS

279. $3^3 - 3 = 24$

280. The boy's address is 196 (the perfect square of 14). Turn the 196 upside down and you get 961 which is the perfect square of 31.

281. $2 + 2/2 + 2^2 = 7$; or $2 + 2 + 2 + 2/2 = 7$.

282. The correct answer is 9, raised to the ninth power of 9: 9^{9^9}

If 9^{9^9} were written as a whole number, it would contain over 350 million digits.

283. $3^3 + 3 + 3/3$

SQUARE ROOT AND CUBE ROOT

284. $\dfrac{I}{VII}$ move this line to make:

$$\frac{1}{\sqrt{1}} = 1$$

285. Using four straight lines in the left-hand side of the equation:

(a) $|| - | = |$
(b) $| \times | = |$
(c) $\sqrt{|} = |$

Using three straight lines in the left-hand side of the equation:

(d) $|/| = |$

XVI. Logic or Mathematical Reasoning

286. By catching a mouse (or having a kitten).

287. George was a juggler — he juggled the pineapples while he was crossing the bridge.

288. They are two of triplets.

289. The dime had more sense (cents).

290. The beggar was a woman.

291. Rearrange the letters of N E W   D O O R in such a manner as to get O N E   W O R D (uses same letters).

292. (*a*) He takes the goose across and leaves it on the opposite side.

(*b*) He returns and fetches the fox, leaves it on the other side and comes back with the goose.

(*c*) He leaves the goose at the starting point, takes over the grain which he leaves with the fox.

(*d*) He returns and brings the goose over.

293. (*a*) One mile in three weeks.

(*b*) 4/5

(*c*) Eight years old. Mars takes twice as long to travel around the sun; one trip around the sun is called a year.

(*d*) 9/10 is under water, 1/10 is on top.

294. The butler was guilty because the pages of a books are even on the left and odd on the right. Pages 133 and 134 were, therefore, on either side of the same leaf. So the butler lied when he said he placed the bill between pages 133 and 134. (Verify by examining different books.)

295. (*a*) Ask him three questions which he will answer incorrectly. Then, say, "Let me see [you are thinking carefully], that's three questions so far, isn't it?" Of course, he will answer "Yes" and lose because he was supposed to have given the wrong answer to four questions.

(*b*) The answer is "0 to 0" or "nothing to nothing"

before the game starts. You said you could tell the score before
the game started.

296. (1) A and his wife go over, and A returns.
   (2) B's and C's wives go over, and A's returns.
   (3) B and C go over, and B and his wife return.
   (4) A and B go over, and C's wife returns.
   (5) A's wife and B's wife go over, and C returns.
   (6) C and his wife go over.

XVIII. Algebra

FORMULAS

297. (a) No homework = 1 red F
   (b) $\dfrac{\text{To learn math}}{\text{the only way}}$ = good class concentration + daily practice on problems
   (c) Math remainder = $\dfrac{\text{never fall behind}}{\text{in your work}}$

298. Two wise you are, too wise you be,

   (YY   U   R + YY   U   B)

   I see you are too wise for me.

   (I C U R   YY   4 me)

SIMPLE EQUATION

299. Let x = number of grapes fox ate the first day
   $x + 6$ = number of grapes fox ate the second day
   $x + 12$ = number of grapes fox ate the third day
   $x + 18$ = number of grapes fox ate the fourth day
   $x + 24$ = number of grapes fox ate the fifth day
   $x + (x + 6) + (x + 12) + (x + 18) + (x + 24) = 100$
   $5x + 60 = 100$
   $5x = 40$
   $x = 8$ grapes
   $x + 6 = 14$
   $x + 12 = 20$
   $x + 18 = 26$
   $x + 24 = 32$

The answers are 8, 14, 20, 26, 32.

300. Let x = cost of cork
Let $x + \$1.00$ = cost of bottle
$x + x + \$1.00 = \$1.10$
$2x + \$1.00 = \$1.10$
$2x = \$ .10$
$x = \$ .05$ cost of cork
$x + \$1.00 = \$1.05$ cost of bottle

The cork cost \$.05 and the bottle \$1.05.

301. Let x = number of cows he had

$$1/4\ x + 1/5\ x + 1/6\ x = 37$$

(multiply by 60) $15x + 12x + 10x = 2220$
$$37x = 2220$$
$$x = 60$$

So, he had 60 cows.

302. Let x = first consecutive odd number.
$x + 2$ = second consecutive odd number
$x + 4$ = third consecutive odd number
$x + 6$ = fourth consecutive odd number
$x + (x + 2) + (x + 4) + (x + 6) = 80$
$4x + 12 = 80$
$4x = 68$
$x = 17$ first number
$x + 2 = 19$ second number
$x + 4 = 21$ third number
$x + 6 = 23$ fourth consecutive odd number

The four consecutive odd numbers are: 17, 19, 21, and 23.

303. Let x = number of apples he had.
$2x + 1/2\ x = 20$
$5/2\ x = 20$
$5x = 40$
$x = 8$ He had 8 apples!

304. $x/.3 = 5/.6$

One solution: (multiply by .6) $2x = 5$
$$x = 2\tfrac{1}{2} \text{ or } 2.5$$

305. Let t = number of feet in height of tree
$3t$ = number of feet in height of pole
$t = 3t - 15$
$-2t = -15$
$2t = 15$
$t = 7\frac{1}{2}$ feet
$3t = 22\frac{1}{2}$ feet

The tree is $7\frac{1}{2}$ feet tall and the pole is $22\frac{1}{2}$ feet tall.

306. 1/4 of 20 is not 5, but 4.
1/3 of 10 is not $3\frac{1}{3}$, but——?

Set up a proportion:
$5:4 = 3\frac{1}{3}:x$
$\dfrac{5}{4} = \dfrac{3\frac{1}{3}}{x}$
$5x = 40/3$
$x = 8/3$ or $2\frac{2}{3}$ (answer)

307. Let x = number of pounds of weight of brick.
$1/2\, x + 6 = x$
$1/2\, x = 6$
$x = 12$ pounds, weight of the brick

308. Let x = number of hours job will take all three men working together.

$$1/6\, x + 1/4\, x + 1/3\, x = 1$$

The first man will do 1/6 of the job, the second man 1/4 of the job, and the third 1/3 of the job. Altogether, they will complete one job.

$2/12\, x + 3/12\, x + 4/12\, x = 1$
$9/12\, x = 1$
$3/4\, x = 1$
$3x = 4$
$x = 1\frac{1}{3}$ hours or 1 hour and 20 minutes required for all three men to finish the job.

309. There is a trick in this problem. "1/2 of them study mathematics, 1/3 of them study geometry . . ." Geometry is a

part of mathematics or included in the general field of mathematics, thus 1/3 is included in the 1/2 listed for mathematics. Really only two fractions are used, one for mathematics and one for chemistry.

Solution A:

Let x = number of Einstein's students
$1/2\,x + 1/7\,x + 20 = x$
$9/14\,x + 20 = x$
$20 = 5/14\,x$
$5x = 280$
$x = 56$ students

If you forget that geometry is part of mathematics, you would use:

Solution B

$1/2\,x + 1/3\,x + 1/7\,x + 20 = x$
$41/42\,x + 20 = x$
$1/42\,x = 20$
$x = 840$ students, which is far too many

310. Let x = number of minutes to drain the tank if all drains are open:

$$x/15 + x/30 + x/45 = 1$$

(multiply by 90) $6x + 3x + 2x = 90$
$11x = 90$
$x = 8\frac{2}{11}$ minutes, or 8 minutes 11 seconds

The tank will drain in 8 minutes and 11 seconds.

311. This problem may be solved by setting up a proportion; however, there is something of a trick to the problem. You cannot compare linear feet with square feet; to compare 10 linear feet with 10 square feet, change 10 linear feet by squaring 10, then do the same for 15 feet:

$$10^2 = 100 \text{ sq. ft.}$$
$$15^2 = 225 \text{ sq. ft.}$$

Now, with algebra set up the proportion.

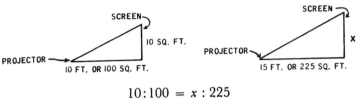

$$10:100 = x:225$$
$$10/100 = x/225$$
$$100x = 2250$$
$$x = 22\tfrac{1}{2} \text{ sq. ft.}$$

The picture will have an area of $22\tfrac{1}{2}$ square feet when the projector is 15 feet from the screen.

312. Let x = George's age. Now, he is 4 years older than John, who is 4 years older than Jim; thus George is 8 years older than Jim and, likewise, 12 years older than Sam.

$$x - 12 = \text{Sam's age}$$

Sam is also one-half the age of George; therefore,

$$x - 12 = 1/2\,x$$
$$(\text{solve for } x) \quad 1/2\,x = 12 \quad x = 24$$

George is 24. John is 20. Jim is 16. Sam is 12.

313. Solve by algebra, setting up a proportion:

(a) If $3 = 5$, then $4 = x$
$$3/5 = 4/x$$
$$3x = 20$$
$$x = 6\tfrac{2}{3}$$

Thus, 4 would be equal to $6\tfrac{2}{3}$.

(b) $1/2$ of $5 = 2\tfrac{1}{2}$
$1/3$ of $10 = 3\tfrac{1}{3}$

Thus, if $2\tfrac{1}{2} = 3$, then $3\tfrac{1}{3} = x$

$$\frac{2\tfrac{1}{2}}{3} = \frac{3\tfrac{1}{3}}{x}$$
$$5/2\,x = 10$$
$$5x = 20$$
$$x = 4 \text{ (answer)}$$

314. Let x = number of bushels ground

$x - 1/10 \; x = 1$ bushel
$9/10 \; x = 1$ (multiply by 10)
$9 \, x = 10$
$x = 1\frac{1}{9}$ bushels

PARENTHESES AND THE SIMPLE EQUATION

315. Let x = number of dollars man started with

$2[2(2x - \$10.00) - \$10.00] - \$10.00 = 0$
$2[4x - \$20.00 - \$10.00] - \$10.00 = 0$
$2[4x - \$30.00] - \$10.00 = 0$
$8x - \$60.00 - \$10.00 = 0$
$8x = \$70.00$
$x = \$8.75$ (answer)

316. $6 \times 8 \div 12 + 3 \times 24 \; -12 \div 6 \; +8$
$= (6 \times 8 \div 12) + (3 \times 24) - (12 \div 6) + 8$
$= \qquad 4 \quad + \quad 72 \quad - \quad 2 \quad +8$
$= 76 + 8 - 2$
$= 82$ (answer)

317. Let x = telephone number. When you follow the steps outlined, your result is:

$$\frac{2[3(60/2 + x - 25) - 15]}{6}$$

$$= \frac{2[3(x + 5) - 15]}{6}$$

$$= \frac{2(3x + 15 - 15)}{6}$$

$$= \frac{2(3x)}{6}$$

$$= \frac{6x}{6}$$

$$= x \text{ (the telephone number you began with)}$$

SIMPLIFICATION

318. Let x = your house number
y = your age

When you follow the instructions, the problem is:

$$\frac{50(2x+5)+y+365-615}{100}$$

$$= \frac{100x+250+y+365-615}{100}$$

$$= \frac{100x+y}{100}$$

$$= x+1/100\,y$$

$= x$ — your house number
$1/100\,y$, or two decimal places, is your age.

319. Let x = the number you started with.

(a) x
(b) $2x$
(c) $2x+4$
(d) $10x+20$ (multiply by 5)
(e) $10x+32$ (add 12)
(f) $100x+320$ (multiply by 10)
(g) $100x$ (subtract 320)
    $100x$ remains
(h) (cross off 2 zeros, same as dividing by 100)
(i) $\dfrac{100x}{100} = x$ = the number with which you began

320. $\dfrac{\text{STOP}}{\text{CUTS}} = $ C   (C is greater than 2)

Another way to write this is: $\begin{array}{r} \text{CUTS} \\ \times\,\text{C} \\ \hline \text{STOP} \end{array}$

If C is 4, you have 5 digits for STOP instead of 4, thus C must equal 3.

$$\begin{array}{r} 3UTS \\ \times\,3 \\ \hline STOP \end{array}$$ S = 9 because $3 \times 3 = 9$

P = 7 because $9 \times 3 = 27$

Therefore:

$$\begin{array}{r} 3UT9 \\ \times\,3 \\ \hline 9TO7 \end{array}$$

The product $3 \times U$ can have no carryover because that would spoil the 9, which we know is S. U cannot be 1 since $3 \times 1 = 3$, and the number must be different because the letter is different. 3 has been used, thus U must be 2.

$$\begin{array}{r} 32T9 \\ \times\,3 \\ \hline 9TO7 \end{array}$$

$T = 3 \times 2 = 6 +$ something to carry, maybe. If we had 1 to carry, the result would be 7, which has already been used. Two is the highest amount that could be carried to the 6, which would make 8. Thus, T must be 6 or 8.

Now, let's test these values in getting the value of O. If $T = 6$, then $6 \times 3 = 18 + 2$ to carry gives 20; however, we can not put down 0 as we were told in the beginning not to use 0's.

If $T = 8$, then $8 \times 3 = 24 + 2 = 26$. Put down the 6 and carry 2 so that $3 \times 2 = 6 + 2 = 8$. Thus, T = 8 and O = 6.

$$\begin{array}{r} 3289 \\ \times\,3 \\ \hline 9867 \end{array} \quad \text{or}$$

$$\frac{STOP}{CUTS} = C \quad \text{is} \quad \frac{9867}{3289} = 3$$

FACTORING

321. You cannot divide by $r-s$, because $r = s$. Therefore, $r-s = 0$, and you cannot divide by 0, which is undefined or infinity (∞).

322. You cannot divide by $5-5$ because $5-5 = 0$ and you can never divide by 0 (see answer to puzzle 321).

323. When you square a positive number and a negative number of the same value, you get the same answer:

$$(-2)^2 = (2)^2$$
$$4 = 4$$

But -2 and 2 are not the same; only their absolute values are identical. Therefore, even though the squares of two numbers are equal, the numbers may be different. When you take the square root of 4, you will get two roots.

$$\sqrt{4} = 2 \text{ or } -2 \text{ because}$$
$$2^2 = 4$$
$$(-2)^2 = 4$$

In $(4-9/2)^2 = (5-9/2)^2$ you are not squaring equals because $4-9/2 = -1/2$ and $5-9/2 = 1/2$. You really have: $(-1/2)^2 = (1/2)^2$. Even though $(-1/2)^2 = (1/2)^2$, it is not possible to conclude that $-1/2 = 1/2$.

EQUATIONS IN TWO UNKNOWNS

324. Let x = number of sheep one farmer had
Let y = number of sheep the other farmer had

$$\begin{array}{l} \text{A} \\ \text{B} \end{array} \left\{ \begin{array}{l} x+1 = y-1 \\ y+1 = 2(x-1) \end{array} \right.$$

Equation A: $x-y = -2$
Equation B: $-2x+y = -3$
(add) $\overline{}$
$-x = -5$
$x = 5$

Substitute x in Equation A: $5+1 = y-1$
$$y-1 = 6$$
$$y = 7$$

One farmer had 5 sheep, the other had 7.

325. Let p = number of problems solved
  Let q = number of problems unsolved
  $8p$ = the money due for correct answers
  $5q$ = the money to be fined for incorrect answers

$$(1)\ 8p-5q = 0$$
$$(2)\ \ p+q = 26$$

Multiply (2) by 5 $5p+5q = 130$
Add (1) and (2) $13p = 130$
$$p = 10 \text{ correct}$$
Substitute in (2) $10+q = 26$
$$q = 16 \text{ wrong}$$

326. Let l = number of inches in length
  w = number of inches in width
  h = number of inches in height

A drawing might prove helpful:

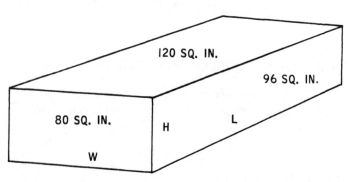

120 SQ. IN.

96 SQ. IN.

80 SQ. IN.

H   L

W

$A = lw$ (area of a rectangle)

Equation A: $lw = 120$ sq. in.
Equation B: $lh = 96$ sq. in.

Equation C: $wh = 80$ sq. in.

(solve for l in equation A)	$l = 120/w$
(substitute for l in equation B)	$120h/w = 96$
(solve for h in equation B)	$h = 96w/120$
(substitute for h in equation C)	$96w/120 \times w = 80$
(solve for w)	$96w^2 = 9600$
	$w^2 = 100$
	$w = 10$ inches
(substitute w in equation A)	$10l = 120$
	$l = 12$ inches
(substitute l in equation B)	$12h = 96$
	$h = 8$ inches

The dimensions of the box are:

$$\text{length} = 12 \text{ inches}$$
$$\text{width} = 10 \text{ inches}$$
$$\text{height} = 8 \text{ inches}$$

327. Let b = number of inches of the fish's body

t = number of inches of the fish's tail

Equation A: $t = 5 + 1/2\ b$
Equation B: $b = 5 + t$

(solve for t in equation B)	$t = b - 5$
(substitute for t in equation A)	$b - 5 = 5 + 1/2\ b$
	$1/2\ b = 10$
	$b = 20$ inches
(substitute b in equation A)	$t = 5 + 1/2 \times 20$
	$t = 15$ inches
	$h = 5$ inches (given)

Thus, the body = 20 inches; the tail = 15 inches; and the head is given as 5 inches. Adding these, the total length of the fish is 40 inches.

328. 16 chicken eggs
       4 duck eggs
       2 turkey eggs

Check: 16   4   2 $.08
           .005   .02   .03   .08
         _____   _____   _____   .06
         $ .08 $ .08 $ .06   _____
                                            $ .22

By algebra: Let H = number of chicken eggs
                    D = number of duck eggs
                    T = number of turkey eggs

(1) $H + D + T = 22$
(2) $.005H + .02D + .03T = \$ .22$

Multiply (2) by 1,000 $5H + 20D + 30T = 220$
Multiply (1) by 5 $5H + 5D + 5T \quad = 110$
Subtract (1) from (2) $15D + 25T = 110$
Divide by 5 $3D + 5T = 22$

Solve for D $D = \dfrac{22 - 5T}{3}$

Now, since D and T stand for duck and turkey, you cannot have a fraction of a duck or turkey and all answers must be in whole numbers. Thus, substituting values of T in this formula, and letting $T = 1, 2, 3, 4, 5, 6$, you can readily see that $T = 2$ is the only value that works, in order to arrive at a whole number for D.

> $T = 1, 3,$ and 4 — give fractional values for D.
> $T = 5$ and greater gives negative values of T which we cannot have.

So, $T = 2$ has to be right.

$$D = \frac{22 - 5 \times 2}{3} = \frac{22 - 10}{3} \qquad \frac{12}{3} = 4$$

$$D = 4$$

Now, go back and substitute in equation (1)

$$H + 4 + 2 = 22$$
$$H = 16$$

The answers are: $T = 2$
                     $D = 4$
                     $H = 16$

and by the check shown at the beginning, you can see these answers are correct.

329. (*a*) Let x = first number
  y = second number
  z = third number

  (*b*) $2x$ (multiply first number by 2)
  (*c*) $2x + 5$ (add 5)
  (*d*) $10x + 25$ (multiply sum by 5)
  (*e*) $10x + 25 + y$ (add second number)
  (*f*) $100x + 250 + 10y$ (multiply by 10)
  (*g*) $100x + 250 + 10y + z$ (add third number)

Rearrange $= 100x + 10y + z + 250$
Subtract 250, leaves

$$100x + 10y + z \quad \text{or}$$

$$x \qquad\qquad y \qquad\qquad z$$
first number   second number   third number

If they gave you:
$$\begin{array}{r} 595 \\ -250 \\ \hline 345 \end{array}$$

Answer: 3   100's
     4   10's
     5   1's

QUADRATIC EQUATIONS

330. Let x = number of inches of the base of a right triangle

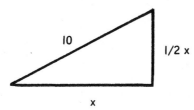

Use the Pythagorean formula:

$$10^2 = x^2 + (1/2\ x)^2$$
$$100 = x^2 + 1/4\ x^2$$
$$5/4\ x^2 = 100$$
$$5x^2 = 400$$
$$x^2 = 80$$
$$x = 8.944 \text{ or } 8.9 \text{ inches}$$

331.

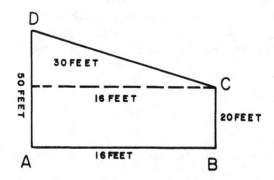

You would have a right triangle at the top of this figure; thus you solve the problem by the Pythagorean theorem.

$$DC^2 = 30^2 + 16^2$$
$$DC^2 = 900 + 256$$
$$DC^2 = 1156$$
$$DC = 34 \text{ feet}$$
$$\text{(square root of 1156)}$$

The rope from D to C is 34 feet long.

332. Let S = number of inches of the side of the square. Use the Pythagorean formula:

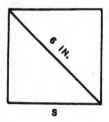

$$S^2 + S^2 = 6^2$$
$$2S^2 = 36$$
$$S^2 = 18$$
$$S = 4.243 \text{ or } 4.2 \text{ inches, approx.}$$

333. The diameter of the log makes no difference. Let x = number of feet the boy traveled. Use the Pythagorean formula:

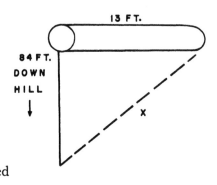

$x^2 = 84^2 + 13^2$
$x^2 = 7056 + 169$
$x^2 = 7225$
$x\ = 85$ feet the boy traveled

334. Let x = one number
y = second number

(1) $x^2 - y^2 = 16$
(2) $y = 3/5\ x$

Substitute (2) in (1) $x^2 - 9/25\ x^2 = 16$
$16/25\ x^2 = 16$
$1/25\ x^2 =\ 1$
$x^2 = 25$
$x =\ 5$

Substitute in (2) $y = 3/5 \times 5$
$y = 3$

Answer: 5 and 3

ANSWERS TO GAMES

(Not all games require answers)

3. (p. 24)

Game A. This game has a pattern the winner must follow: if you are to win, you should be first and select these numbers at your turn:

$$
\begin{array}{cl}
1 & \\
12 & \\
23 & \\
34 & \\
45 & \text{(add 11)} \\
56 & \\
67 & \\
78 & \\
89 & \\
100 & \\
\end{array}
$$

No matter what number your opponent chooses, you cannot lose. Suppose he starts:

	6		
you	12	he	66
he	20	you	67
you	23	he	77
he	33	you	78
you	34	he	88
he	44	you	89
you	45	he	99
he	53	you	100
you	56		

If you don't know the pattern, play it smart and do not go into the pattern of special numbers until the 70's or 80's are reached. That will make it more difficult for the other player to catch on to your trick. He will grow suspicious if you always use the same numbers. Since you have to take 89 to win, the other players after one or two games will come up with, "You always choose 89." They will then try to arrive at 89 first, but you must be one jump ahead and go into your pattern earlier at 78 or even 67. You might have to drop back to 56 and 45 eventually — or all the way back to 12 and 1. When both players know the pattern, only the one who starts and chooses 1 can win.

Game B. This game has a different pattern. Always let the other person go first and, at your turn, you follow this set of numbers:

11	
22	
33	
44	
55	(multiples of 11)
66	
77	
88	
99	

He must say 100 if you reach 99 first, and 88 before that. Again, as he catches on to 88, you must start your sequence earlier:

he	10	
you	11	
he	19	
you	24	(not yet in pattern)
he	34	
you	44	
he	50	
you	60	
he	68	
you	77	(now in pattern)
he	87	
you	88	
he	95	
you	99	
he	100	and loses

When both players know the pattern, the winner must start second and choose 11 on his first turn.

Game C. To reach 100 first, the pattern to follow is to let your opponent start while you choose 10, 20, 30, 40, 50, 60, 70, 80, 90, 100 and win.

Game D. You go first and use the same pattern as in Game A: 1, 12, 23, 34, 45, 56, 67, 78, 89, 99, and he must say 100.

5. (p. 33)

Actually, 11 people were left on the elevator and 18 got off. However, we did not ask for this. The elevator made 8 stops, counting the last stop. After leaving the first floor, the total number of floors passed or stopped at in his travels was 21, counting the last stop. The operator's name is Bill A. Rider, which was given in the second sentence: "A hotel may bill a rider" by the number of times he uses the elevator.

6. (p. 34)

The point of the strategy is that you can always make the number of dots decrease by a total of 4 between one move of your opponent and the next. If he takes 1, you take 3; if he takes 2, you take 2; if he takes 3, you take 1. If you have first move, you take 3 and leave 17 on the paper. Whatever he does, you leave 13 after your second move. After your next move, whatever he does, you can always leave 9. Then you leave 5, and finally you leave 1 — working down by fours: 17, 13, 9, 5, and 1. What your opponent does has no effect upon the result. If he moves first and does not know the secret, you wait until he makes a false move that allows you to leave a winning number. Then you work down by fours in the same way.

8. (p. 53)

To determine the numbers they chose, take the answer given in (*h*) and subtract 250 from it. The remainder is always the first three numbers thought of and in the order in which they were thought of. In the example given:

```
    5 9 5         Try 8, 1, 9, as the given numbers
   -2 5 0
(answer) 3 4 5                    8
                                ×2
   first                        ──
  second                        16
   third                        +5
                                ──
                                21
                                ×5
                               ───
                               105
                                +1
                               ───
                               106
                               ×10
                              ─────
                              1,060
                                +9
                              ─────
                              1,069  (answer he gives)
                              -250   (you deduct)
                              ─────
                               819   (numbers he started with)
```

9. (p. 54)

You get the answer from (h). The last two figures of the sum are the person's age, and the first figure or figures indicate the month. In the example, the sum was 432: 4 is the month (April) and 32 is the age.

10. (p. 55)

To get the answer, always subtract 5 from the number the person gives as the resultant of his calculations. In the example given:

(a) Person selects the 8 of hearts.
(b) Multiply by 2   = 16.
(c) Add 1   = 17.
(d) Multiply by 5   = 85.
(e) Club   6
    Diamond   7
    Heart   8
    Spade   9
      You add 8   = 93.
(f) Person tells you 93.

(Subtract 5, and the first digit is the card, the last digit is the suit.)

$$\begin{array}{ccc} 93 & 8 & 8 \\ -5 & \text{(card)} & \text{(suit)} \\ \hline 88 & & \end{array}$$

Were the answer 127, the card would be the queen of diamonds.

Try this: (*a*)   12
         (*b*)   24   (× 2)
         (*c*)   25   (+ 1)
         (*d*)   125   (× 5)
         (*e*)   132   (+ 7 for diamond)
     132
     −5   (you subtract 5)
     ‾‾‾
     127   (answer) (12 queen, 7 diamonds)

11. (p. 56)

Subtract 250 from the result; the answer gives you the page number first, the line number second, and the position number on the line last. The teacher merely looks this up in the book and finds the word (he always subtracts 250 from the person's number). In the example given:

$$\begin{array}{ll} 28{,}997 & \text{(person's result)} \\ 250 & \text{(teacher subtracts)} \\ \hline 28{,}747 & \text{(teacher's answer)} \end{array}$$

287   page
4   line
7   the word on line 4, which is "editions"

Since you cannot go over 9, the last two numbers will always represent a line and the number on the line respectively. The first digits may have 1, 2, or 3 numbers in them, depending upon the page number. (Example: 2198 means page 21, line 9, word 8). (Example: 326 means page 3, line 2, word 6.)

12. (p. 57)

The teacher gets the information merely by subtracting 250 from the result given him by the person. The example given:

$$\begin{array}{rl} \text{Result:} & 42,170 \\ & \underline{-\,250} \quad \text{(teacher subtracts)} \\ & 41,920 \quad \text{(information)} \end{array}$$

4 for month of April; 19 is the date; 20 is his age.

$$\begin{array}{ll} \text{Take the year} & 1959 \\ \text{Subtract} & \underline{\quad 20} \\ \text{Year of birth} & 1939 \end{array}$$

14. (p. 72)

Start:

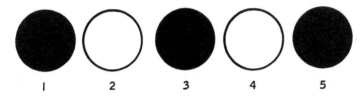

| 1 | 2 | 3 | 4 | 5 |

Move A: move 1 and 2:

    3   4   5   (leave 2 spaces) 1   2

Move B: move 3 and 4:

    5   (leave 2 spaces) 1   2   3   4

Move C: move 2 and 3:

    5   2   3   1   (leave 2 spaces) 4

Move D: move 5 and 2:

    3   1   5   2   4

16. (p. 123)

The second player usually wins. Let the other person go first because normally only six plays can be made and the second player always makes the sixth play.

Also, Player B should try to place his o's in such a way as to take up as much room as possible, leaving only one square open between the marks. When only one square appears, no play can be made here. Six plays is the least that can be played. Seven or even 8 plays may be made if all moves are placed close together, but 7 plays cannot be made if Player B always leaves one space between his play and that of Player A, occupying three spaces per move.

17. (p. 123)

One must learn certain principles for winning:

(*a*) When dots remain on all three rows, remove at your turn a number of dots which will leave the number on each of the three rows unequal. No two rows will have the same amount of dots on it. Maintain this procedure until there is only one dot on two rows:

                •   •

                •

                •

Then, move all but one dot from this top row so you will win here.

                •

                •

                •

(*b*) If, at any time, two rows have the same number of dots on them, remove all the dots from the third row. The two rows left will have an even number of dots and you then follow the rules for (*c*).

(*c*) If there are dots on only two rows, remove at your turn enough dots from one row to make both remaining rows exactly even in number. Continue until there are only two markers on each row:

                •   •

                •   •

Then you have him beaten for sure. If he removes 1 dot, you move 2 from the other row and he loses. If he removes 2 dots or all the dots from one row, you remove 1 from the remaining row and he loses.

(d) If at any time before this 2–2 situation only 2 rows are left, the opponent removes all from one row, you remove all but one dot from the other — and he loses.

If he moves all but one dot from one of the remaining two rows, you remove all from the other row — and he loses.

When you are first, the best move is to remove one marker from any row, but keep all rows uneven. If your opponent is first, try at your turn to put into practice any of the principles (a), (b), (c), and/or (d).

After you have played this game awhile, these rules will become automatic, but at first, play carefully.

18. (p. 124)
One possible solution:

> 4–1, 13–4, 3–8, 10–3, 15–13, 12–14, 1–6, 6–13,
> 14–12, 11–13, 7–2, 13–4, 2–7. One marker
> remains.

19. (p. 136)
This is how 10¾ points were made in Game A:
(Follow the numbers)

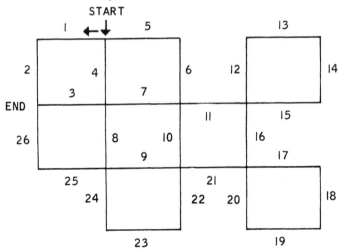

Score: 8 whole
$\frac{3}{4}$
$\frac{3}{4}$
$\frac{3}{4}$
$\frac{1}{2}$
——
$10\frac{3}{4}$ points

This is how 14 points were made in Game B:

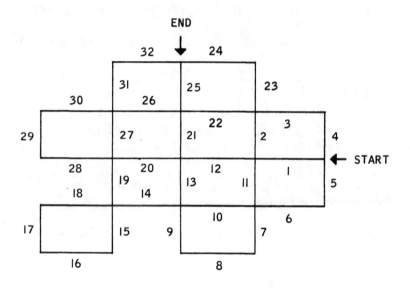

Score: 11 whole
$\frac{3}{4}$
$\frac{3}{4}$
$\frac{1}{2}$
$\frac{1}{2}$
$\frac{1}{2}$
——
14 points

REFERENCES

Here is a list of some of the best sources in the field of mathematical puzzles, fun projects, and games. Teachers and students, as well as the reader, can find additional material in these books. Many of the puzzles included are classics, and the same puzzle may appear in many of the books listed, but differently worded.

Brandes, Louis Grant, *Math Can be Fun*, J. Weston Walch, Portland, Maine, 1956.

Brown, Joseph C., *Easy Tricks with Numbers*, Pelham, N.Y., 1943.

Brueckner, Leo J., Grossnickle, Foster E., Reckzeh, John, *Developing Mathematical Understandings in the Upper Grades*, John C. Winston Co., Philadelphia, 1957.

Burroughs Adding Machine Company, *Fascinating Figure Puzzles*, compiled by Frederick W. Davis, A.A., Detroit, 1933; and *Story of Figures*, 1933.

Freeman, Mae and Ira, *Fun with Figures*, Random House, New York, 1946.

Friend, J. Newton, *Fun, Numbers, and Facts*, Charles Scribner's Sons, New York, 1954.

Gardner, Martin, *Mathematics, Magic, and Mystery*, Dover Publications, Inc., New York, 1955.

Green, Allen V., *Simple Tricks for the Young Magician*, Hart Book Co., Inc., New York, 1955.

Haber, Philip, *Mathematical Puzzles and Pastimes*, Peter Pauper Press, Mount Vernon, N.Y., 1957.

Heath, Royal Vale, *Mathemagic*, Dover Publications, Inc., New York, 1953.

Hunter, J. A. H., *Fun with Figures*, Oxford University Press, Toronto, 1956.

Johnson, Donovan A., *Paper Folding for the Mathematics Class*, National Council of Teachers of Mathematics, 1957.

Kaufman, Gerard L., *The Book of Modern Puzzles*, Dover Publications, Inc., New York, 1954.

Kinnaird, Clark, *Encyclopedia of Puzzles and Pastimes*, Grosset & Dunlap, Inc., New York, 1946.

Kraitchik, Maurice, *Mathematical Recreations*, Dover Publications, Inc., New York, 1942.

Longstreet, Julian, *Brain Teasers*, Page, Boston, 1932.

Leeming, Joseph, *Riddles, Riddles, Riddles*, Franklin Watts, Inc., New York, 1956.

Menaker, Fred, *How Smart Are You?* Sentinel Books, New York, 1935.

Merrill, Helen A., *Mathematical Excursions*, Dover Publications Inc., New York, 1957.

Meyer, Jerome S., *Fun with Mathematics*, World Publishing Company, New York, 1952.

—————— *Fun for the Family*, Greenberg Publishing, Inc., New York, 1938.

Mott-Smith, Geoffrey, *Mathematical Puzzles for Beginners and Enthusiasts*, Dover Publications, Inc., New York, 1954.

Peter Pauper Press, *The Little Quiz Book*, Mount Vernon, N.Y., 1956.

Reichmann, W. J., *The Fascination of Numbers*, Oxford University Press, New York, 1957.

Richardson, Moses, *Fundamentals of Mathematics*, The Macmillan Company, New York, 1958.

Sloan, T. O'Conor, and Thomps, J. E., *Speed and Fun with Figures*, C. Van Nostrand Company, Inc., Princeton, N.J., 1922.

Smith, David Eugene, *History of Mathematics*, Vols. I and II, Dover Publications, Inc., New York, 1958.

Spitzer, Herbert F., *Practical Classroom Procedures for Enriching Arithmetic*, Webster Publishing Co., St. Louis, 1956.

—————— *The Teaching of Arithmetic*, Houghton Mifflin Company, Boston, 1954.

Sticker, Henry, *Essentials of Arithmetic*, Oxford University Press, New York, 1944.

—————— *How to Calculate Quickly*, Dover Publications, Inc., New York, 1955.

Wood, Clement, *A Book of Mathematical Oddities*, Haldeman-Julius Publications, Girard, Kansas.